Winner's Disclosure

WINNER'S DISCLOSURE

An Autobiography

TERRY BIDDLECOMBE

with Pat Lucas

Stanley Paul
London Melbourne Sydney Auckland Johannesburg

Stanley Paul & Co. Ltd

An imprint of the Hutchinson Publishing Group

17–21 Conway Street, London WIP 6JD

Hutchinson Group (Australia) Pty Ltd
30–32 Cremorne Street, Richmond South, Victoria 3121
PO Box 151, Broadway, New South Wales 2007

Hutchinson Group (NZ) Ltd
32–34 View Road, PO Box 40–086, Glenfield, Auckland 10

Hutchinson Group (SA) Pty Ltd
PO Box 337, Bergvlei 2012, South Africa

First published 1982
© Terry Biddlecombe 1982

Set in Linotron Sabon by Computape (Pickering) Ltd

Printed in Great Britain by The Anchor Press Ltd
and bound by Wm Brendon & Son Ltd,
both of Tiptree, Essex
British Library Cataloguing in Publication Data

Biddlecombe, Terry
    Winner's disclosure.
    1. Biddlecombe, Terry.
    2. Jockeys – Biography
    I. Title   II. Lucas, Pat
    798.4'5'0924   SF336.B/

ISBN 0 09 147550 3

Contents

Acknowledgements

So many people have helped in the writing of this book that, for reasons of space, it is impossible to name them all here. They will know who they are and our thanks to them are as heartfelt as to others who have given of their time and thought on our behalf.

We would especially like to express our appreciation to the Biddlecombe family for their memories, and for supplying piles of photographs and newspaper cuttings. Thanks also to Robin, Richard and David Lucas for their support throughout.

Others to whom we owe a great deal include Michael and Mary Scudamore; Mr Peter O'Sullevan and his researcher, Hilda; Jimmy Lindley, Tim Brookshaw, Josh Gifford, David Nicholson; Dr and Mrs Bill Wilson, Peter Smith, Secretary of the Jockeys' Association; Lord Oaksey; Brian Radford and other racing correspondents of *Sporting Life*; Graham Nicholls, Jack Lane, Gary Newbon, Tom Wellon; Mr and Mrs Bryan Jenks; Mrs Mercy and the late Fred Rimell; Mr and Mrs Fulke Walwyn; John Thorne; Julia Bucknall of the Park Street Clinic, London; Bernard Parkin; Mr and Mrs A. Hodgson and Mrs Ann Biddlecombe.

To the long-suffering readers of the book in its original form, who spent many hours rendering it fit for press, we are extremely grateful. Thank you, Jenny, Judy, Pauline, Sue – and the rest of the team in London.

October 1981   Terry Biddlecombe and Pat Lucas

Photographic Acknowledgements

For permission to reproduce photographs in this book the publishers would like to thank: Associated Press, Bespix, Central Press Photos, J. Finlay Davidson, Foto Casti, Fotosports International, Independent Newspapers, Dublin, Frank Meads, P. A. Reuter, Bernard Parkin, Provincial Press Agency, Kenneth Sandalls, Sport and General, and *Windsor, Slough and Eton Express*.

Introduction

Hydra Dor had made no mistakes in the Banbury Novices' Chase at Stratford until we came to the water jump just before the stands. I remember seeing a good stride but he stood off too far, hitting the lip of the water with his forelegs as he landed before going down onto his knees and shooting me up his neck.

I thought he was going to fall, but as I was lying on the ground with the horse half on top of me, he found another leg and scrambled to his feet. As he did so, I realized that my foot was caught in the stirrup iron and the leather which had twisted.

I had one chance as Hydra Dor was recovering and that was to grab the reins, which I managed to do just as he started to trot. But the trot broke into a canter as I was struggling to get back into the saddle, and I let go of the reins. As he gained speed, I could see his hind legs getting nearer and nearer to my head as I tried in vain to hang on to the stirrup leather. Then I felt the saddle slip back a bit and Hydra Dor's hind legs began to crack on my helmet. In that fleeting moment I remembered the next fence, which he obviously intended to jump, but before I could anticipate the agony of having my leg wrenched from its socket, the saddle slipped right round the horse's belly. This enabled him to put his hind hoof squarely on my helmet and kick me over from my back on to my stomach, which untwisted the leather and freed my foot just as he was about to take off at the fence. It all happened very quickly and my head had been banging up and down on the track for about 200 yards.

I had borrowed Bobby Beasley's elastic-ended girths for the race. I had never used this type of girth before and they saved my life. It was a chance in a million that I was not permanently injured.

I vaulted the rails before returning to the weighing room and rode in the next two races but have no recollection of them, as I was suffering from delayed concussion. I was twenty years old and had turned professional eighteen months before. On reflection, that was the most terrifying experience of my racing career.

1
Gymkhana Days – Flyaway, Twinkle and Spot

When I look back I cannot recall a time when horses were not a part of my life.

My mother, Nancy, was born at Westbury-on-Severn and later lived at Dobshill Farm, Staunton Court, near Gloucester. She often rode to hounds with her father and four brothers who were also keen on racing.

My father, Walter, came from Middlezoy in Somerset and was still a boy when he moved with his father to farm at Hartpury Court not far from Dobshill Farm. In his younger days he rode for Harry Dufosee in point-to-points with considerable success and was a good amateur under rules. It was when he brought his horse to school over the fences at Dobshill Farm that he met Mother, and this led to a partnership that has lasted for forty-three years.

After their marriage, my parents first lived at Hartpury Court where my brother, Tony, was born on 6 November 1938 and I arrived on 2 February 1941.

Although general farming was the main livelihood of the Biddle-combe family, there were always horses about the place and when Tony and I were old enough to attend Hartpury School, some two miles away, Dad would either take us by pony and trap or, if he was in a hurry, sling the pair of us up behind him on his horse. We frequently fell off and grazed our knees but he never seemed to worry – and neither did we. We loathed school and hated walking home, especially in the rain. It had its compensations. A school friend of ours had a hoard of chocolate bars stolen, as it turned out, from the nearby agricultural institute, which he hid high in the branches of a huge oak tree. We spent many an evening devouring this rich feast to which we added our own loot of sweet apples, 'scrumped' from local orchards.

Another schoolmate, the son of the local vicar, brought a wad of pound notes to school which we rolled up and smoked behind the toilets. I forget how much money we burned before we were discovered but it was considerable, and most of the vicar's savings had literally gone up in smoke. We were no angels.

In the mid 1940s, Dad bought Lower House Farm, Upleadon, which was not far from Hartpury and where our sister, Sue, was born in May 1948.

The atmosphere at Upleadon was warm and happy-go-lucky. We have always been a close family but at the same time we have felt free to lead our own lives without interference. Mother indulged us all and fed us magnificently. She always had our interests at heart and although our riding activities sometimes worried her, she rarely admitted to this; it was only after Tony and I had been riding in races for some time that I found out she could not bear to watch us. Instead, she spent most of the time at race meetings hiding in the ladies' loo and would ask the attendant whether or not we were all right.

When we were children, Dad was very strict, very kind, and what he said he meant. A quiet man, he taught by example rather than by preaching and his simple maxim, 'Speak up and always tell the truth,' has proved invaluable to me. He was an excellent judge of a horse and one of the finest riders I have ever seen. As a riding instructor he was great. He would put us up on anything and there were always horses in the yard. He showed us how to sit in the saddle, how to keep our hands down, and told us to sit into a horse and go with him. Tony inherited Dad's fantastic hands on a horse which I never really did. Horses which ran away with me would settle for Tony and he developed into a superb horseman. We have always had the greatest respect for each other.

Sue and I used to have quite a few rows as children. Some days I thought the world of her and on others I disliked her intensely because, being the only daughter, she was spoiled to death by Dad and could do no wrong. She is a terrific girl, in fact. She rode beautifully and, apart from our successful gymkhana days, won many prizes show jumping before she had a bad fall and hurt her back.

After that she turned her attention to her boutique in Gloucester and, being a very pretty girl, she had lots of boyfriends. She was later to marry Bob Davies who, apart from being a great character, was also to prove a fierce rival to me in racing. But more of him later.

Sue handled the telephone calls and fan mail which later assailed our home. She virtually took over as our 'manager' and went out of her way to cut out hundreds of newspaper reports concerning our activities and those of our colleagues. She often grumbled at us as sisters do when they have tiresome brothers, but her loyalty and interest in our progress did not go unnoticed by either Tony or me.

In the early days at Lower House Farm there was no electricity supply to the house and buildings. The mains water was connected to the house only, which meant that we had to hand pump water for the cattle and horses and carry it to the buildings in buckets. The cows had to be milked by hand, and Tony and I would help Dad with this before school and on our return. This was a cold job in the winter, with only the light from the hurricane lamps to see by, and in the summer it was all midges, cow muck and cows' feet in the bucket. It was a couple of years before we were connected to the mains electricity, when we bought our first milking machine and were able to replace the Calor gas lighting in the farmhouse.

Mother did her cooking, in those early days, on a huge range fired by a furnace which Dad lit every morning before milking. She did the washing with the old tub and scrubbing board and, like most farmers' wives at that time, she worked exceedingly hard in difficult circumstances with great cheerfulness.

We had log fires in the main rooms downstairs in the winter, and bathed, miner-style, in front of these in an old tin bath. As in all old farmhouses before they were modernized, the bedrooms were freezing, as were the sheets, and we often shivered ourselves to sleep.

It did us no harm. If anything, it toughened us up, and nobody in farming then expected any other way of life.

Haymaking in the summer in the river meadows was usually my job, with hot, sweaty horses and flies that ate you to pieces. If I felt a bit tired of it all I would give up and go to sleep. I was well known for this as I was a lazy little devil and once, during our Hartpury days, I was missing for hours. Everyone thought I had met with a dreadful end but I was discovered by Dad in one of the old disused carts in the cartshed, fast asleep.

When I was quite young I spent every Saturday with Grandfather Biddlecombe, who was a keen shot. I took along my 0.410 shotgun and Grandfather had an old hammer gun which he gave to me in later years. He was a great character. As I remember him, he had white hair, receding a little, and he had about three chins beneath his round face. Grandfather Biddlecombe did not resemble Dad in the least, who has small, neat features, but one thing he did pass on to him was a wicked twinkle in the eye.

Grandfather could be a hard man at times and was known to have a bit of a temper. He drank very little, perhaps a couple of sherries, and he rolled his own cigarettes.

We were walking round the farm on one of these shooting mornings when Grandfather spotted a rabbit squatting in the hedge. He handed me his hammer gun and said, 'Here, have a go with this,' and stood back about 200 yards whilst I took aim. When I pulled the trigger, the recoil nearly knocked me backwards, but I killed the rabbit. It was these memorable little adventures which instilled in me a lasting love of shooting, a sport which has given me tremendous enjoyment all my life.

When Grandfather Biddlecombe retired from Hartpury and sold up, he and Grannie bought a long caravan which enabled them to visit friends and relatives in different parts of the country.

As well as loving his shooting, Grandfather was a keen fisherman and for part of the year the caravan would rest at Beer, near Lyme Regis, where he would enjoy some quiet sea fishing.

He was a man who could turn his hand to anything, an ability which Dad has inherited, and he could tie his own flies or make his own hooks with ease.

When the fishing came to an end, he would move on to stay with my Uncle Jack, who lived close to the Quantocks and had a slaughter-house. Whenever I could, I would go down there and follow the staghounds in the Land-Rover. Grandfather Biddlecombe would take me back to the kennels to meet the old huntsman and drink rough cider, which was powerful stuff. Nevertheless, it loosened the hunts-man's tongue and I would sit there for hours listening to his stories.

Like all kids we looked forward to Christmas. We had a huge lunch on Christmas Day and then another enormous spread in the evening when all the relations joined us. Sometimes there were forty people in the house.

When our grandparents died, the numbers at these Christmas gatherings dwindled, but as it has always been 'open house' at home, the festive season still ends up with the farmhouse teeming with family and friends.

From Hartpury School, Tony and I had moved to King's School in

Gloucester, where Dad had also been a pupil. Academically I was unwilling to learn. Where sport was concerned, I liked football until I missed an open goal. Gymnastics were not too bad until I dropped somebody over the 'horse' and he broke his arm. This put me off completely, and I suspect that it did the same for my victim. I tried swimming, running and cricket, all to no avail, and it was not until years afterwards that I came to appreciate top-class athletics and to love cricket at any standard of play.

Tony left school at the age of sixteen, and I was to do the same. During our school days, as soon as the evenings were light enough we would come home, change and mount up to practise for the summer's gymkhanas. We had some brilliant ponies; Flyaway, a bright bay mare, who stood about 14.1 hands high. Then there was Twinkle, a nearly black pony with a white star, who was not much over 13.2, and Spot, Sue's pony, a much smaller bay with a little white mark no bigger than a cigarette end just below one ear. Flyaway was our star performer and she won over 3000 rosettes for us. When she died at the grand age of thirty-nine we buried her close to the gateway which leads to Lower House Farm.

I revelled in the gymkhanas early on and we were almost unbeatable on our day. Tony was very good. He had that bit more experience than I had but Dad, in his heyday, would walk all over us. Neither of us was in his class when it came to jumping up on a pony, vaulting on at the canter — his speed in everything was incredible, whether it was wriggling under a blanket or getting an apple out of a bucket, and I never saw him beaten at that. He was magic to watch. He competed well into his late fifties and kept a lot of good, keen children on their toes when other men would have been sitting by the fire in carpet slippers. In the musical chairs events, if Dad was in contention with any girls at the critical moment he nearly always gave in to them, and Mother used to go spare. She came to all the shows with us, bringing with her picnic lunches which would have fed an army. We travelled miles every summer and presented quite a formidable team at gymkhanas all over Wales and the West Country. Those were sunny days, full of fun, and we had this terrific will to win.

We also took part in show jumping classes. Dad had some good horses over the years, among them Johnny, who was supposed to be unrideable and cost £17 10s., Billy Budd and Sky Rocket, a horse that Dad had originally sold to Mrs Prue Johnson for show jumping. After Prue's tragic death in a riding accident when exercising a point-to-pointer, Sky Rocket came back to us and Tony had a lot of success with him. He was a very bold jumper and his most glorious hour came at Monmouth Show in 1954. Tony, riding with an injured leg and his foot in a sandal as he was unable to wear a boot, jumped off against Colonel Harry Llewellyn and Foxhunter, who, two years before, had helped to win the only gold medal for Great Britain in the Helsinki Olympics. After three clear rounds apiece, they divided the prize. Tony was fifteen years old at the time and I, the proud onlooker, was twelve.

My best effort was being placed third on Reg Humphries' skewbald pony, Chez Nous, in the Juvenile Open Class at the Three Counties Show. There is little doubt that these youthful experiences helped Tony and me in our racing careers by sharpening our reactions and enabling us to adapt ourselves to individual horses more quickly, perhaps, than some of our fellow jockeys.

In the meantime, I attended one rally held by our local Pony Club and was told by the instructress to adjust my leathers and alter my seat. I politely told her that Dad had taught me to ride in this way and left, never to return. Later I adapted my style to suit myself and I maintain that everybody does this, whether they are a Biddlecombe or a Piggott.

Soon after that disastrous Pony Club rally I became sick and tired of horses. I was almost twelve years old, and felt a bit pressured into schooling and practising for shows. I did not like hard work too much. One day I went to Evesham Show with Dad and Tony, but instead of remaining on the show ground I hired a boat and went for a row up the Avon where, eventually, Dad discovered me. I can see him now, shouting at me from the bank to come and help with the horses. I was in trouble as it was, because I was rowing over the fishermen's lines and making them mad. I stayed on the river for about two hours and Dad was furious. We drove home in our old lorry with its corrugated iron cladding and I was made to go without my usual fish and chips on the way.

During this relatively short period of 'going off' horses I trailed round a few gymkhanas with Dad and Tony. One of these was Middlezoy Show which was held near to where Dad was born. They had staged a little flapping race there. Flapping races are flat races not recognized by the Jockey Club, which take place on established courses with professional and amateur riders competing against each other. It was pouring with rain and a stranger came up to me and offered me a chance ride on a 14.2 pony. I went back to Dad and asked him if I could ride in this race and he said, 'Help yourself, boy.'

I took off my shirt and rode in a pair of old trousers and tennis shoes – and won. It was one of the greatest thrills I have ever had. Afterwards I said to Dad, 'I would like to be a jockey,' to which he replied, 'Maybe you will, one day.'

My father's interest in racing meant that he often took me to Hereford races where we used to go on the course. On one of these outings Michael Scudamore was riding a close finish on the rails and he nearly sliced off my head with his whip. I remember telling Dad that I now had a hero to follow. Michael was a fine horseman of the old school and a member of one of the best-known families in Herefordshire. He was taught to ride by another great horseman, the late Harry Wigmore, who, incidentally, introduced Dad to the excitements of horse dealing. Little did I know then how much Michael was to help me in my racing career and what great times we were to have together later on.

After my success at Middlezoy, my interest in horses was revived and I began to enjoy the gymkhanas again. The greatest triumph which was shared by Tony and me was winning the Ponies of Britain Championship which was held initially at Ascot and later at Peterborough. This championship was awarded to the rider gaining the most points in gymkhana events over three days. Tony won it for two years in succession then, riding in a hurdle race at Wincanton, he slipped up on a bend, broke his leg and was in hospital for a long time. I won the championship for the third year and Tony recovered in time to win the following year. Had it not been for the change of rider we would have won it outright.

Although Dad was an enthusiastic man to hounds, I did not enjoy hunting on small ponies and it was not until I graduated to horses that I came to appreciate hunting properly, although I was thrilled to come third in our local hunter trials on one of Dad's ponies.

At that time Dad had a six-year-old mare called Ascension. Originally she had been trained by Fred Rimell and was sold as 'useless' after she had run through the wing of a fence with Tim Molony at Towcester.

She was a bright chestnut and a rather frightening ride as she stood well off from her hurdles and jumped very flat. She needed hard ground to produce her best form and you could never carry a whip with her. She was one of the fastest mares jumping hurdles that I have ever ridden. She went very well for Dad and he knew her every mood.

I walked the course with him at Hereford one day before he was due to ride the mare and he said to me, 'That's the hurdle I'll fall at – the second last,' and that is exactly what happened.

Ascension had a tremendous turn of foot for about 200 yards. Before that, you had to drop her out and wait on her until the last hurdle and come with one challenge. I had ridden her at home, but watching Dad and Tony win on her at our local racecourses such as Hereford, Worcester, and Wincanton, made me realize that my true ambition was to ride winners over fences.

By the time I had my first ride on a racecourse, Tony had already made his mark as an amateur jockey. He was Champion Amateur National Hunt Jockey in the 1961–62 season with thirty winners and rode not only for Dad but for Major Rushton, Rice-Stringer and many others, before turning professional and becoming first jockey to Ken Oliver at Hawick. Nevertheless, it was the generosity of the local farmers and small permit holders who, in giving us our early rides on their horses, helped both of us to enter the world of racing. I know that Tony will agree with me when I say that without that help and the support we received from the family, we would never have enjoyed the successes that were to come our way.

2

From Amateur to Professional

Once I had decided that I wanted to make a career in racing I was encouraged not only by Dad and my grandfathers but also by a local smallholder, Mr Russell. He was connected with the pony racing at Hawthorn Hill and he gave me a great deal of advice and confidence.

I longed to ride on a racecourse, and the chance to do so, at the age of sixteen, was given to me by Jack Green, whose farm adjoined our own. He had a grey mare called Balkan Flower. She would not walk a step but jogged incessantly. She could gallop and jump, though, and I was invited to ride her in the Beginners' Hurdle over 2 miles at Hereford on 23 February 1957.

I was very excited at the prospect and it was a great occasion for everybody concerned. When we arrived at the racecourse, Dad took me into the weighing room and introduced me to 'Old' Joe Ballinger, who was to be my valet that day. Later, his son 'Young' Joe was my valet for a while, but when he emigrated to Canada his father took over and remained as my valet until I retired from racing. Old Joe was a marvellous man and especially kind to young jockeys. His death in 1980 was a great blow to the many jockeys who had been in his care, and a deeply personal one to me.

The orders that day at Hereford were to go down the outside and keep out of everybody's way. I rode with my stirrup leathers far too long. I managed to complete the course a long way behind the winner, Ken Mullins riding Southbury, and my cousin, Peter Jones, who was third on Pearl White. My racing career had begun.

I next rode Balkan Flower at Worcester on 25 March 1957, unplaced behind my cousin, who won the race, and at Chepstow on 30 March over the longer distance of $2\frac{1}{2}$ miles, again out of contention. On 11 April I rode her in the Leamington Amateur Handicap Hurdle at Stratford. We jumped off and when I rode at the first hurdle, there were the owners and my father frantically waving their handkerchiefs to make sure that I did not run out! With their assistance, or despite it, I managed to complete the course, but was way down the field. I rode Balkan Flower in seven races in 1957. I was gaining more experience of racecourses and race riding but I had not come within a yard of winning.

In between my racecourse appearances and schooling horses at home, I was riding gallops on Burnella, a bay mare belonging to a good friend of the Biddlecombe family, Frank Smith, who lived at nearby Norton Court. These schooling gallops were often attended by a small gathering of interested locals and one day, whilst schooling Burnella with my father and one or two others, I jumped a hurdle and one of my leathers broke. I nearly fell off, but managed to keep my balance and went on to win my first little race at home. This really set me alight, but Burnella was Tony's ride and it never crossed my mind that I would ever ride her on a racecourse.

In the early part of the 1957–58 season on 28 September, I rode Salverino for Mr Russell at Hereford and then I had four rides on Brascos, a horse trained by Tony Winders near Worcester, who also encouraged aspiring young jockeys. I was unplaced in all of these races but, again, they afforded me valuable experience. In addition I was now riding against Dad and Tony which made me even more determined to win.

The day that Tony was to ride Ascension in the Thrown In Handicap Hurdle at Wincanton on 6 February 1958 was like any other race day. Dad drove the box, Mother brought the food and I led the mare up. I will never forget that race. We saw Ascension slip up on the far bend and get to her feet again to continue riderless round the course. We managed to catch her and Dad said anxiously, 'Where's Tony? Is he all right?'

'I don't know,' I said, 'I can't see him from here.'

'Quick, take that bloody saddle off,' Dad said – and he rarely swore unless he was upset.

'Where are you going?' I asked him.

'I'm going to find Tony,' was all he said, and he vaulted onto the mare bareback and galloped flat out across Wincanton racecourse. I have never seen such a feat before or since and the warmth of family concern that pervaded that moment is something I will always hold dear.

Dad reached Tony, who was lying against the rails with his leg bent sickeningly beneath him, long before any ambulance man could get to the scene. Tony's leg had suffered a nasty break and it took a long time to mend. The specialists who looked after him in the Forbes Fraser Hospital in Bath told him that he would have to have the leg operated on and reset when he was older. He was on traction for three months and my parents visited him every day.

With a long convalescence ahead of him, Tony was unable to ride for almost ten months, and it was in these unhappy circumstances that I was offered the ride on Burnella in the Farnham Novices' Hurdle over $2\frac{1}{2}$ miles at Wincanton on 6 March 1958.

I jumped at the chance.

When I arrived at Wincanton I walked into the paddock and cast my eyes over Burnella. She was scruffy, with a long coat, and I thought she would look better pulling a milk float. This was uncharitable of me because I knew she was fit, and you should never judge a horse on its looks. Although this was her first appearance on a racecourse, everybody connected with her was confident that she would run well and stay the distance. There were eighteen runners in the race. We went to post, came under orders and were off.

Burnella was lacking experience with other horses and was off the bridle almost immediately. As we came to the first hurdle she refused, then walked nervously through a gap. I was now a hurdle behind the other runners. The second hurdle was half-flattened and she managed to scramble over this from a trot. The third hurdle was also flat but she jumped what remained of it and began to gain ground. As she did so she steadily passed tired horses and gradually worked her way into fourth place as we turned into the straight.

It was then that I had this wonderful feeling that is so difficult to define unless you have experienced it – the sudden realization that you are going to win. It is a positive, heady exhilaration that never leaves you and once it is in your bloodstream you are thoroughly addicted to racing.

Jumping the last I was starting to fly and set about riding Burnella with all my strength. What my style was like I will never know, but approaching the last hurdle I was gaining on the leader. We cleared it and landed about a length behind him. I could see the winning post and hear the murmur of the crowd gather to a roar as I urged the mare forward to pass the post level with the other horse. It was a very tight finish and I could not tell whether or not I had pushed Burnella's nose in front. As we pulled up I glanced across at my rival and saw that it was Fred Winter. At that time I did not know what his form was, but I did know that he was a highly respected jockey.

Flushed with excitement, I said, 'Mr Winter, do you think I could have won?'

'How the bloody hell should I know?' he retorted, and trotted off towards the unsaddling enclosure just as the winning number was given out over the loudspeaker. I glanced down at my number cloth and realized that *I* had won. I could not believe it. Riding alongside Fred Winter and oblivious to his grim expression I said, 'I've won, I've won!'

But he only gave me a cold look and never once said, 'Well done.' At that moment I could not have cared less. At seventeen years of age I had won my first race on a 20–1 outsider and beaten the champion jockey by a head.

Everybody connected with Burnella had pulled off a tremendous coup, having backed her at a very long price, but I have never discovered just how much money was won. I do know that a lot of money was lost on Piper, the mount of Fred Winter, which had started favourite at 7–4 on.

Throughout the jubilation that followed, with members of both families crowding round and everyone absolutely thrilled to bits, I knew that all I wanted was to be a jockey and relive again and again that glorious moment of winning.

On the way home in the car we were all talking endlessly about the race when we had a puncture. It happened right on a bend and provided one of the funniest endings to a day that I can remember, with everyone a little bit tiddly and struggling to remove the wheel. It was an unforgettable occasion.

I was to ride Burnella to win a few more races before she contracted strangles and died, which was tragic.

On 22 March 1958, just over a fortnight after my first winning ride under rules, I won the Long Distance Handicap Hurdle at Chepstow on Ascension, this time beating my cousin Peter who was riding Pearl White. On 7 April I won with Ascension again at Hereford, beating Verneuil II, a horse that I was to be associated with in the future.

My tactics on Burnella, accidental though they were, taught me more about race riding than any other race I have ever ridden. I felt that you could lose ground at the start and take it easy instead of jumping out of the gate and going flat out over the first three hurdles. If you are sitting quietly at the back you have only two or three lengths to make up between the second last hurdle and the finish. I used to ride Ascension in this way because it was the *only* way to ride her if you were to win the race. I was to be criticized many times in my career for this policy, but I would still try to get my horse relaxed, drop him in quietly at the back of the field and fly at the finish. Until then, he had really done nothing except keep in touch, and I knew that more often than not I would win by holding my attack in reserve.

As I became more experienced I made the running in some races, but my preference over hurdles was to come with a run at the second last, or just before it. Over fences one had to race and be up there to keep out of trouble, and tactics then were very different, but I will always be thankful for those early experiences on Burnella and Ascension. They were to give me my formula for winning races over hurdles from small tracks to Cheltenham.

On 24 April 1958, towards the end of that season, I rode Wild Honey at Ludlow for Alan Mailes, a butcher from Hereford. He was a great supporter of the Biddlecombe boys and usually had a few horses in training with Dick Price at Hay-on-Wye. Whenever I went to horse sales with Dad we would pop into Alan Mailes' shop and he would give us several pounds of sausages, or chops and a couple of steaks. Little did he know that he was helping to ruin my weight for life!

Wild Honey was one of the best little hurdle race horses of his day. He was by Owen Tudor and very fast, with a high head carriage. He was an immaculate jumper and you could never put him wrong at a fence. He would stand off, pop, do anything. He was like Ascension, in that you had to wait with him and come with a long run. He, too, would not race if you carried a whip and you had to throw the reins at his ears and growl – he loved it. During his long career on the racecourse – he was still going when well into his seventeenth year – he was trained by Reg Hollinshead, Jack Yeomans, my father, Geoff Scudamore, Dick Price and Frenchie Nicholson.

When Michael Scudamore was sixteen he rode his first winner on Wild Honey at Chepstow in 1949 soon after his father had bought him from Frenchie Nicholson who had had the horse in training for Lord Sefton. When we had this horse at home we would put him in the barn where he would buck and squeal around. He had a fantastic trick. If you gave him an orange he would peel it very neatly and eat it, just like a human. He was a great character and a wonderful schoolmaster.

I was to win a number of races on Wild Honey and was grateful to Alan Mailes for the opportunities he gave me, not only with this horse but with others, such as Judge d'Or, which he owned in partnership with the late Stan Rees of Cwmbran. Stan Rees and his wife were enthusiastic racegoers and came everywhere with us when we were racing in those early days.

It was at this stage of my life that I came to know Michael Scudamore really well. We had known of each other for many years but he was older than I was and established as a top National Hunt jockey when I was still a struggling amateur. We lived not too far apart and used to travel together to race meetings. He would either pick me up, or Tony would take me to Ledbury to meet him en route.

Michael was retained by Frank Cundell at that time and he put me in for several rides, notably Blackheath, a big, dark brown horse on which I won a couple of long-distance hurdle races.

I remember going with Michael, Paddy Cowley, Rex Hamey and Johnny Lehane to Southwell, and after racing we set off for home. I had arranged for Tony to meet me at Ledbury at about 8 o'clock. We stopped at Chesswood Grange to have a little dinner and I said to Michael, 'I mustn't be late, I've got to meet Tony.'

'Don't worry,' he said, 'we'll be there.'

The four wise men had their gins and tonics and I had never had anything stronger than a 'Cherry B' in my life. They advised me to have a gin and orange, which I did, quickly followed by another. It was sweet and tasted superb but the effect of those two drinks sent me flying outside into the bushes where I was violently sick under a fir tree. Gathering myself together, I strode back into the bar and announced, 'That was great, let's have another,' adding smugly, 'My Dad doesn't know that I drink.'

My companions were in stitches.

Eventually we arrived in Ledbury and there was Tony, fast asleep in the car. It was well past 11 o'clock and one can only say that he was very understanding.

One evening after racing at Folkestone, Michael, Johnny Lehane and I called in at a small pub near Tewkesbury just before closing time to have a quick drink and a natter. Johnny kept insisting that Green Drill, a good horse, trained by Major Bewicke, which had come third in the 1958 Grand National, was the best jumper I had ever ridden. I said that it was not, because I had never ridden it. After a while,

Johnny, who could lose his temper after a few drinks, became worked up, so I picked up the car keys from the table and walked out. Mike and Johnny chased after me and I pretended to throw the keys over some iron gates nearby before walking off, saying, 'If you want the keys you had better go and fetch them.'

They both clambered over the gates and searched around in the dusk for the keys which were in my pocket all the time. Meanwhile, I walked into Tewkesbury, telephoned Tony, who kindly collected me, and went home. At 3.30 in the morning I rang Michael up and said, 'You got home then?' and he hung up on me he was so cross. Then he rang back, laughing, and said that I was of doubtful parentage. Apparently, he and Johnny had had to get a taxi home and it was a long time before Johnny really forgave me.

In the spring of 1959 I had my first and only ride in a point-to-point. W. Silvester offered me the ride at the Croome and West Warwickshire Hunt fixture on his horse Merry Courier. I was thrilled to be asked to ride and duly turned up at the course at nearby Upton-on-Severn in new breeches and boots for the occasion. I thought I looked great compared with the other 'Indians' in the race with their old baggy breeches and everything else falling apart. The race was murderous. I went round on this superb jumper and everybody kept coming and knocking hell out of me – just because I was poking my way up the inside. I banged my knees, and was nearly brought down twice – it was quite a rough ride. I dead-heated with Roger Guilding on Black Andrew II and the judge's decision did not go down very well as Roger felt sure he had won. Give me a steeplechase with professional jockeys riding in it any time.

The October meeting at Cheltenham brought tragedy. Dad had purchased a lovely French-bred grey thoroughbred called Or Massif from Trevor Jenks for show jumping. Originally trained by Ryan Price, this little horse showed such talent over hurdles that he was given to me to race and it was decided that I should ride him in the Hawling Hurdle on 14 October 1959.

In the race he ran very well but when we were going past the water jump I heard an almighty crack. I did not think much of it at the time but suddenly he felt strange under me as he ran to the last. He crumpled up on landing and when I got to my feet I saw that he had shattered a foreleg. The horse was down and I took the saddle off. The vet was there almost immediately and, as I walked away with my saddle, I heard the sharp snap of the bullet and knew my horse was dead. I was heartbroken. As I grew older I became more resigned to this sort of thing, but whenever a horse I have ridden has had to be destroyed it has crucified me. I have never felt that it was one of those things in racing and that it did not matter. It is one of the sad aspects of racing that every jockey has to face in his own way.

As I had ridden Blackheath successfully over hurdles for Frank Cundell, Michael Scudamore secured the ride for me on Aliform in the Rosy Brook Chase at Newbury on 22 October 1959. Aliform was owned by A. Summers, who also owned Blackheath, and for whom I was to ride a number of winners.

My first steeplechase was a nerve-racking affair to say the least. I went into the weighing room feeling scared to death. 'Young' Joe Ballinger sensed my nervousness and said, 'You'll be all right – you'll win.'

I said something like 'Don't be bloody silly,' but he was right. I kept Aliform well behind the rest until the second last when he just sailed on to win easily by six lengths. I was both relieved and overjoyed when I rode into the winner's enclosure with another 'first', this time over fences. I never lost those pre-race feelings in the whole of my career as a jockey. I was frightened, for want of a better word, until I was actually on the horse, when all apprehension left me and all I wanted to do was to make a good job of riding my race. I always wanted to win, and win well, and this, I feel sure, is what spurred me on above all else.

I have been sentimental about the majority of horses I have ridden. I can honestly say that I have disliked only about five horses – and they disliked me. But you cannot dislike animals that have given you so many thrills, and spills, over the years. Horses have taken me into all walks of life and, being a farmer's son, I never imagined when I was a boy that I was to get as much pleasure as I did through being associated with them, or to meet such a cross-section of people.

In my early racing days, I took any rides that were offered to me, which meant that I had to ride all sorts of horses. Bad, big, green animals that had been poorly schooled or maybe hated the job. They taught me more, I suppose, than the good horses. They showed me how to get out of mistakes and when trainers sometimes said to me, 'This horse can jump big houses,' I used to reply warily, 'Never mind about the big houses – can he jump hurdles?'

Nine times out of ten I would get orders in the paddock, never having seen the horse before. I would listen to the orders, but I hope it does not sound arrogant when I say that I could usually weigh up the horse by walking him round the paddock and cantering to the starting gate. This would tell me more than any owner or trainer could possibly know on the day.

Each horse has been an individual to me – it has had to be. Some are knowledgeable, some are dreadfully ignorant, which could be the result of rough breaking in or some incident which has scarred a horse's mind somewhere in his life. From the tension in a horse I could tell immediately whether he was in love with racing or not. Michael Scudamore used to say that no horse is a 'rogue' unless there is something hurting him. I tend to agree with this. Naturally, you come across some bad horses, but one could have a headache, another could have a stomach ache, or a bad leg. An intelligent horse with a suspect leg will try to save it by changing legs and hanging badly. This gives him a poor name in the eyes of the racing public which is wrong. He is not a 'rogue', but in having the sense to know that there is something wrong with him he does not turn in his best performance – a jockey knows this, and trainers find out afterwards, but the punters frequently write off such a horse as a 'non-trier'.

I learned not to be too brave. Every young jockey has to take what rides he can when he is starting and needs to be noticed by the press if he is to get others. As I became more successful I was offered better horses and could then avoid the bad ones, but I never underrated the experience I gained from riding them.

The 1959–60 season provided me with a number of good rides for a young amateur. Major Geoffrey Champneys, of Upper Lambourn, whose horses were fit but fat, was a gifted trainer and he offered me some decent horses to ride such as Valiant Spark, my first ride at Aintree, and Domaru, a nice horse by Domaha. He was a very quick jumper, owned by Dick Bazell, who became a friend of mine, not only when I rode his other horse, Riversdale, but also when I became really enthusiastic about my shooting. Dick and I had met at a shooting party organized by Stewart Tory at his home in Dorset, and we were to be comrades in arms at many other such parties, especially during the foot and mouth epidemic when racing came to a halt.

That season I also rode Young Hinds, Birinkiana and Balkan Catch for Bill Wilesmith, of Powick, near Worcester, who offered rides to both Tony and me for a number of years.

When I rode Birinkiana in the Yuletide Novices' Hurdle at Birmingham on 14 December 1959, I was just behind Jimmy Lindley on a chestnut gelding called Mosterton, who slipped up approaching the first and half-refused before scrambling over the hurdle. I jumped past him and finished way down the field. Afterwards, a frustrated Jimmy Lindley flung himself into the weighing room, having had an awful time on Mosterton, who had propped before every hurdle before climbing over the final obstacle to finish last.

Jimmy was a fine rider over hurdles, winning some thirty-six races, many of them on the flamboyant Retour de Flamme, on which he came third in the 1958 Champion Hurdle. Whilst still a jump jockey, he rode a few flat horses for 'Towzer' Gosden at Lewes, notably Aggressor, which he rode to win the King George VI and Queen Elizabeth Stakes at Ascot in 1960 for Sir Harold Wernher, beating the Aga Khan's flying filly, Petite Etoile.

After sampling the flat racing scene, Jimmy eventually decided to stick to it and he joined Jeremy Tree in 1961 to ride many Classic winners. When he retired from racing to become a television commentator for the BBC I had nothing but admiration for the way in which he refused to be moulded into anybody other than himself. For my own part, his enthusiastic, distinctive style reflects both his knowledge and love of horses and horse racing.

He and I have remained friends over the years. We used to shoot together and occasionally, when I went to Newbury in later years I would stop off at Jimmy's home and use his private sauna box. He was a smashing fellow to me and after I had been in there for about an hour and a half he would come in with a glass of champagne. Sometimes I shared Jimmy's sauna with other flat-race jockeys, such as Joe Mercer and 'Flapper' Yates, and we had some good times.

On 21 November I rode Blonde Warrior at Doncaster in the Badsworth Chase for David Machin, who trained near Lincoln. He was an excellent trainer and had a pet badger which used to run alongside him in the woods when he was riding out and then come in the house at night and sit down, just like a dog.

Blonde Warrior was a dark bay horse with a terrific jump in him and at Doncaster that day he unseated me. I managed to remount and take third place, but this was in my younger days when I instinctively remounted. As I grew older and more experienced I found that it was better to push myself as far away from a falling horse as possible and curl up until everything else had gone on ahead. There were occasions when I remounted and finished a race, but they were very few.

After riding Balkan Catch to win at Chepstow on 12 December and scoring on Domaru at Wincanton five days later, I was booked to ride Rough Night for Frenchie Nicholson at Wolverhampton on Boxing Day in a 3-mile chase in which we started favourite. Johnny Lehane was riding Prince Seppal for Fred Rimell and this horse was a notorious front runner. He set up one hell of a gallop and Rough Night just could not lie up with him. Turning into the straight I must have been a fence and a half behind when the old horse suddenly started to run with me, just as he always did when David Nicholson rode him. At the finish I was beaten by two lengths. The stewards held an inquiry and they had Frenchie Nicholson and myself called before them. They said to Frenchie, 'Nicholson, are you satisfied with Biddlecombe's riding?'

To my astonishment he replied, 'No.'

I was only a kid and I had not done anything wrong. I could not have done more. The horse made up his own mind when he wanted to go and that was it. I was severely cautioned for 'riding an injudicious race' and I was stunned. After that incident I never called Frenchie Nicholson 'Guv'nor' or 'Sir' again, just 'Frenchie', to indicate my lack of respect. I had had my first taste of being wronged and this was something I was to hate for the rest of my career.

I was really getting into my stride from the outset of 1960. On New Year's Day I rode Rue Raspail for David Machin to win at Manchester. Why that man did not train more winners I will never know because he was such a good trainer and certainly knew his horses. He was hardworking, straightforward and charming, but he was not the sort of man to seek out owners. I think that he just ticked along with a few very good horses which won when he said they would. Rue Raspail was one of them.

Through Dave Machin I met Leslie Little, a man whose family had owned a fleet of about eight trawlers at Grimsby. Knowing that I was keen on shooting, he frequently asked me to stay with him to shoot duck and sometimes Tony came with me. He became a friend of the family and we used to call him our 'fish punter'. Every Friday or Saturday he would telephone us, telling us that there was a box of fish waiting for us at Gloucester Station, and that if there was anything running that day would we kindly put a couple of quid on it! He was a kindly man who often came to shoot with me at Upleadon. We were saddened when he died, and the Purdey gun which I have now I bought from him for next to nothing.

I rode my first double ever on 30 January at Warwick where in the Dunsmore Chase I rode The Sapling for Reg Hayward. Reg was a local farmer who trained trotting horses. He always turned out The Sapling to perfection and ran him in an enormous white sheepskin noseband. This horse was a very hard puller and was usually Tony's ride because he could hold him. When I won on him at Warwick, he ran away with me but he went from fence to fence without touching a twig. I followed this blood-stirring ride with a win on Birinkiana, beating Tony in the process!

Bill Ransom, another Lincolnshire trainer, gave me my first ride for him on Not a Link, which I rode into second place at Doncaster on 6 February in a hunter chase, and I snatched first place from my brother again with him on 23 February at Birmingham. Blackheath had put on one of his spectacular displays of hurdling to win at Newbury on 10 February and my last win as an amateur was at Warwick on 27 February 1960, riding Clear Profit, trained by the late Lance Newton. This strapping horse gave me a fantastic ride, one of the best I have ever had in a 3½-mile steeplechase.

I was thoroughly enjoying myself, riding not only horses that I knew well but unfamiliar ones that were winning races for me and, as an amateur riding against professionals, I was becoming a little conspicuous. The press had drawn attention to my activities and the Jockey Club had been following my progress closely.

At the end of February 1960, I was asked to attend a meeting of the National Hunt Stewards in London. I did so and was courteously reminded of the fact that I was taking quite a few rides and therefore depriving professional jockeys of their income.

I had already discussed the possibility of turning professional with Dad and he felt that it was time I made up my mind. Racing was already my whole life and I therefore advised Messrs Weatherby that I intended to take out a professional licence. It was a decision I have never once regretted.

3
Not All Glamour

Now that I was a professional jockey I became totally dedicated to my job. I knew that I had to go out and make my own life and my own living. My parents, who had done so much to help me and taken me to different tracks all over the country when I was an amateur, were no longer responsible for me, although I always had their full support. When I told Dad that I was joining the professional ranks he said, 'Well, you're on your own now, and the best of luck.' That was it.

My rate of pay when I first turned professional was £7 10s. a ride, with no percentage of the prize money. Generous owners would give cash or presents of some kind if I rode a winner for them, and a successful jockey at that time could make a good living. Out of my income I paid £1 to my valet, plus his expenses. Added to that was my own expense of getting to racecourses and at the beginning of my career I had about £5 clear per ride.

This improved over the years and today jockeys receive £36 per ride, plus a percentage of the prize money, and a valet's fee is around £4 for each ride he services.

Trainers then, as now, were responsible for the colours, but your valet would take your saddle, boots, and breeches and have them clean, ready for racing the next day. Every jockey had to supply his own saddles, girths and other equipment. The saddles I owned would fit any horse and varied in weight from 1 to 12 pounds. I also carried a sheepskin wither pad and a full-sized numnah, plus a weightcloth, which I often did not require.

It was a great feeling to be a professional jockey. I wanted to be more than a good jockey – I needed to achieve something outstanding, and my ambition then was to be champion National Hunt jockey. Making my own mistakes taught me a lot, but I sought advice from older, more experienced jockeys like Michael Scudamore, Tim Brookshaw, Dennis Dillon and Johnny Gilbert.

Johnny was a brilliant hurdle race jockey. He and Dennis would walk round the track before racing, marking the best going with little lollipop sticks. They also walked the track before racing, pushing hurdles down from the take-off side with their feet. This was not illegal and did not alter the height of the obstacle but it did save a lot of falls because when hurdles are first driven in they are a bit stiff. If you got too close to them there was the danger of turning over. I have sometimes 'loosened' hurdles, but never bothered with the lollipop sticks!

The professional jockeys of my day were a fantastic bunch. They were helpful, good fun, gave no quarter and were terrific men to be associated with both on and off the course. Early on I watched the tactics of the older brigade, Michael, Tim Brookshaw and Paddy Broderick; they were good, tough jockeys who sat deep in the saddle and asked their horses to stand well off from their fences, but they got results.

Then there was Stan Mellor, who was in a category all by himself, a superb all-round horseman and jockey and always a danger in any race. Jimmy Uttley was much the same as Johnny Gilbert over hurdles, always up there and very stylish. Pat Taaffe was brilliant in the country and I never saw him ride a bad horse. Riding for Tom Dreaper, he rode big, strong, well-bred horses, usually of Gold Cup standard and they would carry him round. If I had to make one criticism of Pat it would be his finishing ability from the last fence to the winning post – he was an 'Indian'. In jockeys' parlance this means that a rider lets his horse's head go and throws the reins at its ears; he looks as if he should have a spear in his right hand; he sits in the back of the saddle and bumps up and down as though he had no stirrups. In other words, stick a feather in his cap and you have almost got the picture.

I have often compared Pat to Tommy Carberry in this respect, but they both rode hundreds of winners and that is what counts.

When riding styles changed, jockeys such as Johnny Haine and David Mould emerged and Haine, in particular, was beautiful to watch. They represented a new breed of jockey which was stylish over both hurdles and fences.

Josh Gifford was a horseman in his own right. He had everything: style, ability, judgement and sheer guts. I am not one to pick holes in any of these men because my own style was, from the outset, condemned by many of the experts. Although I was tall, I rode comparatively short and people would question this. I maintained, and still do, that if a horse is balanced and going forward for you there is no need to kick him in the belly. If you can get your own balance right and keep your hands down – hands are the most important thing of all, combined with balance and rhythm – if you can get all these together, then nothing else matters. I used to poke my toes down a bit but riding that much shorter enabled me literally to kneel on my horses which freed any weight from their loins and so distributed it over their forehand. I loved to ride on a lightweight saddle when I could feel the muscles of a horse moving under me and I could just squeeze him with my knees and send him forward. I developed a habit of kicking with my right leg only, which was an idiosyncrasy I shared with Peter Pickford, and I never flopped around in the saddle if I could help it. I would lie up on a horse's neck rather than bump around on his back. I soon learned that in order to win races one had to be strong in the body, gentle but firm in the hands, and have a good sense of rhythm. A quick reaction was essential. To be able to slip your reins in mid air and pick them up again before landing only comes with experience, falls – practice! I used to give horses all the freedom I could when they were about to fall, slipping them a lot of rein when they made a mistake because I could almost hear them say, 'Oh, give me a bit of rein, let me get my legs out, please,' and, unless they had blundered really badly or could not see where they were going, they would often manage to find a leg and stand up. It did not always work that way, but there were many times when it did.

My first winner as a professional was Blonde Warrior in the Otby Handicap Chase at Market Rasen on 5 March 1960. It was a pleasure to ride again for Dave Machin, and Blonde Warrior was to beat some good horses in his time.

After the Cheltenham meeting that spring, when I finished second on Birinkiana in the Gloucestershire Hurdle on 9 March, I was faced with the tingling prospect of riding at my first Liverpool fixture. Major Champneys had booked me to ride Valiant Spark in the Topham Chase on 24 March; I was to ride Birinkiana in the Coronation Hurdle the following day and, in the Grand National afterwards, my partner was Aliform.

I fell at Becher's with Valiant Spark. He failed to get out his landing gear and that was that. I have only fallen at that fence twice in my life and on this occasion I was in another world, never having ridden over the Aintree course before.

In the Coronation Hurdle I drove Birinkiana with great determination to come third to Fred Winter on Davy Crockett. As I came back into the weighing room I met Willie Stephenson at the entrance.

'Biddlecombe,' he said, 'I've been watching you – come back here when you're weighed in, I want a word with you.'

He had noticed something which I thought nobody else could have known except me. Halfway up the run in I went to give my horse a belt and missed him. My arm went over the top of his quarters and this screwed me round so far in the saddle that I nearly fell off.

Willie was waiting for me when I came out of the weighing room.

'Go home, sit in a chair, backwards, and try pulling your whip through,' he suggested.

'What do you mean?' I asked him.

'You missed your horse just now, didn't you?' he demanded, in his high-pitched voice.

'No – yes, I did, sir,' I mumbled.

'You just do as I tell you,' squeaked Willie.

I never did try his method, and I never could pull my whip through, but I respected his advice. He was a sharp man and I was to ride several winners for him.

Years after I had retired from racing, and Sir Harry Llewellyn was hunting regularly with the Ledbury, he and I were riding alongside at the back of the field, trotting along the road near Pendock, where hounds had been checked short of the motorway. We had stopped for a quick port and were chatting together when he said to me, 'The trouble with you young professional jockeys is that you don't know how to pull your whips through, turn them in your hand and change them to the other side – as I was taught to do by our stud groom who came from Newmarket.'

Sir Harry started to demonstrate what he meant, but he had thick hunting gloves on and his whip flew out of his hands and landed on the road. I jumped off, collected his whip, and handed it to him trying to keep a straight face.

'Here you are, Sir Harry,' I said. 'I'm afraid I wouldn't have time to do this for you in a race.' He had to smile.

It is difficult to define my feelings before my first Grand National. The only person who had told me anything about Liverpool was Michael Scudamore. He had a great record in the National in which he rode for sixteen consecutive years, finishing second in 1952 on Legal Joy, third on Irish Lizard in 1954 and winning on Oxo in 1959.

I remember that the night before the 1960 race we had a light dinner; then everybody else went out and I was the little boy who was left alone in the hotel. I lay in bed, half-asleep, thinking about what I was going to do in the race – as I was to do before other Grand Nationals. I was there, going to the last with no chance, wishing that the horses in front would all fall and I would win the race! Then, I'd been brought down and remounted, and at that point in my fantasies even to have been second would have been great. These things raced through my mind all night, and I woke up in the morning feeling ghastly.

The routine that followed was fairly predictable with all the ensuing Grand Nationals in which I rode. Schooling on the track in the early morning at Liverpool has never ceased to exhilarate me. Even in my later days when I had no ride in the race I would go and watch the horses work. There is a bit of dew on the grass; the stands are empty; the air is fresh and clean and there are very few people around.

After schooling I would nip into the weighing room to see what weight I was and then knew how much breakfast I could have or, better still, drink half a bottle of champagne in the baths while shedding a few pounds. Most of us stayed at Southport, especially those who were wasting, and after breakfast we would go into the Turkish baths where we would fool around a bit, pretending to argue as to who was to buy the first bottle. This helped everyone to forget the bad dreams of the night before. There would be at least ten or twelve jockeys in there who really had to get the weight off. If you did not have to lose any yourself, you still went in to help the others and share the champagne.

There was one little steam room at Southport about as big as an old-fashioned wooden-seated lavatory, with a whistling draught coming in under the door which made your feet cold and stopped you sweating. In my day, we had an old masseur who never stopped running and bustling about like a busy old lady, pushing bowls of hot water under the door for you to put your feet into and thereby keeping your body temperature high.

When you went from the steam room into the hot room it always seemed that you were not losing weight as the perspiration dried on your skin as soon as it appeared. This sometimes made you panic and go for a swim, only to find that your body had re-absorbed water, so it was back to the hot room again.

The masseur would go out at about 9.30 in the morning and bring back some champagne or fresh orange juice, which refreshed everybody. Then we would all have to leave by 11 o'clock because we had to check out of our hotels before noon on the morning of the National. These sweating sessions were enormous fun, talking, laughing and generally relaxing before the big race.

After leaving the baths we would go to the course and into the weighing room. I usually rode in a hurdle race before the National as a warm-up. Michael Scudamore disapproved of this because he felt that the risk of injury before the big race was too great.

Then came the National itself. The weighing room was so quiet. There were no jokes then, and the only character in my day who could be lighthearted was Johnny Lehane, and I suspect that he had had a few more brandies than the rest of us. It was impossible to get into the lavatory because it was full of jockeys. I have never seen so many trying to have a last 'go' – if you had held a tablespoon under them they could not have filled it. The weighing room was filled with tension. Some jockeys would light a cigarette, just before being called out, and then immediately extinguish it. Others did not speak. Lord Sefton would come in and deliver a little speech, asking us to go steadily at the first. I suppose we took a bit of notice, especially in later years after the great pile-up of 1967. When you walked out into the paddock and got a leg up it was suddenly like any other race. There was the thrill of the parade, going to post, and lining up, trying to edge into your chosen plaace, but I think I speak for everyone when I say that my own thoughts then were only that I had a job to do. There were tens of thousands of people watching but, apart from hoping that they had put their money in the right place, I used to go out and enjoy myself.

My first ride in the National on Aliform was very exciting. I had just turned professional, I was riding an old favourite and he jumped those Liverpool fences perfectly. I asked Michael Scudamore how to recognize Becher's Brook and he said, 'When you come to the straw path, keep kicking.' I crossed the straw path the first time round and

Aliform cleared Becher's like a bird. It was a great feeling. Before this, just to make sure that I knew where the fence was, I had asked 'Taffy' Jenkins during the race to tell me when we were approaching it. We had just crossed the straw path at the time and his reply was, 'It's the fence after this one.' 'This one' was Becher's itself and as we landed I shouted at him, 'We've just jumped it, you fool!' Taffy never knew where Becher's was and he was the one man who should as he had worn out more pairs of boots walking back from it than most of us.

The second time round my horse was tiring. I started kicking after crossing the famous straw path, but he landed on his head at Becher's and my first Grand National was over. As I lay on the grass, slightly winded and feeling a bit choked at falling, who should be there but Scudamore, who had fallen at the fence the first time round and had waited there to watch me. He gave me an almighty kick in the ribs and said, 'Come on, get up, you're not hurt.'

I could have murdered him.

I was to get my own back later on at Newton Abbot when he fell at the last fence on a horse called Archavon. I was the spectator then and seized my chance. I gave Michael a kick which he has since said was harder than any horse could have dealt him and said, 'Get up, you silly bugger, you are all right,' and he had to laugh.

It was one of my chief delights when we were racing together to know that if he had fallen in front of me he would be curled up waiting for the rest of the field to pass, and if I happened to be the last to jump the fence, which was often the case, I could shout at him as I sailed overhead, 'It's all right, Scu, you can get up now!' which used to infuriate him.

He once told me that he never minded me winning 'cleverly' but that when I did so and got up by a head or a neck and turned round to grin at him, he longed to ram his whip down my throat!

Michael was a sincere friend to me all the time we were racing and has remained so since. We used to argue like hell in the car. He would criticize my tactics, and tell me that I tended to lie out of my ground. I would defend my every action, but a lot of common sense came out of these heated exchanges.

When we went any distance to meetings we found some excuse to stay in London. It was something I have always done since, but I swear that I learned the habit from Michael.

It was he who introduced me to Wheeler's fish bar, and Jules Restaurant, places beloved by wasting jockeys in particular because of their proximity to the Turkish baths in Jermyn Street. It was great to stop off there on our way home from meetings like Wye, Plumpton or Lingfield, especially if one of us had had a winner. There would probably be three or four of us on the train, playing cards on the way to racing and again on the way back to London. After a good meal we would roll out and catch the train home. Time and again we overshot the station at Gloucester and ended up at Cheltenham.

My height of 5 feet 11 inches with a frame to match meant that I put on weight easily and, from the beginning, I had a problem where this was concerned as I had a splendid appetite. When I started racing, I would often join Michael in the Turkish baths at Gloucester, and these almost became my second home. When I became a regular visitor there, often five mornings a week, the staff were so good to me that they virtually gave me a 'season ticket'.

After a cup of tea, I would get to the baths at 7 o'clock in the morning. They were usually deserted but the steam would be ready so I would switch it on and then weigh myself. I could lose up to 6 or 7 pounds in a couple of hours – sometimes more, moving from the steam room to the hot rooms, ending with a quick dive into the cold plunge pool, which was exhilarating.

At about half past nine, Bill, the manager, or his assistant, John, would come in and ask me if I wanted anything. I would ask for 'the usual', which consisted of a Worthington 'E' and a port and Babycham. I would pour out exactly half of the beer before going back into the baths and going through the same routine, then I would come out and finish the beer. A quick shower, wash and change – I could change in about two minutes flat – into the car and off to the races. Once in the car I would sip my port and Babycham which made me feel great. I never stopped to dry myself and, in all the years I kept up this routine, I never had a cold as a result.

If I was still a few pounds too heavy, I resorted to diuretics or 'pee pills' which removed still more moisture from my body, and if that failed, then I took a strong dose of laxative. Later on, I took appetite suppressants, and had a daily injection of vitamins B and C, which was the equivalent of 7 pounds of liver.

I tried special diets and low-calorie programmes but I used to get so depressed that I preferred the rigours of wasting. The only fortification I had after the session at the baths would be a quick 'livener' on the way to the races – if I had a companion with me – but it was not until the evening that I could enjoy a good meal. This usually put back all the weight I had struggled to lose at the start of the day but dedicated starvation would have been unbearable.

If I had not stuck rigidly to my routine at the baths I would never have been able to carry on riding. I imposed this discipline on myself and, if I was stopping overnight anywhere, I knew exactly who I was staying with, where I could get some weight off and what parties, shooting or otherwise, might have been arranged, so that I could take these into account.

I was the only member of the family with a weight problem. Dad and Tony remained at under 10 stone without difficulty and I found it doubly hard to keep my weight at a constant 11 stone, which sometimes had to come down to 10 stone 7 pounds or under.

Christmastime was murder. Nobody understood what I was going through and Mother, with the best of intentions, would encourage me to eat. Most Christmas Days I spent in my own sweat box, a contraption which Dave Dick had sold to me for £25 and which I installed in the cellar at home. Dave was with Bryan Marshall at the time and I drove down to Newbury to collect the box and met Bryan in the yard.

'I've come to collect Dave's sweat box,' I told him.

'What do you mean, Dave's sweat box?' demanded Bryan, 'it's my sweat box, but you can have the damned thing anyway.'

I brought the box home and, come to think of it, I never did get my money back from Dave.

Dave Dick was one of the most amusing men in racing and even now I only have to meet him to start laughing. He was one of those individuals who are almost larger than life; very masculine, courageous and capable, but always game for a boyish prank. He was more of Fred Winter's era than my own and yet for the few years that I rode with him, and the experiences I shared with him at parties, on holidays and other various occasions, I can only describe him as hilarious.

Tall, with dark, swept-back hair and a swarthy complexion, he rode successfully for the rich and eccentric Dorothy Paget when she had her horses with Fulke Walwyn.

I had seen this strange lady shortly before her death in 1960 and been astounded at her vast size. Her habit of dressing in dowdy coats and hats and her voracious appetite were well known, as was her dislike of men. She only seemed to respect those who showed no fear of her and Dave Dick was one of them. He won the Cheltenham Gold Cup on her Mont Tremblant in 1952, among other good races, and when he broke his leg on a protruding rail at Cheltenham later that year, Dorothy Paget not only sent him quantities of gourmet food but also played a vital part in obtaining compensation for his injury from the Cheltenham executives.

Dave taught me a lot and I say that advisedly. He was a fine jockey and an outrageous teller of unrepeatable stories during a race, and these were usually against himself. He was full of energy, wit and fun, and completely unpredictable. He came to stay with us once at Upleadon and I discovered that he was a compulsive picker of food. He loved to go into Mother's pantry and sample her pickled onions. When he was taking the physic 'Regulet', to lose weight, I have seen him eat about ten pickled onions at the same time. He also had a passion for elvers, of which Mother also kept a good supply, and I could never make him understand that baby eels could only be caught once a year, when the spring tides enabled them to swim up the rivers Severn and Wye.

The sweat box I 'bought' from him has quite a history. It originally belonged to Charlie Smirke, who passed it on to Bryan Marshall. Charlie was small and fitted into it easily, but both Bryan and I had to be careful getting in and out because the heat was generated by bare 150-watt bulbs with special bamboo filaments. I lost count of the number of times I burned my backside on them. I would sit in the box in a deckchair, wearing my customary sweatsuit, goggles and a pair of old suede shoes. Sometimes I would read for a bit but if it got too hot inside I could stick my head out of the lid in the roof and gulp down some fresh air. I had an old carpet on the floor to absorb some of the sweat and to say that this became a bit 'high' is an understatement.

I recall one Christmas in particular. I was shunning all company, and the sumptuous spread in the dining room, to sweat off the pounds for racing on Boxing Day. Johnny Lehane was staying with us and he kept coming down to the cellar to comfort me with a glass of champagne.

'Keep it coming,' I said 'it's great.' The sweat was pouring out of me. I had a little bowl in the box that I used to step into at intervals, pull the leg of my sweat suit away from my leg and let the water pour out. It was just like turning on a tap.

Johnny kept bringing the champagne, and I felt terrific. When I was ready to come out, Johnny fetched me some towels, I went upstairs to my room with my sweatsuit still on and passed out when the cold air hit me. Mother was absolutely furious and Johnny told me afterwards that I had drunk three bottles of champagne in about three hours. Dad never found out about this and certainly would not have approved as he neither drank nor smoked.

As well as Gloucester baths and my own little box at home, I should think that I have been in every Turkish bath in the United Kingdom. There have been some funny incidents in these rather unusual surroundings and I was to meet some colourful characters there over the years.

During the spring of 1960, I was going by train to London to try the Savoy Baths in Jermyn Street. I was sitting in the railway carriage, minding my own business, with my saddles and other equipment in the rack above me, when a smooth-talking Jewish gentleman who was sitting opposite struck up a conversation. I had never set eyes on him before and, when he introduced himself to me, I was still none the wiser. He was, I discovered subsequently, a well-known punter who, like many others, took an interest in young jockeys who showed promise. He asked me where I was going and I told him I was heading for London and the Turkish baths. He offered to take me there and added, 'If you ever want any money put on, just tell me and I'll put it on for you.'

I was frightened of the man but tried not to show it.

'I don't bet – and I haven't much money anyway,' I told him, and he said, 'Well, if you lose it doesn't matter. If you like, I will get you a ride at Ludlow.'

He was so confident and disarming that I was half inclined to believe everything he said. I had come from a farming background, not a racing stable, and knew nothing of punters and the way they operated. I was relieved when we parted company outside the baths and thought little more about it until he asked me to ride at Ludlow. He had secured the ride for me and I came third.

I rode the same horse several times afterwards but was not to win on him. I was no richer but I was a little wiser after my first encounter with a professional punter whose motives were not entirely honourable.

There was an occasion in my amateur days when I was asked to ride a horse at Stratford. The trainer came up to me in the paddock and said, 'We're not trying today.'

'Oh, aren't we?' I answered, angry inside, and won the race easily. I was not popular but I could not have cared less.

Professional punters and crooked bookmakers who try to corrupt young jockeys who are keen for rides and therefore vulnerable have always sickened me. It is so easy to be led astray by men much older and more worldly than you are in a game like racing, where so much money is involved.

I was once in a London club, soon after I had turned professional, and a well-dressed, respectable – or so I thought – man came up to me and asked me if I would ride a horse at Wye for his friend. Eager for fresh rides I agreed, and then he said he would pay me £500 to stop it. I went to the races scared and worried. I had mentioned this proposition to Mother and she was horrified. Dad had always said, 'Never stop a horse, Terry,' and his words kept running through my brain.

In the paddock I said to the trainer, 'I'm afraid I can't stop this horse – I can't do it,' and he replied, 'We thought you'd change your mind, so we've stopped him for you.'

So, having turned down £500 I went to the first fence and the horse felt blind drunk under me. He crashed through it; I picked him up, sent him on again and he refused at the next. The amazing thing was that although the horse started odds-on favourite there was no inquiry and no dope test afterwards.

But that was the best thing I ever did in my life. I can honestly say that I have never in my career stopped a horse for money. I may have given a green or unfit animal an easy race, and I pulled one out at the gate because it was lame, but that is a very different matter.

Ironically, I was asked later to stop a horse at Leicester and although I was trying like hell on him, I was beaten by a short head. When I dismounted the owner handed me a racecard.

'You were brilliant,' he said to me, 'please take this racecard.'

'But I don't need a racecard, sir,' I answered.

'Take it,' he insisted.

I took it and, in the relative privacy of the weighing room opened it to find £75 in notes tucked inside. And I had tried to win! I always tried to win. For me, racing was all about winning, and yet to this day that owner will think that I am a 'bent' jockey and that by coming second as he had wished, I would be prepared to do the same for other owners.

On the other hand, there is no denying the fact that most jockeys have friends who like to back horses and who will ask them if a horse is likely to win. Jockeys are often regarded as bad tipsters, but if one of my horses was successful and I had indicated to anyone that I thought it had a good chance, I was often sent boxes of fruit, or as in the case of Leslie Little, crates of fish, or some such commodity. Most trainers behave in exactly the same way, and I have never understood why jockeys are condemned for supplying casual information when trainers get away scot-free. The supplying of information and gambling coups are part and parcel of racing. Without it, there would be no racing, and none of its uncertainties. What I absolutely abhor is the truly unscrupulous individual who will persuade a jockey to stop a horse or deliberately not win a race, for financial reward. That to me is criminal, and any jockey worth his metal will have nothing to do with such a person, however tempting the offer may be.

At Ludlow I also rode Little Corporal for Dick Price of Clyro. This was a hard-pulling little bay and we were odds-on favourite in a novice chase. Paddy Cowley was on my outside on The Pylons and as we went round past the stands towards the sixth fence, my horse cocked his jaw and tried to run out.

'Keep him in, keep him in!' yelled Paddy.

'I can't,' I shouted back, and carried Paddy and The Pylons out across the tarmac road that ran by the track and onto the adjoining golf course. Somehow we managed to swing back onto the racecourse and rejoin the other horses in time to jump the correct fence and then rode a desperate race to dead-heat for second place.

Two days later, I rode Little Corporal to win at Bangor-on-Dee and finished the season with another win for Dick Price at Hereford, riding Eaton Belle.

That autumn I had my first ride for Jack and Percy King who were wonderful owners and loved to gamble. They were in farming and did quite a bit of cattle dealing. They were also fond of their shooting and when I rode more winners for them later they gave me many invitations to their shooting parties.

Baldachino was a horse belonging to them and trained under permit by Tim Hamey, and I rode him in a selling hurdle at Cheltenham on 13 October 1960, which he was not expected to win. There were seven runners in the race and coming round the last bend I was upsides Michael Scudamore with my horse pulling like a train.

'What do I do?' I asked him. 'I'm not off the bridle.'

'If you stop that you'll be warned off for bloody life,' Mike replied, and I went on to win by ten lengths, not trying. I was not popular again, but I had remained true to my convictions. If a horse wanted to go on and win I never disappointed him, whatever my orders before the race might have been.

The first ever contact I had with Fred Rimell was when I was about seventeen years old. I had a message asking me to telephone him as soon as possible. I tried to ring him from home but the telephone was out of order so I tore down the road to the public telephone box and dialled the Kinnersley number.

Fred Rimell asked me if I would ride Tokoroa for him on the flat. I accepted, and walked on air for days. To be asked to ride by one of the most famous trainers in the country was something every young jockey dreamed about, and it had happened to me. I was soon brought down to earth by another telephone call from Fred Rimell, telling me that the horse was injured and unable to run, and apologizing for the loss of the ride.

After the initial disappointment I forgot all about it. Then, on 26 November 1960, I rode for him for the first time on Joe Tustin's chestnut gelding Red Ember at Warwick, in a 2-mile handicap chase with a 10-pound penalty, and finished a poor third. Joe Tustin, who lived at Upton-on-Severn, had several good horses in training with Fred Rimell, most of them carrying the 'Joe's' prefix, and he remained loyal to me all the time I was riding. Red Ember was to be my first winner for Joe Tustin when I rode him at Worcester on 15 November 1961 in the Kippax Handicap Chase.

One of those people who absolutely make racing for me, he was fair to his jockeys but not wildly so. I will never forget the day Bobby Beasley rode two winners for him and Joe Tustin, characteristically, gave him some potatoes and a chicken, together with some cherries which, he told Bobby, would cost him half a crown!

I went to Market Rasen on 26 December to ride another Rimell horse, Flame Royal, which should have won the selling hurdle but pulled up lame.

My inauspicious start with Fred Rimell's horses was compensated by an easy win in a novice chase at the Market Rasen meeting that December on the Tim Molony-trained Condor. Tim was a congenial man. I remember riding with him at Stratford in a novice chase when I was a young amateur. Michael was in the same race and he said to me, 'You go upsides Tim, and I'll be on the other side of you,' because he knew my horse was a chancy jumper. At the first fence I made a mistake and was falling off when a hand reached from nowhere, grabbed me, put me back in the saddle and a voice said, 'Hey up, matey – you nearly went there!'

It was Tim Molony. He was one of the iron men of racing, a great champion, and never too big to give advice.

The first time I had laid eyes on Josh Gifford was at Hurst Park on 18 December 1959, when he fell at the last fence in the Christmas Rose Hurdle with Scarron, trained by Ryan Price and a stable companion to the winner, Cortland, ridden by Fred Winter. Josh broke his collarbone in that fall and broke it again within about a fortnight. I remember him coming back into the weighing room after it had happened, laughing it off and telling everyone not to worry about him. I thought to myself then, 'Well, this is a good, brave sort of guy,' and I was right. Everybody in racing had been talking about this boy, Gifford, who had served his time with Sam Armstrong and was reputed to be one of the best apprentices to come out of Newmarket.

Although I rode against him for some time, it was not until he had trounced me in 'Biddlecombe country', when riding Red Alley to victory at Hereford in November 1961, that I came to know Josh really well. There was a small party in the weighing room after racing and it was then that we realized that we were somewhat birds of a feather. We have been firm friends ever since and, during our racing days, were almost inseparable. Josh stayed with us many times at Upleadon, particularly over the Cheltenham Festival Meeting, an arrangement which has lasted for over twenty years.

Just as Josh was one of the family at Upleadon, I was treated the same whenever I went to stay with his parents in Huntingdon. It was home from home really, and I thought the world of his parents who are no longer alive.

Mrs Dinah Gifford made the most fantastic jugged hare, which Josh, his brother Macer and I loved. Tom Gifford was a star man too, and I can see him now sitting by the fire, with his old dog on his lap, sipping a little gin and winking at Josh, urging him to have a drop. When Josh's uncle died, the farm was left to him and Macer and it was Macer who took over the farming side of things, riding as a very good amateur, whilst Josh pursued his career as a jockey and trainer. Their sister, Sue, married a very nice chap, Don, who used to play football for the Peterborough first team. I always say that several good people came from Huntingdon – Joe Bugner, a footballer and a jockey – all first class.

When Josh moved to Findon to ride Ryan Price's jumpers, he lived first of all in what I can only describe as a converted deep litter house. I often called in to see him if I was racing at Plumpton or anywhere nearby. Josh's hut was about 200 yards from Ryan Price's place and while he was there 'Buck' Jones looked after Josh like a nanny-cum-nursemaid. I used to watch, amazed, as Buck carried on with the cooking and cleaning without question. He would wash Josh's underpants, which were always full of holes, as though he had been a laundrymaid all his life.

Buck's father, Davy Jones, had been a first-class lightweight on the Flat and had also won the 1945 Cheltenham Gold Cup on Lord Stalbridge's Red Rower.

Buck, too, was a good jockey and rode several winners for Ryan Price, including some owned by Lord Denning. Later, he bought some land near Findon and combined farming and training quite success-fully.

Paul Kelleway was another character down there who kept every-one in fits of laughter. He was an exceptional jockey and, like Eddie Harty, he shouted and roared in a race so that you could always tell who was coming alongside. He rode with a good length of stirrup and reminded me of a larger edition of Sir Gordon Richards in appearance. Although he was a great joker, Paul was a difficult man to beat.

Later on, Josh moved into a flat with some friends nearby, and I frequently stayed there. We had some very good times at Findon.

When Josh was riding for Ryan Price he met Joe Sullivan, a scrap merchant who had a horse in training with Ryan Price called Beaver II. Joe was a colourful character with an infectious laugh which, when he let it out, he too found so funny that he would roll about in tears. He was small and stocky, built like a tank, with short, strong legs, and arms to match. He was very muscular, with a round jolly face, black hair and eyes that danced with mischief. He would deal in anything and make a profit. Soon after I met him he bought a massive sea wall near Southampton harbour for rubble, and later on went to France to buy a dozen cranes. He had a scrapyard full of all sorts of strange things.

We went to a club in Worthing with him one night and in one of the downstairs lounges there was an aquarium full of exotic fish. Joe nudged Josh and whispered in his ear and the next thing we saw was a 'French letter', smuggled from the cloakroom, full of water and tied at one end, floating among these spectacular fish. It absolutely intrigued them and they kept swimming up to this thing and 'pinging' at it with their noses.

I was now riding more horses for Fred Rimell to whom Stan Mellor was then first jockey. On 14 January 1961, at Birmingham, I rode Mrs Leonard Carver's Culleenhouse in a 2-mile novice chase and was up with Stan Mellor on Tokoroa when I made a mistake and finished third. Watching Stan riding Tokoroa over fences for the first time I noticed the horse's speed and ability to pull. Dave Dick had come second on him in the 1958 Champion Hurdle and Tokoroa stood off his fences a very long way indeed, as I was to find out for myself.

He gave me a thrilling ride at Hurst Park on 4 February, when he nearly pulled my arms out of their sockets, with Pat Taaffe on Mountcashel King beating me for first place on the run in.

In the meantime I had ridden my first winner for Fred Rimell when Voleur, a big, tough chestnut, also owned by Mrs Carver, won the Studley Novices' Hurdle at Warwick on 28 January. Mrs Carver, whose horse E.S.B. won the 1956 Grand National with Dave Dick after the Queen Mother's Devon Loch and Dick Francis had slipped up yards from the winning post, had several horses in training at Kinnersley, and I was fortunate enough to ride most of them.

I rode Culleenhouse again in a 3-mile novice chase at Sandown in February and was pushed under the iron rails by the stands by Peter Pickford on Galloping Green. I objected on the grounds of 'bumping and boring' and was awarded the race. In the heat of the moment I had been whip-happy on poor Culleenhouse. As he was a very thin-skinned horse, the marks showed up like fingers on his quarters. When I saw them I felt ashamed because I realized that I had been much too hard on the horse in my enthusiasm to win. The stewards did not question my riding but there was no doubt about it that I should have been fined for excessive use of the whip. I soon found that whipping unnecessarily lost more races than it won. After that incident I rarely set about a horse unless he was really idling. I might give him a reminder out in the country and then not again until I made my challenge when I would give him one down the shoulder before the second last. If he responded, I knew he would find some more if I hit him behind the saddle, and before the last I would maybe give him one going into it and one going away from the fence. Most of the time in finishes I would be going through the motions. I have always maintained that if a horse does not respond after two blows with the whip he won't produce any extra however much he is punished. Excessive whipping is a cruelty I have attacked many times since I retired from racing but, knowing that I have been guilty of it myself, I can in part understand the reasons for it.

Take the case of an Irish jockey who was hauled before the stewards and asked why he had hit a horse about.

'Jesus,' he replied despairingly, 'I'm in trouble now. I'm in trouble with the stewards, and if I'm not in trouble with the stewards I'm in trouble with my trainer, so what am I supposed to do? I'm sorry – I followed my trainer's orders.'

This is an impossible situation and there is another aspect to whipping which is understandable if not forgivable.

A lad has been in a stable for some time and he has looked after a horse for perhaps three years – mucked him out, ridden him out, strapped him down, taken him to the races and been livid when other jockeys have laid the whip on him because he thinks the world of that horse. Then, suddenly, he has a licence to ride, and he does exactly the same as the other jockeys. He wants to win a race. He does not want to hit his horse but knows that he will probably have to do so. It is a question of mixed emotions. Rather like beating your wife! Nevertheless, I still hold that if a horse will not go for two cracks he will never go for ten, and I have never condoned whipping for whipping's sake.

After a crashing fall at Plumpton on 13 February on H.T. Smith's Chinese Rose, when I damaged the point of my shoulder, I went to Market Rasen to ride Pandate for Lance Newton, who also owned the horse, in the Kilvington Handicap Hurdle on 4 March. I fell at the first and brought down one of David Machin's horses, Limsol, who trod on my shoulder, broke his leg and had to be destroyed. This was the first bad fall I had had and I was carted off to the ambulance room feeling shaken up and half dazed. Afterwards, I was taken to Market Rasen hospital where I lay in a corridor for what seemed like hours.

I felt dreadfully cold, could not move my shoulder and had no feeling in my hand.

It was warmer in the X-ray room, but I have an aversion to X-rays which is almost phobic. Whether it is the pain or the coldness of the plate against my skin I do not know, but I have always suffered from this and invariably pass out. After the X-rays had been taken I was put into a ward where I felt very alone and a long way from home.

After a while a lady doctor came in and told me that I would probably have to have my shoulder blade removed as, according to the X-rays, it was smashed to pieces and had actually pierced the skin.

I nearly died of shock! I refused to let anybody touch me and in the morning another doctor came to see me. He had also read the X-rays and he told me that although my shoulder blade was broken in three places the break in the skin had been caused by the tip of Limsol's shoe, or even his caulked heel. So they strapped the shoulder up and there was no more talk of an operation.

I felt a new man after that. When the night nurse came on duty I could not believe my eyes. She was blonde and very beautiful. I think we both fell in love because she was very attentive and when the ward was quiet she gave me a few cuddles to ease my pain.

While I was there I was visited by David Machin and also the Ireland family, for whom both Tony and I had ridden and, delightful people that they were, they took me all the way to Cheltenham races to meet up with my family as it was too far to expect my parents to collect me from Market Rasen.

My shoulder was straightened out by Bill Tucker in London, that brilliant rejuvenator of jockeys and, apart from wearing a sling to support it while it mended, I was soon fit to ride again.

It was on my first visit to the Park Street Clinic that I met Miss Jeannie Cooper. She was a first-rate physiotherapist who looked after me for several years before setting up her own private clinic near Sloane Street.

Jeannie, with her trim figure, and hair either drawn into a bun or a neat pony tail, was most professional and efficient, yet had time for a lark in that she would wire you up for a faradism, which sent electric charges through your body and energized your muscles, and ask you sweetly, 'Does this hurt?' When you answered, 'No,' she would turn the power up to its full strength and you would nearly go through the roof. In her time, Jeannie eased the aches and pains of several good jockeys, including Fred Winter, Dave Dick, Dick Francis and Michael

Scudamore. Henry Cooper was another of her clients. She was a cheerful person whom we all missed when she left to make her own career.

I have had the same family doctor looking after me since I was five years old and I do not know what I would have done without him.

Dr Bill Wilson had been a surgeon in Ireland and was on his way to London to carry on with this work when he heard of a position in the local practice at Staunton which was available for six months. The salary was good, he applied for the post, was accepted and, thank heaven, he never went to London.

Not only is he a close personal friend, but he is a brilliant doctor who has patched me up and kept me in the saddle when others in his profession would have written me off. He thoroughly understood my weight problem and helped me in every way possible to keep it under control, while at the same time allowing me to enjoy life.

I had such faith in him that rather than allow racecourse doctors to treat any of my injured associates, I would bring them home to see Doc Wilson, which sometimes drove him to distraction. Johnny Lehane broke some ribs in the Grand National one year and I locked him in his room on the Saturday night, thinking that he might get up to all sorts of things if I did not, before bringing him back on the Sunday morning to Doc Wilson's house. He found Johnny in a state of shock on the back seat of my car and when he got him to hospital they aspirated almost half a gallon of blood from his lung. Doc was rather severe with me over that!

I also brought Josh Gifford back to see him after he had been hurled into the rails at Wolverhampton and smashed his jaw. He had also torn his lip badly, and this had been hastily patched up before he left the racecourse. Doc Wilson took the plasters off his face and decided that the wound needed several stitches. Both Tony and I were there, egging Josh on to be brave and, to be fair, he let Doc stitch up the wound with no anaesthetic without flinching. Then Doc asked him if he had had an anti-tetanus injection. Josh said he had not, and with great bravado told Doc to shoot the serum into his arm. When Doc produced the hypodermic Josh took one look at it and passed out cold!

I frequently asked Doc Wilson to go racing with me, not only for the pleasure of his company and his delightful sense of humour, but also because he too loved racing. He enjoyed going all over the country and exploring. I would get him in free of charge at race meetings, telling the powers that be that he was riding in the next race. It was always nice to have him with me and he looks after my well-being to this day.

The injury I had sustained at Market Rasen had happened dangerously close to the Liverpool meeting where Fred Rimell had again asked me to ride Tokoroa in the Mildmay Chase, and I was also to ride Kingstel for Major J. 'Ginger' Dennistoun in the Grand National.

In order to prove that I was fit enough to ride at Liverpool I had to put in an appearance on a racecourse beforehand and I had three unsuccessful rides at Uttoxeter on 18 March, just fourteen days after my fall at Market Rasen.

I adored riding at Liverpool, and I was leading jockey there for many years. The fences were different, although in the Mildmay Chase in those days they were relatively easy except for the second which was one of the original Grand National fences.

Tokoroa, as I have said, was a tremendous puller and a bold jumper – in short a hair-raising but exciting ride; the kind of horse that if you were successful on him would bring you to the notice of the racing public.

There were eight runners in the Mildmay Chase on 24 March 1961 and before we went to post Fred Rimell said to me. 'Do what you can, try and settle him and don't go too fast.'

Going to the first fence there was no way that I was going to hold this horse. I tried to settle him and dropped him in nicely in about fifth place, but he soared over the fence to land in second place. Having seen daylight, he stormed towards the next which loomed larger and larger as we approached it. I saw a good stride, but Tokoroa had seen an even bigger one before that and took off so far away from the fence that he landed in the bottom of it, turned over and broke his neck. I was knocked unconscious and came to in the ambulance room with my head pounding and pain beginning to jab in my wrist.

There was a marvellous Irish doctor at Liverpool then who took great care of all of us and often gave us a little nip of brandy which was against the rules, but most welcome. He was worried about my concussion and I had not told him about the pain in my wrist. After a lie down, I went into the weighing room and my wrist was really hurting. I ran the cold tap in the washroom and held my hand under it, trying to ease the swelling. I was still concussed and stood there, hardly aware of what I was doing, when in came Josh Gifford.

He gave me a swift look and said, 'Are you all right?'

'Yes, thanks,' I said, 'but I've hurt my wrist a bit.'

'Let's have a look,' Josh said, then, 'Christ – you've broken the bloody thing!'

'No, it's all right – and anyway, I've got a ride in the National tomorrow,' I answered, peering at my wrist as I did so and seeing for the first time that it was bent right round and swelling by the second, with the feeling in my fingers nonexistent.

I do not know whether Josh reported me or not, but the upshot of it was that I was sent to Liverpool hospital where they put such a tight plaster on my wrist it was unbelievable. I had a thumping headache from the concussion and was glad to return home. On the morning of the National I was having my wrist reset and plastered by Bill Tucker. My horse, Kingstel, was ridden in the race by George Slack. He fell at Becher's the first time round but Fred Rimell won the race for the second time in his career with Nicolaus Silver, ridden by Bobby Beasley.

After that fall I was grounded until the second week in May, missing the Cheltenham spring meeting and also my ride at Wincanton in the Fonthill Novices' Hurdle on 20 April 1961 on Dad's horse, Mumbo Jumbo, a colt whose performance over hurdles had shown a steady improvement that season.

I gave Dad the leg up on Mumbo Jumbo and his orders.

'He'll stay,' I told him, 'best of luck,' and let him go.

I had £20 in cash in my pocket and, feeling certain our horse was going to win, I had the largest bet of my life and, as far as I can recall, the last, at 7–1. I then stood in the stands to watch the race.

At the second last Dad had gone clear, having ridden a lovely race, and as he jumped the last I was already counting my winnings when I saw Roy Davies on Kington Dome absolutely flying up the straight. Dad was standing in his stirrups, pulling up, with 'I've won' written all over his face when this horse flashed past him to get up by a short head.

I went to lead Dad back in and I was furious.

'What did you drop your hands for?' I raged at him. 'You should have won.'

He thought it was a huge joke, but that put me off betting for life. I have often lost money playing cards but betting on horses is not for me. Twenty poounds, then, was a lot of money.

At Towcester on 20 May I rode Free Agent to win a novice hurdle for Arthur Thomas who trained just outside Warwick. Arthur Thomas had two yards, one of which was used by Paddy Sleator's team whenever he sent class horses over to England for the big races. They were looked after by a very good head lad by the name of Jim Leigh, and Arthur Thomas trained these horses under licence for Paddy Sleator. He had some first-rate gallops there which consisted of hundreds of tons of sand from the local foundries.

Arthur was a large man with a little hat set on his bald head, rather like 'Kojak'. He manufactured porcelain lavatories and when people asked me what he did for a living I used to say, 'He makes bogs!' He was thrilled when I won on Free Agent because he used to bet quite heavily and when I rode in he said, 'Lester Piggott's got nothing on you,' which flattered me immensely.

I won for him again at Stratford on Intercede on 25 May and, just when I was thinking that winners were coming my way more easily, I rode Cacador's Lassie in the last race of the season at that meeting, the Latecomers' Hurdle, with both Dad and Tony in contention. There were fifteen runners in all and Stan Mellor won by four lengths on Jules Verne. Tony was second on Midanne, Dad was third on Pearl White and I was on the ground, nursing my pride after falling at the fourth.

Nevertheless, I ended the 1960–61 season with eighteen winners. I had ridden some fine horses for Fred Rimell, winning enough races to show him that I had the makings of a good jockey and losing even more which proved that I still had much to learn.

Having tested my potential and weighed this up in his mind, he asked me if I would ride as second jockey to Bobby Beasley the following season, with a retainer of £200. I was absolutely delighted and accepted his offer gladly. At the close of my first season as a professional, I had been asked to ride for one of the most successful National Hunt trainers in the country. It was a wonderful opportunity.

4

Second Jockey to Fred Rimell

I was to have nine enjoyable years with Fred and Mercy Rimell. I liked Fred's easy-going manner and, if we had a disagreement, which was rare, we would forget it within a couple of days.

Mercy Rimell impressed me with her strength of personality, her incredible knowledge of horses and form together with her ability to run the Kinnersley stables single-handed if need be. She rode out every morning and appeared at the breakfast table later looking as chic as a fashion model. I admired her for that, and it reflected her attention to detail in everything else.

Fred Rimell was a highly successful trainer. He had learned much of his skill from his father, Tom, who had sent Forbra out to win the 1932 Grand National ridden by Tim Hamey. Fred inherited the Kinnersley stables when Tom Rimell moved to Lambourn following the death of his wife. Although Fred Rimell was not lucky in the National as a rider, he was Champion National Hunt Jockey four times: in 1938–39, 1939–40, 1944–45, when he shared the title with Frenchie Nicholson, and again in 1945–46. His big race triumphs included winning the 1945 Champion Hurdle on Brains Trust, trained by his brother-in-law, Gerry Wilson, who was also champion from 1932 to 1938, and in 1940–41, and who will for ever be remembered for his partnership with Golden Miller. A couple of falls, in which Fred broke his neck on each occasion, compelled him to take up training, and he had sent out a stream of winners from the outset. Together, he and Mercy proved a formidable team in the world of National Hunt racing.

When I took up my appointment as second jockey at Kinnersley Fred Rimell had already headed the National Hunt trainers' table in

1950–51 and in 1960–61; he was, in my view, at his peak from this period onwards.

The routine at Kinnersley ran like clockwork. I would leave home once or twice a week and drive to the stables which were about eighteen miles away, set in lovely rolling countryside a few miles from Worcester. I arrived just before 8 o'clock as a rule, when the first lot of horses would be tacked up and ready for work. I rode work, schooled over a few hurdles and fences and then came home for breakfast.

In the early days I rode out the second lot as well, when I usually joined Fred and Mercy for a sherry afterwards, or maybe I would have a chat with the head lad, Ron Peachey. He was a fantastic man who had a special empathy with horses; he died in 1979 after some twenty-five years' service at Kinnersley. His wife, 'Mick', remained as secretary at the stables and ran the office with supreme efficiency. I never knew her to panic in any circumstances which, in a yard coping with up to fifty horses, can vary from minute to minute.

Then I would have a word with Jack Kidd, the travelling head lad, who rattled away at me in his thick Irish brogue, before I ended the morning by joining some of the lads for a drink in the local pub.

There was an excellent loose school at Kinnersley and on some schooling mornings we would put the young horses in there and send them round over poles about 2 feet high, jumping absolutely free. Then they would be asked to jump wicker hurdles, and I would watch each horse, noting how it would need to be ridden. One might be a bit free, another would indicate you needed to sit still on him, and yet another might require sending on. I would memorize these young horses and I learned a good deal about them by observing them in the loose school.

One rather warm day I was in the school with Fred and we had a novice in there which refused to jump round left-handed. He would go well enough in the other direction but he was definitely 'right-handed' and proving very difficult.

Fred had been given a huge bull whip which he used to crack – the horses were never hit – and I had a smaller whip, a 'Long Tom' which also cracked and sent the horses round. On this particular morning we were at different ends of the school, and the more this young horse resisted, the shorter Fred's temper became. Suddenly he gave his smart new whip a twirl which should have resulted in a crack like a pistol shot. Instead, the thong wrapped itself around Fred's ample body and he lay on the floor, moaning with pain.

We left the loose school on normal mornings and went to the schooling ground with maybe ten or twelve young horses and two lead horses to give them confidence. I would take the Land-Rover, jump a couple of horses over fences, then drive down to the hurdle track to school two or three horses there. This kept me quite fit, but I did not make a habit of doing it every day because there was the danger of becoming 'one of the family' and being expected to take on too much. I never undertook any part of the stable routine but just handed over my saddle and bridle when I had finished schooling.

By the same token, I never rode work on the gallops because I was rather too heavy, and I left this to the work jockeys. Sometimes I would go into the house for breakfast, which for me would consist of a cup of coffee, and the telephone would be ringing non-stop with calls from owners.

Fred loved his breakfast and, if I was wasting, it was agonizing to watch him load his plate with kippers, or eggs, kidneys, bacon – everything! We would use these breakfast times to discuss the previous day's racing, or the racing to come; this horse and that horse, and it was often quite fun. If I had ridden a bad race there would be silence, with Mercy looking severely at me over her glasses while I sat there agreeing with everything. I do not think that I ever argued at these breakfast sessions. I have always made it my policy not to disagree with employers. Dad said to me when I first went to Kinnersley, 'Never answer back, no matter how much anybody cusses you,' and this was sound advice.

We certainly had our ups and downs, but throughout those nine years together we built up a deep understanding. I rode some outstanding horses and Kinnersley was to provide me with some of the greatest moments of my racing life.

As second jockey to Bobby Beasley I was fortunate to be released to ride for other trainers if my services were not needed by Fred Rimell. In addition to riding for my previous trainers, such as Dick Price, Bill Wilesmith, Major Champneys and Arthur Thomas, I had my first ride for Edward Courage at Cheltenham on 11 October 1961. This was Noble Pierre, a big chestnut and a typical 'Courage' horse. He was beautifully bred and carefully schooled and he ran well for me in the Rodborough Hurdle to come second. To be asked to ride for Edward Courage was a great compliment and this was the first of many opportunities he was to offer me.

That autumn I rode one of the best long-distance horses I have ever encountered, called Nosey. He was owned by old Jack King and trained by George Todd at Manton. George Todd was a very good trainer of long-distance horses, both under Rules and on the Flat, and he had a distinguished collection of horses in his yard.

I rode Nosey for the first time in Birmingham on 13 November and he just trotted up in the Stoneleigh Hurdle. He galloped with his head held very low, but if you could settle him you just had to sit there. Nosey, Penharbour and Two Bucks were all brilliant long-distance hurdlers owned by Jack King and trained by George Todd.

Early in 1962 a truly superb horse by the name of Trelawny came to the Kinnersley stables. Owned by Mrs Carver, he was a lovely dark brown with a good shoulder, beautiful head and masses of scope. By Black Tarquin out of Indian Night, he was bred by the Astor Stud and bought from Mr J.J. Astor as a three-year-old. As a four-year-old he had won the Chester Cup and the Brown Jack Stakes before being sent to Fred Rimell to see how well he took to hurdle racing.

He had a gentle, relaxed temperament, but beneath his rather sleepy exterior rested a wealth of talent. In the loose school he too refused to jump left-handed, but he was a joy to watch.

I was given the ride on him in his first hurdle race at Warwick on 27 January 1962. He was a natural and never made an error. I gave him an easy race to come third to Derek Ancil on Eastern Harvest. After that, Bobby Beasley rode him to take second place in the Tudor Rose Hurdle at Hurst Park, the Gloucestershire Hurdle at Cheltenham and the Coronation Hurdle at Liverpool.

The following season he was sent to George Todd at Manton and he proceeded to win class races on the Flat. In total he won eleven of them, including the Goodwood Cup, and twice winning the Queen Alexandra Stakes and the Ascot Stakes. I was not to know when he left us that he would return to give me a taste of his true brilliance over hurdles.

My twenty-first birthday party at Staunton Village Hall was terrific. As if from nowhere, just about every friend I had turned up, and jockeys came from miles away. I had piles of presents. One of them, a gold signet ring, given to me by Fred's daughter, Scarlett, and Sarah Crump, I wear to this day. Sarah Crump, daughter of trainer Neville Crump, was my first real girlfriend and at that time she was gaining experience as a chef at Kinnersley. I remember that we had a whale of a time, with Johnny Lehane losing his false teeth halfway through the evening and crawling round the floor looking for them. The family certainly gave me a party to remember and the only nasty moment came when I nearly drove into a ditch as I was taking Sarah home afterwards.

It is well known that I have been very fond of the opposite sex from an early age. As a jockey, travelling round the various race tracks, I soon realized that, as in other sports, racing had its own band of admiring female followers.

I would be lying if I denied taking advantage of the pleasures offered to me. I indulged my rather passionate nature to the full, and loved every moment of it. Women have given me lots of enjoyment and laughter. A man has to be mad not to like them!

Following my successful run on Arthur Thomas' horses at Warwick, he asked me to ride Another Flash in the Blacknest Hurdle at Windsor on 3 February 1962. Bobby Beasley had ridden this horse to win the Champion Hurdle in 1960, trained by Paddy Sleator under the auspices of Arthur Thomas, and was placed on him in that race in 1962 and 1964. As first jockey to Fred Rimell, Bobby was engaged elsewhere, and I was his lucky deputy.

It was a condition race, with four runners, including Josh Gifford riding Most Unusual for Bill Ransom. We both had orders to wait until we went to the second last. So, as the gate went up, nobody wanted to make the running and we absolutely crawled. I was on this super horse and I remember pulling up my leathers and thinking how great it would be to beat Gifford so easily when, at the second hurdle, Another Flash landed through the top bar and smashed it to smithereens. I heard Josh laughing and then he made a mistake! We were both still upsides, hack cantering and not daring to move. Approaching the second last I was still waiting, and so was Josh; I thought, 'Well, somebody's got to go, for God's sake, but it isn't going to be me,' when suddenly Josh started his run. I went with him and I have never been so fast going into the last hurdle. We both picked up a mile off, landed together and I was still reluctant to move on my horse and so disrupt his rhythm. I just squeezed him and hoped as we went for the winning post. I had drawn clear by half a length and was sitting there trying to look pretty, when Josh came back at me on the line and we crossed it together. When the number went up, I had won by a head and Josh was outraged. Dad was there that day and he was not too pleased either.

'Don't you do that again,' he said to me afterwards. 'I nearly had a heart attack.'

Josh was responsible for Terra Nova being bought out of the Armstrong stable to be trained at Kinnersley. He was a sweet little horse by Tulyar and I do not think he would have measured 15 hands. Josh had told Fred that he was a stuffy individual who needed a lot of work and he was right. Terra Nova was very thick through the shoulder and a strong ride. He went well for me but I had to perch right on his withers and really work on him. He could never carry big weights but he could really fly. He was a smashing jumper but when you went to a hurdle the top bar would be about 6 inches above the top of his head which was a bit unnerving as he used to get very flat at the obstacle then squat and jump it like a hare. He never fell with me and won many races before being retired to stud as a successful pony stallion.

Having won with Two Bucks and Penharbour in the spring of 1962 for the Jack King and George Todd combination, I rode Nosey in the Birdlip Hurdle at Cheltenham on 14 March.

I went out of the paddock chatting to the travelling head lad. We had had quite a few winners together and I thought him a decent chap. George Todd had previously checked the girths which were elastic and rather ancient, and he said to me, 'Don't touch these when you get to post, they're all right.' It was a quirk of his that a horse might be over-girthed at the start by an inexperienced starter's assistant.

When I got to post, the assistant came up to me to check the girths and I said, 'Pull them up,' just to be on the safe side. He went to do so, but when he saw the name 'Todd' by the buckle he said, 'It's more than by life's worth to touch these – Mr Todd and his head lad are watching me from the stands.'

'Oh, all right then,' I said, 'leave the bloody things.'

I was carrying 12 stone 5 pounds on Nosey, who was second favourite, and he pulled hard going up the hill. Going down the hill he was only half settled in about eighth place. He was still pulling like hell and at the first hurdle down the hill he stood a long way off. As he landed, the saddle and weightcloth moved up on to his shoulders. The next hurdle came very quickly as I wrestled with the saddle, trying to push it back into place and by this time it was on Nosey's neck. I was upsides Joe Guest and I said to him, 'Hell, Joe, my saddle's going to bloody go.'

He had a look and agreed that I looked a bit perched up! At the next hurdle, Nosey stood way off again and once more the saddle moved. Again I said to Joe, 'This is going to go for sure.'

Galloping to the last two hurdles on the first circuit my saddle was almost in its correct place but I had passed one or two horses and Nosey had seen daylight. He began to pull for all he was worth and I turned to Joe and said, 'Don't take me on, please,' as by now the saddle was nearly by the horse's ears. Passing the winning post for the first time I said to Joe, resignedly, 'I'm going to have to pull up,' which is what I did past the stands.

When I came in I was sitting behind the saddle on the horse's quarters. I dismounted and was met by Wally, George Todd's travelling head lad.

'What's happened?' he asked

'You can see what's happened,' I retorted.

He took a good look at me and the horse.

'God!' he exclaimed, 'would you believe it!'

'Well,' I said, 'you told me not to touch the girths.'

'That's the Guv'nor,' Wally said.

We undid the girths, put the saddle in position and walked back into the unsaddling enclosure. Up strode George Todd in a blazing temper.

'What the bloody hell's happened here?' he demanded. 'Why did you pull that horse up?'

'The saddle slipped up his neck,' I replied. 'Couldn't you see, sir?'

'That saddle never moved,' he snapped.

'You ask Wally,' I countered, 'because he's just helped me to put the thing back – tell him, Wally.'

Wally said, 'No, sir, the saddle was all right.'

I just looked at him and walked away.

There was a Stewards' Inquiry. They had Todd and myself in and I told them what had happened but there was no need for they had seen it for themselves.

I found out afterwards that George had gambled heavily on Nosey and, to give him his due, he did telephone me that evening to apologize. Everything was all right between us after that.

I had a dream of a ride on Blonde Warrior in the 1962 Grand National. He jumped every fence with great fluency to finish twelfth behind the winner, Fred Winter riding Kilmore. After that performance I decided that Blonde Warrior would have made a first-class show jumper.

He confirmed my opinion of him when I rode him in the Molyneux Chase at Liverpool on 1 November 1962, when he went under by one and a half lengths to Pat Taaffe on Domacile, who was receiving nearly 2 stone.

I was unplaced on Lizawake in the Watney Mann 'Red Barrel' Chase at Market Rasen on 12 May, but he deserves a mention. This big, long, almost black horse was trained by Pat Moore at Newmarket and had won over hurdles and fences when ridden by his owner, George Hartigan, and ran in the 1964 and 1965 Grand Nationals. Lizawake was then sold to Mrs Mary Marshall and Tom Brake show jumped this horse for her from 1965. Later she gave Lizawake to Tom and he went from strength to strength.

I have known Tom Brake for years, through both his show jumping and racing activities. He owned several racehorses and had been a good point-to-point rider in earlier years. Lizawake had an enormous jump in him and was to clear 7 feet 3 inches at the John Player High Jump Championship at Nottingham in 1971. I knew what a tremendous feel this horse had given me way back in 1962 and it was a standing joke between Tom and myself that I had taught this super horse to jump for him!

Little Terra Nova rounded off my first season as second jockey at Kinnersley with a spanking win at Hereford on 11 June 1962. I felt that I had the world at my feet.

5
Honour Bound

Fred Rimell liked to start the National Hunt season early on in those days but later he changed his policy, possibly because he did not have so many horses in the yard that preferred the top of the ground. In late summer the going on some of the West Country courses could be rock hard.

When we went to these meetings we either stayed at Salcombe or at a little guest house at Newton Abbot which we called 'The Warren' because it was a maze of passages and small rooms. Sometimes up to fifteen of us would stay overnight and the proprietors fed us well and were very tolerant of our all-night card games.

One night we awoke to cries of 'Fire! fire!' Smoke was billowing out from beneath Johnny Lehane's bedroom door. He had thrown a smouldering cigarette end into his wastepaper basket which was blazing merrily while he slept. Luckily, one of us was making love not many rooms away and smelt something burning. If everyone had been asleep that night, upwards of a dozen jockeys could have been incinerated in a short time.

We were usually up to some pranks when we went to Salcombe. I was dared to climb to the top of the flagpole of the hotel where we were staying and, having had a few jars, I set off up to the top. It was raining hard and coming down I started to slip, finally sliding from top to bottom at great speed. I bruised certain parts of my anatomy and could well have broken my neck.

My first winner for Edward Courage was Little Oracle which won the Potterspury Chase at Towcester on 27 October 1962. This was a spare ride for me. I loved wearing the Courage colours – yellow and maroon halved – and to win with them was a bonus. There was always a lot of 'paper talk' about the Courage horses which, in my early days, centred around his great chasing mare, Tiberetta. Edward Courage was a charming man, and his horses were trained, under his supervision, by his excellent head lad, whom I always knew as 'Morgan'.

At the end of my riding career, Edward Courage gave me his game mare, Lira, with a foal at foot by Precipice Wood.

Tony and I both rode for Fred Rimell in the Ansell's Brewery Chase at Worcester on 3 November 1962. I was to ride Icanopit and Tony was asked to ride Lady Lyons' horse, Jungle Beach.

Fred took us to one side before the race.

'Now then', he said, 'don't stick up each other's backsides, will you? Keep well clear.'

Tony was on the outside and I was somewhere in the middle of the field, nowhere near him and certainly not behind him, when he fell left-handed in front of me. I could not get out of the way and bang – we were both on the floor. We got to our feet and glared across to see who was at fault, only to burst out laughing.

'Oh, Christ!' Tony exclaimed on seeing me, 'not you!'

Fred's language was blue afterwards but it was a pure accident.

Following the meeting at Newbury on 23 and 24 November 1962, Tony and I arranged to meet Michael and Mary Scudamore for dinner at Ross-on-Wye. We had all the time in the world. I was driving and as I followed the familiar road out of Newent I reached the top of a bend and saw a car pulling straight across my path. Tony had his head down, fiddling with the radio and I just had time to shout, 'Look out – we've got him!' before swerving to the right to miss this vehicle. In that split second I saw another car behind the one I was trying to avoid so that all I could do was to swing the steering wheel down left-handed. I hit the first car broadside. I banged my head and was a bit dazed for a second or two and then I looked down at Tony. There was blood on his face and he was motionless. 'Christ,' I thought, 'he's dead,' then he began to groan and move slightly. I got out of the car and two witnesses came over and told me that they had seen everything and that there was nothing I could have done to avoid the collision.

The driver of the car we had hit was still inside it, and he was pretty badly hurt with blood everywhere. The horn was blaring non-stop and it was all very unpleasant. We went to hospital in the ambulance, feeling a bit shaken. Tony had a few cuts and bumps. I had lost a tooth and fractured the roots of three others.

Although my mouth was painful I did not want to miss the ride on Red Thorn at Haydock on 28 November in the Wigan Novices' Chase. He was owned, as was Terra Nova, by Mrs L. Brown, whose husband had had him in training with Dan Moore. When Red Thorn came to Kinnersley he had been coughing consistently for twelve months. Fred Rimell gradually got him right and he developed into a super horse. He was a big, chestnut baby with a tremendous jump in him. He was a beautiful ride although he was quite a strong puller. He loved to run away with you and when a horse does that it is better to let him think he is getting his own way – for a while. It humours him and he takes more interest in his work.

Red Thorn had a good chance at Haydock so, with my mouth plugged with cotton wool, I went to post. He jumped like a stag to win easily and I knew I was riding a quality horse.

I was not so happy when I rode Flamingo Feather for Frank Cundell in the Calne Novices' Chase at Wincanton on 6 December. She was a well-bred mare and started second favourite. We were three fences from home and going well when she began to wobble under me. She lost her legs and started to gargle, and I thought, fleetingly, that she must be doped. I jumped off her and removed the saddle, but she was dead. Apparently she had broken a blood vessel and bled to death internally.

I have rarely known when a horse has been doped. It is not for a jockey to say, really, it is for the trainer to know. I have ridden horses which I thought could have been doped in that they ran badly, or lost their form over a period, but you have to ride a horse to find out if he has been 'got at', which is the hard way of going about it. I think most jockeys, including me, would be guessing, as so many factors come into play, especially these days when so many poor performances are caused by virus infections which are not only difficult to isolate, but even more difficult to treat.

I had seen Lieutenant-Commander Lockhart-Smith's Sartorius beaten at Ludlow and noticed that Fred Winter and Joe Guest had failed to win on him, so I asked the owner if I could ride the horse when he next ran. He agreed, and added, 'If you win on him I will pay for you to have a new tooth.'

I thought this would be great and really set Sartorius alight to beat David Nicholson on Black Caprice at Windsor on 12 December 1962.

The owner was as good as his word. I had a spanking new tooth fitted which looked fine until I bent it out of shape in a fall later on.

At Sandown, on 14 December, I had my first ride on Honour Bound, a grand little colt owned by Mrs Katie Gaze of Ross-on-Wye and trained by Fred. He was bought in Ireland and was a racing machine in his own right. He was lovely. A red bay with black points, he had half-lopped ears, galloped close to the ground and jumped very flat. Several people had turned him down because he made a 'noise', but it was nothing to worry about in fact. He was a real character of a horse who spent a great deal of his time asleep in his box. He had a superb temperament and I thought a lot of him.

In the Regent Novices' Hurdle that day at Sandown, Johnny Haine thought he had the measure of Honour Bound in Buona Notte, another great horse, but it was not to be and again, as with Red Thorn, I knew I had under me an animal of terrific potential.

Christmas promised to be yet another mixture of fun and starvation in readiness for racing at Kempton on Boxing Day but it started to snow, and snow and snow. The hard winter of 1963 had set in.

My cousin Peter, Dave Dick and I arranged to pay a visit to the Boat Show at the invitation of Max Aitken, then to go from there to Scotland for a few days' shooting. The severe cold and heavy snowfalls everywhere meant that racing would be off for quite a while and it seemed a heaven-sent opportunity for a bit of sport.

We caught the midnight train and arrived near the Solway Firth in a very happy mood. We had rented a cabin close to the estuary and it was bitterly cold. Peter and I were pretty tired, but Dave Dick was a very active man at all times. We had had about two hours' sleep when there was a loud banging on the door. Dave had decided that it would be a good idea if we went down to the dunes and waited for the duck to flight over. Wearily, we dragged ourselves outside and into the car we had hired for the holiday, Dave driving flat out with Peter and myself half hung-over. Going round the first bend in the road the brakes jammed, as they were frozen up, and how we survived I will never know.

Eventually we reached the dunes and clambered out of the biting wind to nestle in a sandy gulley.

'Right,' Dave said, 'stay there and listen, we'll be in for some sport just now.'

The hours ticked by and we were frozen. Just as dawn was breaking some people walked down by the water's edge with their guns and dogs. There were hundreds of duck and geese feeding by the estuary and they all took off. The noise of the guns as these people let fly was incredible and so was Dave's language.

'That's screwed that up,' he growled, and shot a seagull out of spite.

We had black pudding for breakfast and were warming ourselves up when Dave said, 'We'll get a boat and row across the estuary to get some flighting on the other side.'

Off we went to the opposite bank where we walked for miles, poached for miles and there was nothing about whatsoever. It was colder, if possible, than it had been that morning, so we decided to return to our own side of the water. Having negotiated the icy depths we stood in the dunes, cold and disillusioned, only to see another boat going upstream with two people aboard. We were sheltering by an old tin shed, and some low-flying widgeon came down river towards us. The idiots in the boat immediately picked up their guns and let go with a left and a right. They missed the widgeon but the shot rattled round our tin shed nearly deafening us. I was so enraged that I fired back at our attackers – and then ran!

We were thoroughly browned off by this time, but the indefatigable Dave knew a family who had an estate nearby. He told us that he would telephone and ask if we could have a day of proper driven goose shooting on their land. This was all arranged for the following day and with an idle afternoon on our hands we set off for nowhere in particular.

'Stop,' Dave said, 'there's a pheasant in that field.' He stopped the car, I got out, the pheasant got up and I shot it. I picked it up and ran back to the car. We all thought it was great fun – poaching! Then we went on to an orderly estate across the moors which Dave felt sure was full of promise. He saw nothing, neither did Peter and neither did I. All at once, Dave yelled, 'Run, run!' and we all went like hell. When we stopped to have a look round we saw Dave fast in the clutches of a gamekeeper. It seemed for an awful moment as if he was going to lose his gun and equipment, but he managed to talk his way out of his predicament and we returned thankfully to base.

In the morning we arrived at Dave's friends' estate to shoot driven geese as promised and up came the keeper to be introduced to us.

'This is Mr Jones – Mr Biddlecombe – and this is Mr Dick.'

On seeing Dave, the keeper stiffened. He was the very man who had caught Dave by his coat tails the day before.

'I believe we've met before,' he said stonily.

It was very funny; but we had driven geese afterwards which was great. We shot about twelve between us and that night the old keeper came down to the pub with us. Dave kept filling him with booze and he was absolutely pie-eyed when we left him. Then, more than merry ourselves, we boarded the train home in the morning, lugging our guns, cases and, of course, the geese. We must have looked a sight. Dave gave a couple of geese to the train driver and told him to get us home safely, and one to the guard to ensure that he woke us up at the right station.

It was quite a memorable trip. I hung my goose for about three weeks and Mother cooked it for lunch. It was so solid from the hard weather and so tough that we could not eat it! I will never forget that little expedition.

The cold weather went on and on and, despite the shooting, and tobogganing at Scudamore's, with Lehane and others, seeing who could stay on the longest before hitting the hedge, we were all glad when racing started again.

I came back with a winner at Newbury on my old friend Sartorius on 8 March 1963. I soon realized that whenever I was laid off, for whatever reason, it was politic as far as the press was concerned, and indeed my own self-confidence, to return to the racecourse if possible with a winner. Sometimes it happened by accident, but as I became more astute in these matters I tried to ensure that I rode a winner after being side-lined. It made good headlines! Racing is a precarious occupation in more ways than one and reputations can be killed overnight by biting press reports. I have seen several good jockeys maligned by the press and subsequently ignored by trainers as a result. I was determined that this would never happen to me.

At the Cheltenham Spring Meeting I had a superb ride on Honour Bound to win the Gloucestershire Hurdle. He was such a good horse, with a tremendous turn of foot, and he skimmed the last hurdle like a swallow, beating Bahrain, ridden by Tommy Carberry, and Super Fox, ridden by David Mould.

Michael Scudamore put me in for my first ride in the Cheltenham Gold Cup on King's Nephew. Trained by Frank Cundell, this was a fine, upstanding horse full of ability, which loved to stand well off from his fences. I can feel the power of him under me now. For me he

was another Mill House and had everything you could wish for in a
3-mile chaser. I was simply cruising on him and going to the third last I
saw a long stride. I had that super feeling, 'Oh, Christ – I'm going to
win!' – when he just touched the top and crumpled up on landing. I
was bitterly disappointed. It was the dream of my life to win that race,
more than the Grand National, which I always considered to be
something of a lottery, and more, even, than becoming champion
jockey. My turn had not yet come.

The first Schweppes Gold Trophy Hurdle was run at Liverpool on
28 March 1963. I was riding Honour Bound in the race with a 12-
pound penalty in a very big field of forty-one runners. We lined up and
I saw Stan Mellor take up his position right on the outside on Eastern
Harvest. Everyone went like hell. I was on the middle to outside with
Stan well in my sights. At the second hurdle Eastern Harvest fell and as
he got up he put one of his feet on Stan's head.

Josh Gifford won the race on Rosyth, and I finished nowhere, but
when we came back to the weighing room we heard that Stan had
been hurt and was in hospital.

After racing, I went with Bobby Beasley and his wife to see him. We
walked through the ward which had about ten beds on either side of it
and passed Stan as we did not recognize him. His head was swollen
like a football and he could breathe only with difficulty. Hospitals
have a terrible effect on me. The smell of ether and the sight of Stan,
unable to communicate except by writing messages on a pad, made me
dizzy. Luckily, Bobby's wife had some smelling salts with her and
these brought me to when we left the ward.

Miraculously, the surgeons pieced Stan's fractured face together
again and he was as much a favourite with the ladies after his accident
as he had been before.

In the Grand National I rode Loyal Tan for Arthur Thomas. By the
time we had reached the Canal Turn for the second time he was tiring.
Josh Gifford had fallen on Out and About at the third last and when
he stood up he saw me making my weary way home. He ran towards
me and the next thing I knew he was hanging onto my leg, laughing.

'Get off, you silly bugger,' I said, and gave him a push. He was still
giggling as he lost his balance and fell to the ground for the second
time. It was one of those ludicrous incidents that happen in Grand
Nationals.

I think that it was on the evening before this National that I invited
our attractive hotel receptionist out for a drive. We borrowed Johnny

Lehane's car and drove down to the beach for a night of passion in the back seat. After a while, we drifted off to sleep and I was awakened by a slapping sound on the front wheels. I sat up and realized that the tide was coming in. I tried to start the engine but it just croaked, and I had to run about a mile to gather a rescue team together to pull the car out of the sea. When we got there the water was up to the car bonnet and I was out of favour, both with my new girlfriend and Johnny afterwards.

Honour Bound ran a magnificent race in the Prestbury Handicap Hurdle at Cheltenham on 9 April 1963, beating Salmon Spray ridden by Johnny Haine. It was satisfying to beat Johnny because he sat so correctly on his horses and he was such a stylist. He had one little giveaway – once you saw his hands start to go into action you knew he was off the bridle and, if your horse had anything left, you could go and beat him. He was inclined to be a bad loser. He never said much but his expression spoke volumes.

The following day at Cheltenham, Jungle Beach won the Gratwicke Blagrave Memorial Challenge Cup for Lady Lyons, who loved her racing and was a very sporting loser.

Jungle Beach had ability and always did his best but he had a habit of swallowing his tongue. We tried to prevent this by putting a lump of dirt in his mouth before the start of a race to make him salivate. If this did not work we covered his tongue with olive oil to make it slippery, so that if he did swallow it there was a chance that it would slide back into place again. This also was a short-lived cure but he still won many races.

I had ridden Pillock's Green several times for Teddy Tinkler, who owned a garage in partnership in those days and later became President of Tewkesbury Golf Club, but I had not won on the horse. Fred had seen Pillock's Green walking round before a selling race at Warwick and when the horse won he bought him for a few hundred pounds. On arrival at Kinnersley, Pillock's Green roared like a bull – his wind was so bad. Fred had him successfully Hobdayed and when the horse was fit again he won the first ever Victor Ludorum Hurdle at Haydock in 1962, ridden by Bobby Beasley.

I was to ride Pillock's Green again at Manchester on 13 April 1963, in a 2-mile hurdle. Teddy Tinkler had a super Aston Martin which Fred drove to the races, with me crouched in the tiny back seat behind Teddy. Fred was longing to see how fast this car could go and put his foot down. When the speedometer reached 135 miles per hour Teddy turned round and looked at me, and I was cowering in the back, terrified.

Still in a state of shock, and oblivious to Fred's orders, I rode Pillock's Green in the race, knowing that Teddy had a nice bet on him and, as I jumped the second last, I glanced across to my left and saw a figure racing up the tarmac path alongside the course. It was Teddy Tinkler, with his glasses banging up and down on his chest and his form books clutched in his hands, shouting at the top of his voice at me, 'Come on – keep him going, keep him going!' It was an astonishing sight and incredibly funny. Pillock's Green won easily and we had a carefree journey home in the Aston Martin. Teddy maintains to this day that the scare Fred had given me on the way to the races had made me forget everything except riding my own race, and winning.

Ever since Nicolaus Silver had won the Grand National in 1961 I had itched to ride him in a race. I had only sat on him briefly at Kinnersley and I was flattered when Fred asked me to ride him in the Scottish Grand National at Bogside on 20 April 1963.

On the morning of the race I was up early walking the track and I put up a fox, a real beauty, which must have had its lair in the heather in the centre of the course. I hoped it was a good omen, being mindful of Tony's warning to me, having ridden for Ken Oliver in the north himself, that it was not always safe to get beaten on a favourite at Bogside as far as the punters were concerned. When he had done this on one occasion he had had bottles, cans and turf thrown at him, which was quite extraordinary. This does happen once in a while. I remember a quite frightening scene at Fontwell when Bobby Beasley failed to win on the favourite and had to have a police escort to the weighing room.

When I had the leg up on Nicolaus Silver for the Scottish National he felt superb under me. He was a made horse, silver grey in colour, and during the race he moved like a well-oiled machine. I managed to get a good run on the inside when, just past the stands, the old horse 'put down' before the fence, missed it entirely and that was it. One ride, one fall – and he had won the Liverpool National! My pride was hurt but there were no other injuries.

At the end of April, I went to Ireland for the first time. Honour Bound, which was entered for the 2-mile Martin Mahony Champion Novices' Hurdle at Punchestown on 30 April, had been kicked shortly before he was due to leave England, and it was touch and go whether or not he would run. However, all was well and Katie Gaze, Mercy,

Fred and I flew to Ireland the night before. We had a slap-up dinner that night. I have never seen such enormous steaks in my life and it was quite a party.

On the morning of the race, Fred decided he needed a haircut. Having discovered the whereabouts of the nearest barber he told me that I had better have one too, as my hair was hanging down over my collar.

We went into the barber's shop and Fred sat in the chair, leaving me reading the newspaper and listening to the radio. I could not hear Fred's conversation but apparently he said to the man with the clippers, 'That's my son behind that paper – you give him a right haircut and no bloody messing about.'

Knowing nothing of this, I sat down for my 'trim' and when the fellow had finished he held the mirror up for me to see the result. I was aghast. He had nearly taken the lot off. Fred was killing himself laughing and said it was the best haircut I had ever had, a remark which incensed Dad when I got home, as he had been cutting my hair at intervals for years.

The weather was cold and wet as we lined up for the start and there were surprisingly few people on the course. I tucked Honour Bound in behind the leaders and did not move on him until about four hurdles from home when I asked him for his effort. He drew clear approaching the last and had the race won long before the winning post.

Bobby Beasley was to have ridden Scottish Memories in the next race, the Drogheda Handicap Chase, but as he had been injured I was offered the ride instead, and was thrilled to partner this exceptionally good horse which had won a lot of races in England, where he had been trained by Paddy Sleator's team under the guardianship of Arthur Thomas. We were up against some good class horses in this race, especially Ben Stack, ridden by Pat Taaffe, and Highfield Lad, which had won the previous year.

Coming into the last bend there was one fence to go. I was on the rails with Francis Shortt on Dandy Hall on my outside and Pat Taaffe with Ben Stack on his outside. I was so close to the rails I could not move and then I heard Pat shout across, 'Your inner, Francis, your inner!' – and with that Francis came and nearly crucified me against the rails. I thought he had broken my leg and I have a photograph showing the white paint on my boots and my horse's quarters. I managed to pull out and get up to beat Pat by half a length and although I knew I had been 'hampered', as the newspapers stated afterwards, I hesitated to say anything on my first visit to Ireland.

The stewards had seen my horse nearly pushed over the rails, however, and they ordered an inquiry.

'We consider,' they said, 'that Francis Shortt should be warned off for foul riding.'

Then they asked me to explain what had happened.

'Well,' I replied, 'I've never ridden round the track before over fences and I should not have taken the liberty of coming on the inside.'

The expressions of relief that spread over Pat's and Francis' faces were marvellous to behold. There is no doubt that they deserved suspension, or worse, and the stewards were prepared to deal out some harsh punishment. Afterwards, both men thanked me for letting them off so lightly. Pat is a great guy and I like Irish jockeys – but they can be good at bumping people!

By winning with Honour Bound and Scottish Memories we had made history. It was the first time that English-trained horses had been successful at the Punchestown meeting and to beat the Irish on their self-styled 'Cheltenham of Ireland' made the victory doubly sweet.

A fortnight later, Honour Bound won the Yorkshire Cup when ridden by that great flat-race jockey, Doug Smith, which only served to emphasize this horse's versatility.

6
First Jockey to Fred Rimell

When Britannic fell with me at Hereford on 3 June 1963, I broke my left wrist again. Bill Tucker suggested that I ride with a fairly rigid support around this wrist and a leather gauntlet on the right one, so that I could continue in my profession without undergoing surgery. I had the rest of the summer in which to wear these about the farm and they certainly helped to strengthen my increasingly mis-shapen bones. Doc Wilson has often commented that I do not need cutlery as I have a 'dinner fork deformity' in both wrists!

Back in 1960, I had met a man by the name of Chummy Gaventa when I celebrated my nineteenth birthday at one of his clubs in London with some other jockeys. He was a commission agent, passing bets from his clients to a wide range of bookmakers, but there was a good deal of mystery about him which I never penetrated.

A racehorse owner himself, he loved anything to do with the sport and was particularly kind to any jockeys who were injured, visiting them in hospital and taking them anything they needed. Over the years he had three drinking and gambling clubs which were restricted to members only, but his hospitality extended to the racing fraternity and he would give excellent meals to any of us in his restaurants, or supply us with tickets for any special event in the sporting or social calendar.

Naturally, he would pick up what information he could from the conversations that took place in these circumstances, but he never once asked me to stop a horse or do anything that I felt was in any way wrong.

It was through him that I met George Raft, the American actor, who adored his racing, and also Charlie Tucker, another American who was agent both for Julie Andrews and Jimmy Tarbuck.

Whatever other people thought about him, I had a respect for Chummy which he did nothing to shake. I am one of those who speaks as he finds and I found nothing wrong in my association with a man who was to prove nothing but a friend to me.

The highlight of that summer was when Chummy invited Josh and me to join his party to see the historic fight for the World Heavyweight Championship between the then Cassius Clay and Henry Cooper on 17 June 1963 at Wembley Stadium.

We had seats in the third row from the ringside and a first-class view of both boxers. Quite early on in the fight, Henry's eye was cut and we could see that he was anxious to finish the bout before he was cut again. With Clay backing off, Henry had to come in and take the fight to him when, as everyone knows, he caught Clay with the renowned 'Henry's Hammer'. Christ, it was a punch! Clay went down like a stone. It is old history now but there was a bit of delay in Clay's corner after the bell went, which was highly criticized afterwards. When Clay came out for the next round, however, it was quite unforgettable. He hit Henry right and left, opening up his eye again, and the blood squirted out. Every time he had the chance, Clay went for Henry's damaged eye and the spatter of blood was quite horrifying. It sprayed all over us in our evening dress whenever the two boxers came round to our side of the ring, and I do not think that Clay missed once.

Henry Cooper is one of the most superb men you could wish to meet – strong and brave – and he fought like a tiger, hitting back and hitting hard. Josh and I were stamping and shouting, thinking that we were the only ones behaving in this way, but when we looked around us we saw that everybody else was doing exactly the same. It was a tremendous fight and although we thought that Henry had been unlucky when he floored Clay just before the bell, there is no doubt that in Cassius Clay we had seen a boxer who would join the ranks of the immortals of the sport.

My interest in boxing began when I was a small boy. Grandfather Biddlecombe, Dad and Mother used to listen to the big fights on the radio before the days when most people had television, and I would listen too. My great hero was Bruce Woodcock and when he lost the World Championship I cried! I was no boxer of any account myself. I put the gloves on against a boy at school once and he hit me all over the place. That was it as far as I was concerned.

The first man I knew in boxing was Terry Spinks. I met him in the Savoy Baths when I was wasting, having seen him fight a couple of times. He loved his racing and was, I believe, involved with the Epsom crowd of racing men. After a fight he would sit in the baths with us, drinking gallons of lemonade, with his face swelling until sometimes his eyes were invisible.

Howard Winston was another fine fighter whom I knew quite well, and also Terry Downes, who was a tough, hard man.

Boxing was a feature of the many functions I attended in London. It was an excuse to put on your evening dress, have dinner, puff cigars and watch some boxing, usually featuring up-and-coming fighters. In the early days the bookmakers ran round the ring giving odds to anyone who wanted to bet. This no longer happens in that it is not seen, but it opened my eyes at that time. I still go to the Stable Lads' Boxing Championships. They are totally different. Some trainers teach their own lads to box – Ian Balding is one – and it is one of the traditions of racing stables which I hope will continue. Several good lightweight boxers have emerged from these contests and it is a fine way to keep fit. Marshalla 'Taffy' Salaman, who won the Championship three times, hated hurting his opponents and retired from the ring. He was a successful jockey and trainer, but he was an excellent boxer.

I had several holidays in Majorca, the first being in the summer of 1963 when Josh Gifford, Johnny Lehane and I flew out to join Mercy and Fred Rimell's party which consisted of their daughter, Scarlett, Neville Crump and his wife, and Sarah, together with Ken and Rhona Oliver.

We were having drinks at the bar one night and everyone became a bit merry. Rhona Oliver ran up the trunk of a palm tree like a monkey and I chased her into the foliage. When we came down, Ken was standing at the foot of the tree, looking a bit worried, but he took it in good part as one of those holiday pranks.

The argument I had with Neville Crump afterwards became a bit heated. I had told him that, given level weights of $12\frac{1}{2}$ stone, I would ride lighter than he would because he rode like a bag of spuds. He was so enraged that I thought it diplomatic to swim back across the bay to our hotel, and Josh dived in with me. Johnny Lehane was frantic with worry because armed guards were on the lookout for anybody who might be smuggling, and it was said that they would shoot on sight. We arrived at our own beach safely, if a bit frightened, to find

Johnny waiting for us with the car. He delivered a long lecture on stupidity before we all went to bed.

The next night, Johnny was driving us to a little restaurant and he nearly killed a man who was standing in the middle of the road. How we missed him I will never know. We swerved to the left and the right of him and on the next bend hit a wall and burst a tyre. We drove on to the restaurant, having burned the tyre to pieces, and went inside for a drink to calm our nerves. We made friends with the locals while we were in there, explained our predicament, and in a trice they poured outside, lifted the car bodily, changed the wheel, and away we went.

That holiday, Josh and I water skied for the first time, sitting on wooden lavatory seats and being pulled through a rough sea, thinking that we were both rather good.

I rode forty-one winners from 287 mounts in the 1962–63 season and Josh Gifford was champion jockey for the first time with seventy winners. That was his bonus. Mine was being asked to ride as first jockey to Fred Rimell as Bobby Beasley had decided to renew his previous association with the Paddy Sleator–Arthur Thomas partnership. Ken White, a close neighbour of mine, was to be second jockey at Kinnersley. He was a good horseman, quiet and sympathetic, and I liked him a great deal. He was able to do the lighter weights more easily than I could and the arrangement was satisfactory all round.

The 1963–64 season started with the usual West Country meetings which were an excellent way of getting fit after the summer break. The Renfrees were quite a force to be reckoned with in that part of the world, and although they were farmers as opposed to racehorse trainers, they and the Bassetts would notch up a lot of winners. You could never dismiss them lightly when they were racing against you.

I had so much in reserve when I rode Jungle Beach in the Berrington Chase at Ludlow on 19 September that I just sat there, and this was nearly my undoing. I had glanced over my shoulder and was easing up as the nearest rival was some fifteen lengths behind me. I started talking to my horse and tried to look like a model jockey when I had another quick peep behind and saw this horse coming like an arrow towards me. I was barely 20 yards from the winning post and I dared not move on Jungle Beach. As we passed the post to win, I saw a flash of blue and grey colours pass me, going like holy smoke. It was Paddy

Farrell riding Prudent Barney for Mrs Lerline Brotherton, whose colours I was to come to know so well myself.

Fred went beserk.

'Who the hell do you think you are?' he demanded as I dismounted, 'Bloody Piggott!'

There was a Stewards' Inquiry afterwards and I was lucky to keep the race.

Edward Courage had asked me to ride Border Flight in the Grand Sefton Chase at Liverpool on 2 November. I had won on this smashing horse at Sandown on 14 December 1962. He was a big, long-legged individual with a raking stride and he ran his usual bold race, sailing over his fences with great zest. Again, I made the mistake of looking over my shoulder to see what opposition, if any, there was. I was just coming to the second last as I did so and Border Flight over-jumped and fell. The next morning Dick Francis gave me some 'stick' in his racing column in the *Daily Express*, stating something to the effect that young jockeys should not look over their shoulders thereby unbalancing their horses and causing them to fall.

On 21 November 1963, at Kempton, I rode Spartan General to win the Vauxhall Novices' Hurdle over 2 miles. He was a mighty sort of horse by Mossborough which Fred had bought off the Flat. He had finished quite close up in the Derby of 1962, which was won by Larkspur, after several horses including the favourite, Hethersett, were involved in a pile-up near Tattenham Corner. Spartan General had jumped over one of the fallers and I often wonder if this could count as his first 'school over obstacles'.

He was a thick-necked, powerful liver chestnut and quite a hard puller. For a colt he had a marvellous temperament. He could jump very well but he had a tendency to knock hurdles out of the ground if he met them wrong, or even run into them, but he was a clever individual. When I first sat on him I knew I was astride a real racehorse. He was like a bull – a big bull. He loved to gallop and jump and when he won the Speen Novices' Hurdle at Newbury on 30 November, he took one hell of a hold, smashing a few hurdles; but I knew that he was very, very good.

He was owned by Madame Maureen Logut, who was the European Champion water skier; her husband, Phillipe, was World Champion at this sport at that time. She was a lovely lady, English by birth, and although she and her husband lived in England, they had a house in France also.

Johnny Haine and Salmon Spray reversed the placings with me on Honour Bound at Newbury on 30 November in the Berkshire Hurdle. Honour Bound had been off for some time with leg trouble and he ran well enough for us to have high hopes of him returning to top form.

He was strongly fancied for the Gillette Handicap Hurdle on 7 December at Newcastle. The race was worth £5560 and run over 2 miles and a few yards. We started favourite and when we set off I could not hold one side of him. He stood off so far at the second last that he landed a bit heavily and the tendon went on his off foreleg. It was tragic because he would have won cantering. He was to come back to racing again, at Kempton and Fontwell, and then at Cheltenham in 1965, when he broke down for the last time with me in the Spa Hurdle, and subsequently retired to stud. He was a brilliant horse, one of the greatest I have ever ridden, and when Dad wanted to breed some good horses he asked me which stallion I thought he should use. I immediately recommended Honour Bound, who proved himself an outstanding sire, among his progeny being Tied Cottage, who lost the 1979 Cheltenham Gold Cup at the final fence, and was disqualified when he did win in 1980. Honour Bound's premature death was a severe blow to racing.

My trip to Newcastle was not without its compensation for I was offered a chance ride on Prudent Barney by Mrs Lerline Brotherton in the John Eustace Smith Trophy Chase. Prudent Barney flew in to win and I knew then from the speed he had under his bonnet just why Paddy Farrell had nearly caught me in that earlier race at Ludlow. This was the beginning of a long and happy association with Mrs Brotherton and her trainer, old Bobby Renton, who had his establishment at Ripon.

Mrs Brotherton was perhaps best known as the owner of Freebooter, winner of the 1950 Grand National. She knew a great deal about racing. I once visited her home in Yorkshire and the walls of her entrance hall were covered with horseshoes belonging to her winners. There must have been hundreds of them. Bobby Renton was almost her private trainer. The son of a parson, a keen hunting man and a natural horseman, he was a cheerful little character and shared her passion for a game of cards, which they would play for hours.

Meanwhile I had won the Christmas Cracker Chase at Liverpool on 4 December on Border Flight – and I do not think I looked round – and the Holly Hurdle on Arctic Gittell, who had the worst legs I have ever seen on a horse, having broken down three or four times. They resembled gateposts.

During the Holly Hurdle I saw the late Tim Brookshaw take the most horrifying fall when his mare, Lucky Dora, crashed through the wing at the fifth. Tim fell straight onto his chest and his legs jack-knifed upwards towards his head. It was not until afterwards that I learned he had broken his back and his horse had been destroyed. Tim was one of the toughest, bravest men I have ever come across, and the fact that he fought paralysis for years to recover sufficiently not only to be able to ride again, but to take out a licence as a trainer, speaks for itself.

Spartan General was beaten twice before Christmas 1963. In the Yuletide Hurdle at Birmingham on 9 December we thought he was a certainty, but young David Wales, one of today's leading point-to-point riders, simply cantered over us to win on Black Diamond. I thought Spartan might have had an off day, but when he was left in third place at Cheltenham on 14 December, I found him very slow under me. He was a horse that you had to keep working at and he should have won many more races.

I had won on Thelma's Kuda at Warwick on 25 January 1964, and wasted hard on that occasion to do the weight. She was trained locally by Jim Perrett and his son, who owned a coach firm near Cheltenham, and they were keen gamblers. The Weald Chase at Lingfield on 21 February was Thelma's Kuda's next objective and I had to waste desperately to do the weight of 10 stone 6 pounds. I spent the whole night in the baths in Jermyn Street and had about two hours' sleep all told. I only carried 1 pound overweight in the race which I won, beating my brother Tony in the process, which was great.

The Savoy Baths were totally different to those anywhere else. There was usually somebody you knew there. In my day it could have been Dave Dick, because he lived in London then, Rex Hamey, Arthur Freeman, Michael Scudamore and a host of others, as well as some of the flat race boys, especially Charlie Smirke.

If I was staying in London overnight with other jockeys we would perhaps go to a club or to the pictures and then return to the baths to lose weight for the next day's racing. The management was appreciative of tidy people, and I think most jockeys come into this category; if you were there in good time they would keep some cubicles for you, each with two bunks inside. Having secured these, we would go down for a sweat and ask the man in charge to give us a tap on the shoulder in the morning at about 5 o'clock or 6, so that we could have yet another session.

There were a lot of queer people in the London baths. Sometimes you would go into the wrong cubicle and disturb them and at other times they would stare at you or follow you around. After a while you took no notice of them. I remember Gerry Scott saying to one fellow who was pestering him, 'If you jump in the cold pool with me I shall just sit on your head and drown you!'

If you were late getting into the hot rooms in the morning, the smell was quite awful. So many people congregated down there during the night that the aroma of stale sweat went up your nose and into your mouth so that you could taste it. Dave Dick, of course, had the answer, as he scrubbed out the hot rooms with Dettol. This not only killed the smell but it also shifted more weight.

It was a habit I copied if I felt energetic at some of the other baths, not, I hasten to add, from the cleanliness point of view, but because it shed a few more pounds.

To stay in London was expensive, but at the Savoy Baths we had marvellous service for about £1 10s., which included a doss down in the bunks, the use of the steam and hot rooms and a shave in the morning from old Bill, the barber. The masseurs there were all good, but one of them was outstanding. If I was too tired to sweat I went into the steam room to get really hot and then to the massage room. There they had slabs of marble which were sprayed with hot water to keep your body temperature up and the masseurs would get to work.

This particular man had an old sock which he put on his hand before beginning to rub my back, my backside, legs, thighs and stomach for half an hour, non-stop. The sweat used to pour out of him and I would lie there, half asleep and think to myself, 'Christ – I'm in the wrong job, I should be doing that!' In half an hour he would rub up to 3 pounds from my body.

Frankie Jordison was a delightful owner. He owned a group of hotels and thoroughly enjoyed his racing. His best horse had been Unconditional Surrender, winner of twenty-seven races, and I had ridden another horse he had in training with Fred called Young Ferryman, which had come third to a good horse in Samothraki that February at Newbury. Frankie liked nothing better than to give his jockeys absurd orders, with instructions, sometimes 'not to be opened until you get to post'.

Tim Brookshaw arrived at the gate with one of Frankie's notes one day which read, 'Go like hell to the first, jump it, get off your horse, set fire to the fence and then go on and win, nobody will ever catch you!'

At the end of February, I was schooling Young Ferryman on some marshy land we had at Kinnersley, when suddenly he whipped round and I sat down on my hand, squashing my fingers. I was in agony and when we went back to the stables I said to Mercy, 'I've broken my finger.'

'No you haven't,' she said, 'it's only a bruise.' I took off my tie and wrapped it round my finger which was then hurting like hell. Afterwards I went to Gloucester Hospital where they found I had crushed the bones in the middle finger of my left hand. It was strapped up so tightly that I could not ride, so after leaving the baths I took the plaster off and tried to wrap my finger up again by myself. I drove to Ludlow where I was to ride Irish Reel for Willie Stephenson and during the race I hit my finger. It was excruciatingly painful and I had to pull the horse up. Fred was cross because I had not ridden one of his horses in any case, and he told me the following morning not to ride again until my finger was right. It took from 26 February until 5 March before I was able to ride on a racecourse again. I went to Bill Tucker who put two splints on the finger but by then the damage had been done. I can still move that finger out of joint but it no longer hurts me. Fred Rimell was right to stop me riding because Cheltenham was drawing near. I spent my time shooting.

Prudent Barney gave me a wonderful ride in the National Hunt Handicap Chase at Cheltenham on 5 March 1964, to give me my first big win on this course. He was a lovely old horse and a bold jumper on his day. You had to wait with him, literally, as he did all the waiting and you had to sit there and suffer. When he went into overdrive in this race it was sensational. We went to the last and he was really scorching on – I think that is the fastest I have ever been going to the last fence at Cheltenham. He sailed over and I was out in front, still running on. There was a terrific roar from the crowd and I knew that nothing could come and beat me. Prudent Barney beat Francis Shortt on Aussie by five lengths. Winning any race at Cheltenham has meant more to me than winning a race anywhere in the world, but that was a special day for me, and it was one race the Irish were certainly not going to claim, which was always a feather in your cap at Cheltenham. I have always adored that course and loved winning there.

I rode quite a few horses for Eric Cousins and one of them, The Pouncer, was my ride in the Juliet Hurdle at Stratford on 12 March.

During the race I dropped my whip. Turning into the straight I asked one of my fellow jockeys if I could borrow his whip and he said, 'No.'

'I'll give you a tenner for it,' I offered. 'No,' was the reply, so I grabbed his whip out of his hand and sent The Pouncer on to win. After the race, this jockey came and asked me for the tenner and I said, 'I offered you £10 during the race and you let me down, so you're not having it now!' I think I won by a head and I should have won by ten lengths – I was lucky.

The 1964 Liverpool meeting was a mixture of events. Jungle Beach fell at the first ditch in the Topham Trophy on 19 March. He was not really a Liverpool horse as he jumped rather precisely and could never 'fiddle' his fences.

In the Grand National on 21 March, Red Thorn was jumping magnificently, loving those big fences, when he weakened suddenly and I had to pull him up with a broken blood vessel four fences from home.

It was a tragic race in that Paddy Farrell fell with Border Flight at the Chair fence and broke his back. After this dreadful accident, added to the injury already sustained by Tim Brookshaw, the Brookshaw–Farrell Fund was started to help the dependants of these two jockeys. This, in turn, led to Tim and Paddy suggesting that a fund to help others, who might suffer as they had done, be set up, and this resulted in the inauguration of the Injured National Hunt Jockeys' Fund, with Lord Oaksey, Fred Winter, Brough Scott, Colonel John Barstow and Bob McCreery as its present trustees, and Edward Courage as chairman. This Fund has received tremendous support not only from jockeys but from members of the public who enjoy their racing.

During my time as second jockey to Fred Rimell, I had ridden a few horses for northern trainers with some success, particularly for Denys Smith of Bishop Auckland, and John Barclay of Lockerbie. They were to prove faithful to me to the end of my racing days, and I loved to go up to the northern tracks to ride their horses, especially to Perth, which I have always considered to be one of the loveliest racecourses in the British Isles.

These men gave me credit for knowing a bit about horses and how they should be ridden. They did not give me a string of orders but merely said, 'You know the horse – ride him how you like.' If I was new to the horse, they would obviously tell me anything I needed to know, but I felt that I was respected in my own right.

I had my first win for John Barclay when I rode his Vulmidas in the Wigston Handicap Hurdle at Leicester on 6 April. This was a little darling of a horse, a brilliant jumper which was to prove a prolific winner for several seasons.

As I have said, Josh Gifford and I were fierce rivals on the racecourse and the best of friends when off it. At Cheltenham on 9 April I rode Nosey in the Stayers' Handicap Hurdle and the race developed into a contest between Josh, riding Man of the East, and me. Going to the second last hurdle I pushed Nosey along on Josh's inside and he glared at me and said, 'Don't you bloody well come here, Biddlecombe, or I'll put you over that fence.'

I honestly did not believe him until I realized that I was indeed about to go over the fence as promised and I said to him, 'Gifford, you mean it!' – and he did. I changed gear on Nosey and got to the post a length and a half ahead of Josh, who was furious. I could understand his reaction. I should not have come where I did and it looked bad from his owner's and trainer's point of view to be seen to allow another jockey to come up on the inside. Friendship must never be taken for granted when racing.

On the final day of that Cheltenham meeting, 11 April 1964, Fred Winter rode the last race of his career as a jockey on Sunbeat in the *Sunday Express* Chase. I was on Border Flight and, like Fred, not really in with a chance as we both jumped the water. I seized the opportunity to say to him how much I had enjoyed riding with him over the years and wished him luck as a trainer. We had a laugh together, which covered a good deal of nostalgia. When a great jockey leaves the game it is a sad occasion.

Cartmel was a fascinating figure-of-eight track with a fairground in the middle. Fred Rimell sometimes took horses there and on 16 May Terra Nova and Spartan General trotted up in their respective races.

I always enjoyed the trip to the racecourse by ferry across Lake Windermere, and also the hound trailing which took place on the Sunday morning before racing on the Bank Holiday Monday.

Specially bred hounds followed a man-laid trail of aniseed for some miles over the mountains, jumping over the stone walls while their owners shouted and whistled them home. It was a most unusual sight, and the betting was fast and furious.

It was at about this time that Johnny 'Tumper' Lehane came to live with us at Upleadon. Having known him and travelled about the country with him and Michael for several years, I thought of him as one of the family. Initially he had ridden for Bill Marshall, and then Major Bewicke, and had shared a flat with Paddy Cowley in Cheltenham before moving to other lodgings and then staying with us for a few years. He was an emotional man and so generous that many people were unscrupulous enough to take advantage of this. He was a sincere friend, but he took life seriously from time to time and was sensitive to a degree. If he had a run of losing rides he was really depressed and I sometimes took him by the shoulders to shake him out of it.

How he came by the name 'Tumper' I am not quite sure, but I think it was through his habit of addressing everyone and everything with the word 'tumping'. He would call us 'wicked tumpers' and, being shortsighted, he liked to be well up with the field as he could see the 'tumping' fences better that way! He had a gift for mimicking people's expressions, and if he and Paddy Cowley had had a few jars and then danced together, it was side-splitting.

He liked nothing better than to give people nicknames, especially jockeys. Josh Gifford was dubbed 'Heifer'; Macer was called 'Buller'; David Nicholson was known as 'The Duke'; Paul Kelleway was christened 'Girl', which infuriated him; Peter Pickford was named 'Poacher' as he was inclined to take one's ground; Stan Mellor was 'Bounce', which described his punching method of riding; and Bill Rees was known as 'The Parson' because of his immaculate style of dressing and good behaviour. Johnny, at great risk to our friendship, decided that I should be known as 'The Blond Wog'!

He also called Tim Brookshaw 'Brown Cow' as Tim, for years, had addressed everybody with the greeting 'How now Brown Cow', irrespective of the occasion. He overdid this a bit in 1959 during the celebrations following Michael Scudamore's victory on Oxo in the Grand National. Leslie Hutchinson, the celebrated coloured singer and pianist, whom Tim knew well, was present at the party at the Adelphi Hotel that evening, and Tim, more than full of goodwill, sauntered over to him and putting an affectionate arm round his shoulder said amiably, 'How now, brown cow' – before he realized the enormity of the insult. There was a silence, but Hutch laughed off what could have been a very embarrassing moment.

Dave Dick decided that Michael Scudamore should be known as 'Bumble' because he was pigeon-toed and waddled around the weighing room in a bumbling sort of way. But it was Johnny Lehane who labelled most of us. His most outraged target was Fred Winter.

Johnny had read an article by Peter O'Sullevan in which he mentioned that Fred had been a lieutenant in the Paratroopers during the war. This amused Johnny no end and at Kempton one day he saluted Fred, saying, 'Hi, Lieut.' Fred was most annoyed and told him to grow up, with the predictable result that Johnny referred to him as 'Lieut' from then on.

All in all, we jockeys were excellent friends both on and off the racecourse. There is a comradeship in National Hunt racing that I have not found anywhere else. We all take part in a dangerous but thrilling sport and there are few jockeys who would deliberately think of riding against you in such a way as to harm you. Any rider who tries such tricks consistently is soon ostracized by the rest. As one old stager remarked, 'If you "do" me today, I will only "do" you tomorrow,' which is somewhere near the truth. There is too much at stake in any race without the added hazard of a malicious rival.

In the early days of my racing career, Michael Scudamore and a few others, including me, formed a cricket team to challenge anybody who felt like a game. This was really an excuse to drink beer as, for every wicket that fell, half a pint of beer was carried out to the players. Michael was captain in those early days, and we had some great Sunday matches, playing against local teams, with Michael's god-father, Neville Shaw, as umpire.

Anthony Porter, who had a horse called Carnelian in training with Fred, hosted many of these cricket matches at his home near Birlingham, not far from Worcester. He did all the cooking and laid on lunches for us, as well as the anticipated beer. He was a very kind man and when he gave up riding he became a handicapper. It was from Anthony that I bought my 12-pound saddle which must have carried me to victory over 400 times. It was made in Australia and I paid him £25 for it. Anthony is now in the saddlery business himself at Hawick and I still buy bits and pieces from him.

For some time the northern jockeys had been urging the southern-based jockeys to form a similar association to their own, which provided some insurance for a rider who through injury was unable to earn his living. Nobody did anything about it until Tim Brookshaw was cornered one day when he was riding up north and asked about the proposed association. He said that one was in the process of being formed, naming a few of us as committee members, but in fact all we had done was talk about it. Fred Winter came to hear about this and was very cross as he was very anti-union and thought that a union and not an association was going to be formed, which was not the case.

Things were reaching quite a pitch and it was at one of Anthony Porter's cricket matches that a meeting was held and a committee formed as the nucleus of the Southern Jockeys' Association. Stan Mellor was appointed chairman, Michael was vice-chairman, David Nicholson was secretary, and the rest of the committee was made up of Paddy Cowley, Johnny Lehane and myself. After about a year, David Nicholson found he could not cope with the secretarial side, and a friend of Michael's, Peter Smith, who kept The Tump Inn, near Hereford, at that time and was a racecourse announcer, took over as secretary for no fee. When the association was amalgamated with that of the flat-race jockeys in 1968, Peter was appointed secretary, with a salary, and still holds this post at the headquarters in Newbury.

From those early cricket matches the Jockeys' XI developed, with David Nicholson as captain and Tom Wellon as umpire. When we started we made no money at all, as that was not our intention, but under David's captaincy, and following the injuries to Tim Brook-shaw, Paddy Farrell and others, charity matches were laid on where money for the Injured Jockeys' Fund was raised by means of raffles, sponsors and, with luck, donations from well-wishers.

The jockeys' team did not consist entirely of jockeys. We had some good outsiders to help us knock up the runs such as Jim Meads, the sporting photographer, Ian Arthurs, a Gloucestershire auctioneer, and Andrew Wates, a racehorse owner and amateur rider. Jeff King was probably out best batsman among the jockeys, and other members of the team included the Dartnall brothers, Josh and Macer Gifford, Jeremy Hindley, Dick Wellon, and any others who were prepared to play. It varied quite a bit. I was a superb wicket-keeper throughout!

Tom Wellon, our umpire, was a bloodstock breeder and wholesale butcher, who had known me for years, and we had a lot of fun at these matches. Once we had established a team which could more or less cope with the local opposition we went farther afield, playing Burton Ales on their own ground, returning in twos and threes due to the special brand of beer they had brewed for the occasion. Our greatest success was when we beat Joel's XI at Newmarket where they had drawn up the equivalent of a Test team to play us as it included Dennis Compton, Gary Sobers, Frank Tyson and Ian Mackenzie. I do not think that Ian Mackenzie thought he would be up against such big men in our team because he said to Dennis Compton, 'I don't know any of these jockeys batting here – what weight do they ride at because some of them must be about fourteen stone!'

We thought that the match against the Bookmakers' XI at New-market would be a walkover, envisioning a team of portly, cigar-smoking novices. They hit hell out of us.

After we had played for several seasons we went 'abroad' – to the Isle of Wight. The first time we went by hovercraft and I managed to persuade the pilot to let me have a go at the controls. I had a glorious time but everyone else was seasick and I was physically restrained from taking over on the return journey.

We played the Cowes Police XI on one visit, and when Tom called out the Jockeys' XI for the great match the day after our arrival, only about five members of the team turned up; the others, including me, were sleeping it off in the pavilion. Tom routed us out and we had a great match against the constabulary before returning to our hotel with them and having a high old time. Late in the evening, Tom Wellon was appalled to see me, clad only in a pair of lady's tights, clinging to the top of a lamp post, with an irate constable standing on the pavement below demanding that I should come down. Tom came to the rescue.

'Who is that up there?' asked the constable, pointing to my practically naked figure desperately embracing the lamp bracket.

'Oh,' replied Tom, 'that's Biddlecombe, he's been playing your lot today at cricket.'

'Leave him up there then,' said the constable. 'They've just pub-lished an account of his injuries – he's broken so many bones that he won't be any trouble!'

We went to the Isle of Wight several times and, later on, we asked Sir Martin Gilliatt if we could be permitted to wear the royal colours on our jerseys and caps. This was granted, and the colours are worn proudly by the Jockeys' XI to this day.

7

Champion Jockey

I began the 1964–65 season with a nice run of winners, not only in the West Country with Fred Rimell's horses, but also by taking as many rides up north as I could with Denys Smith and John Barclay. In fact I took every ride that was made available to me because I sensed that the championship could be within my grasp.

I won the Barle Hurdle at Newton Abbot on 13 August with Lord Roberts. This was a fair horse trained by Bill Marshall; he was raffled for a good cause at the Fontwell meeting a fortnight later, when I again rode him. He went well in the Alec Baker Novices' Hurdle until falling at the last. Strangely enough, the person who won him in the raffle was later to become my brother-in-law, Bill Tyrwhitt-Drake.

Bill Marshall was quite a character. I first met him when I was still an amateur and he drove me to Fontwell with one of his owners, Paddy Cowley and Johnny Lehane. On the way to the racecourse he narrowly avoided hitting a car which drove straight across his path and I was amazed at the speed of his reactions.

He had been awarded the DFC for his bravery as a fighter pilot in the war and was successful over fences both as an amateur and a professional, taking out a trainer's licence in 1950. He could produce horses to win under both sets of rules but is perhaps best remembered for his training of My Swanee and Raffingora, who won thirteen races between them on the Flat.

I was to ride quite a few winners for Bill. He could be quite abusive after a few drinks; some people would cringe under these verbal onslaughts. This was just one side of Bill Marshall that you had to accept if you rode for him. If you won, he wanted to give you the world. He was a fine trainer.

In a two-horse race at Sedgefield, on 22 August, I rode Greek Scholar for Denys Smith in the Bishop Auckland Chase against Pat McCarron on Mount Gable.

Greek Scholar was a big, chestnut horse with a white blaze, and a fine head carriage. He really needed 3 miles to be at his best. It was his magnificent jumping that used to win him his races over 2 miles. He ran quite free and if you rode him hard into his fences he would stand off a mile. If you just sat and caught hold of his head, he would merely pop. He was an intelligent horse and never took more out of himself than was necessary.

Sedgefield was a bit sharp for him. Pat and I chatted all the way round and at the finish Pat just found that bit of extra speed to win. Sedgefield is unique in that the last fence is an open ditch and I would take a bet with anyone that few people in racing today know that! I have ridden a few winners round this track and in my day the runners would come out of the last bend, gallop through a flock of free-range hens and sail on into this open ditch. I think I have only ever seen one horse fall at it because somehow you always met it just right.

Greek Scholar came out again at Market Rasen to win on 5 September, and then again at Southwell on 7 September beating Mount Gable, ridden this time by Larry Major. Larry had a pub at Catterick and we called it our 'Catterick Base'. On our way up to meetings at Sedgefield or Perth, we would stop over at Larry's on the way and have a game of golf at the weekend. He was a great guy, who unfortunately fractured his skull later on in his riding career and had to give up.

Having begun the season with a nice run of wins, which filled me with bouncy confidence, I was put in my place by Reg Hollinshead at Ludlow on 22 October. He was getting on in years and although he rode in hurdle races he wisely avoided novice chases. I was riding Terra Nova, who was favourite and cracking along in the Cleehill Hurdle with Reg just behind me on Ashbyhill. I turned round and said to him waggishly, 'Good God – I thought you'd retired!' and he was so mad he came and beat me by a short head, which served me right.

Eddie Harty also got the better of me at Newbury on 24 October, when he set up one hell of a gallop on Hopeful Lad in the Capital and Counties Hurdle and I had no chance of getting near him on Spartan General.

Eddie was a colourful character. Always jovial and never at a loss for words, he was an extremely lively man. He prided himself on the fact that he never swore. He would say 'bucking hell' or 'bucking' this or that, but I never heard him actually swear. He was a devil for shouting at you when you went to the first fence, and I think that this was some kind of release for him.

I was leading the jockeys' table, with Josh Gifford, Roy Edwards, David Mould and Stan Mellor close on my heels by the beginning of November. The press was busy advertising the fact and the big bookmakers were laying odds as to who would be champion. I have never approved of betting on who will or will not be champion in a game as risky as racing. I think it is a bad thing to gamble, in effect, with human lives. So much can happen to a jockey, but although I have had my share of injuries, the old superstition held by many riders that if you have not had a fall for a long time, you are due for one, I feel, is ridiculous. Who on earth wants, willingly, to go arse over head in order to get it out of his system so that he can get up and think, 'Right, now I can have a few more rides without any falls!'?

Even if you marry young, and I did not, and you have responsibilities to your wife and children, if you are truly dedicated to your job then you still go ahead and do it. I would have done exactly the same if I had married at nineteen. If I had a real 'stopper' it was my weight, but never my responsibilities. All I ever wanted to do was to become champion jockey, ride winners and enjoy life.

The trophy for the winning jockey of both the Stanley Tools Handicap Chase and the Dormer Drill Novices' Chase at Doncaster on 21 November was a silver penknife. I collected one knife when Prudent Barney, coming with a long run, won the first of these races, and the other after Spartan General, having his first run over fences, ran brilliantly to win the second. He broke the track record in that race only to have it shattered by Paddy Broderick riding Hya in the race which followed.

Some years later, when I was competing in the jockeys' show jumping class at Wembley, my house was burgled. The thieves, who broke into my home at the same time as I entered the ring in London, took several thousand pounds' worth of property, including my safe and its contents. Two years after the robbery, the Thames Police were conducting a routine search of the river bed and recovered the safe in their trawl net. It was a chance in a million. Inside there were a few of my treasures which had been left because they had my initials inscribed on them and among these were the two silver penknives I had won with Prudent Barney and Spartan General in 1964, and I have them to this day.

There was a great gamble on Come Blow Your Horn, the horse I rode to victory for Denys Smith at Nottingham on 30 November. That was an unlucky meeting for Josh Gifford, who fell in the Southwell Chase on Reverando, breaking his right leg, which put him out of action for the rest of the season. He had no sooner recovered when he broke the same leg in a car crash the following summer after one of our charity cricket matches, which again stopped him riding for some months.

I rode my fiftieth winner of the season when I won the Snowball Chase on Quick Approach at Liverpool on 3 December. He also belonged to Madame Logut, the owner of Spartan General, and had won several races for me earlier in my career.

I was surprised to find that Quick Approach was so good round Liverpool. I believe this was his first visit to the course and his jumping on other tracks was so neat and clean that I feared the bigger fences would daunt him. He confirmed my view that if a horse is a good jumper he can usually cope with Aintree.

After his outstanding debut over fences at Doncaster, Spartan General ran in the Oxfordshire Chase at Newbury on 4 December, when he took off with me. His enthusiasm was his undoing because he dived at the last open ditch, landed on top of it and, being an entire, hurt himself where it hurts most. Many horses would have fallen after something like that, but, being such a robust horse, he managed to keep his feet to finish a poor third. The mishap upset him, naturally, and he never raced over fences again.

Just as Quick Approach had surprised me at Liverpool with his ability to cope with big fences, so did Pillock's Green at Newbury on 5 December. He was not a big horse but he showed me how brave he was that day. I thought it was ridiculous to run him at Newbury but he jumped very well to win the Clanfield Novices' Chase.

I sometimes disagreed with Fred Rimell's views on training, although we seldom argued about this for, after all, he was one of the top trainers and had been turning out winners for years. I approved of the loose school, which was excellent, but when it came to schooling the chasers I felt that the younger ones needed more time spent on gaining their confidence. Sometimes they would jump six to nine fences before racing, and the old horses would not be jumped at all.

The hurdlers would have perhaps two schools over a flight of hurdles before a race and prior to that might only have jumped them six or eight times in all. If I schooled the novice chasers and jumped six fences on them, that was all I had to do. Perhaps it was my fault that they did not do more, because Fred would say, 'All right, you've got to ride the thing – OK?' and I never disagreed. When these young horses raced for the first time, if the jockey was brave enough and gave them a good ride, they would go out and jump well. The second time, more often than not, they would be carrying a penalty for their initial success and they would lose a bit of confidence, especially if they ended up on the floor. I felt they would have benefited from more experience at home, and Pillock's Green was a prime example.

Although he had won his first race over big fences at Newbury, it had frightened him. He was given a penalty when he ran at Windsor on 10 December and made several mistakes before falling two fences from home. He did not have a school between races, his confidence had gone and he was being asked to race on a different track with more weight to carry. I am not questioning Fred Rimell's stature as a trainer; I am merely stating my own view on the training of novice horses and I could well be wrong.

On the racecourse, Josh Gifford was as good a jockey as one could find, but shooting was never his strong point.

We were once both invited to Guy Harwood's estate at Pulborough, Sussex. Josh had retired as a jockey then and was training at nearby Findon. I had two other friends with me, James Langmead and Robert Green, and Josh turned up very late. We were all standing around waiting for him and he was most apologetic.

Guy Harwood came out, saw that we were all ready to go and said, 'Right, guns, – load up,' and those of us who knew the shooting routine climbed into various Land-Rovers and set off across the fields. Unseen by me, and completely misunderstanding the instructions, Josh obeyed the command in his own way by literally loading his gun with cartridges! This was seen by James Langmead who could not find an opportunity to tell me about it before we left. Completely unaware of what had happened, I removed the gun from Josh – who had pointed it at me once or twice whilst we were in the Land-Rover – and placed it in the rack on the side of the vehicle. We were bumping and crashing over the fields to where the pheasants awaited us. When we climbed out at our destination, James tapped me on the shoulder and said, 'Er – your friend – you've got to tell him.'

'Tell him what?'

'Look,' he whispered, 'he's got two cartridges in his gun,' and the full realization of what had happened dawned on me.

'Listen, Heifer,' I said to Josh, 'when they said "Guns load up" just now, it meant that all of us who were shooting today were to get into the Land-Rovers, not put live cartridges in our guns.'

Gifford was terribly apologetic and jittery, wondering what he was going to do wrong next. I was drawn next to him, and in one particular drive the pheasants were streaming over us. The gun on Josh's left was killing behind him, and I was having one or two, while Josh was banging away until his barrels were red hot. Every time a pheasant dropped he cried, 'There, I got another one – did you see that?'

It was a most entertaining day.

The highlight of the Cheltenham meeting on 7 January 1965, for me, was winning the Fred Withington Handicap Chase on the erratic Pappageno's Cottage, trained by Ken Oliver, who had produced him to win this 4-mile marathon the year before. 'Swanny' Haldane, his jockey on that occasion, had broken his leg and I was asked to deputise for him, with my brother, Tony, riding the other Oliver contender, Happy Arthur. I let Pappageno's Cottage run on in front and he won comfortably from What a Myth, who was receiving 21 pounds, with Tony in third place. It was gratifying to win this stamina-testing race which was not without its prestige.

Spartan General trotted up at Haydock on 9 January in the White Lodge Hurdle and I was relieved that his nerve had not been shaken after his painful experience over fences.

I have never been very keen on objecting to the riders of horses that have beaten me unless there has been something dangerous or dirty involved. I have relied far more on the stewards at any meeting to hold their own inquiry if the evidence merited it in their view.

At Leicester on 11 January, Quick Approach won the Harrington Handicap Chase, beating Major Champneys' horse, Buttery Bar, ridden by Vic Haslem, only to lose the race afterwards on the grounds of 'crossing'. I was mystified because going to the last fence I must have been five lengths clear of Buttery Bar and was going so easily that I won pulling up. I was disqualified because the stewards considered that I had jumped across Buttery Bar at the last fence, even though I was a good way in front. Technically I had infringed the rules, and that was the end of the matter for a while, although I felt nettled because Quick Approach had run such a good race and it seemed unfair.

He got his own back on 20 May at the evening meeting at Wincanton. In the Clematis Chase, Jack Cook on Slave Dancer was several lengths in front of me going to the last fence. He ran down the fence a bit before jumping it and going on to win. Pulling up afterwards I said, 'Well done, Cookie,' when the loudspeakers announced a Stewards' Inquiry. I could not understand it. Fred said, 'What the bloody hell's that for? What have you done wrong?' I said that I had not done anything wrong.

Jack and I stood in front of the stewards and they said, 'What happened, Biddlecombe?'

Feeling blank, I turned to Jack and said, 'What happened, Cookie?'

'Well, sir,' Jack said, 'I ran down the last fence a bit, sir, and may have taken his ground but I don't think it has made any difference to the result.'

Then they turned to me and asked me for my version. I thought quickly and said, 'Well, he crossed me, sir, and took my ground at the last, and I had to snatch up and it cost me the race,' which a blind man would have known was not the case.

Jack and I left the stewards' room and they awarded me the race! There was no way that I should have got it, and I felt sorry for Jack Cook but, conversely, there was no reason why I should have lost that earlier race at Leicester on Quick Approach in very similar circumstances.

Afterwards Fred exclaimed, 'Well, that's English justice for you – you lose one bugger and they give you one back!'

I experienced one of the saddest moments of my life when Red Thorn fell in the Great Yorkshire Chase at Doncaster on 30 January 1965. One look at my horse told me that he would have to be destroyed, having broken his foreleg. It was even worse when, walking away from him and feeling absolutely choked, I saw Johnny Haine coming towards me in tears. His horse, Buona Notte, had fallen and broken his neck at the next fence. Johnny was very upset and there we stood, not speaking, but each knowing that we had lost two of the best horses one could ever have wished to ride. Buona Notte was of Gold Cup standard and Johnny was especially fond of him as he had 'ridden him away' at Bob Turnell's as a two-year-old. As far as Red Thorn was concerned, I not only knew that I had lost a superb partner over fences but felt that it was such a dreadful waste. To my mind he was capable of winning one or even two Grand Nationals and he was only a nine-year-old when he died.

I was usually lucky on my birthday, and on 2 February I had a treble at Nottingham. Two of them, Crockfords and Tibidabo, were trained by Thomson Jones and Arthur Freeman respectively at Newmarket, and the third, Dicey, was trained by Fred for John Liley, who had several horses at Kinnersley. I liked riding for the Newmarket trainers because they seemed to have a character all of their own and when I went down there to school I met a totally different type of person.

The owner of Tibidabo was a Mrs A. M. Gibson who lived at Newmarket and was deeply involved with racing. I rode out on the gallops there one morning for Arthur Freeman, her trainer, while Mrs Gibson watched the horses work. I was often in trouble for not keeping my hair short and she said, 'Who's that girl you've got riding for you, Arthur?'

'I'm afraid that's our jockey – Biddlecombe.'

'Oh,' replied Mrs Gibson, looking most surprised, 'with those golden curls he looks just like a little girl.'

Having won with Tibidabo on 2 February, I rode him in the Aldermaston Novices' Chase at Newbury a fortnight later.

He was a little French-bred individual with a will of his own. He had a tremendous pop in him, although he was so light framed, and throughout this race he jumped impeccably. Going to the third fence from home there were only three of us in contention and one horse fell, leaving Bill Rees alongside me on Arch Point, giving me something to race against. At the second last, Arch Point fell, leaving me alone in front. I was two fences ahead of anything else and Tibidabo had to have company if he was to race. Going to the last he suddenly put on his brakes and refused. There was nothing I could do about it and I had had the race sewn up until then.

I was convinced that the punters would have it in for me when I returned to the unsaddling enclosure but instead they were most sympathetic There were calls of 'Bad luck' all round and I could hardly believe my ears. Funnily enough, Basil Thwaites' Dramatist, trained by Fulke Walwyn, refused in identical fashion at Newbury in 1980, and I did so sympathize with Bill Smith who was in the saddle when it happened.

Having shown consistent ability over hurdles, Spartan General was aimed at the Schweppes Gold Trophy Hurdle at Newbury on 20 February, which then carried prize money totalling £7821. I jumped out of the gate and the horse dwelt with me. I was left some two to three lengths and in a race of that quality, with a handicap, it takes maybe ten lengths to get back into contention. I managed to get into the race again but, with top weight of 11 stone 12 pounds, it took all my skill to drive Spartan General into third place, beaten one and a half lengths and two lengths by David Nicholson on Elan, and Johnny Gilbert on Rosyth. At one point in the race I thought I might win, but it was not to be, though that was a race that I ought to have won and I knew it.

Spartan General ran well in the 1965 Champion Hurdle on 10 March but, there again, I should have made sure that he won it. As it was, I let Dave Dick come up on my inside on Exhibit A. He, in turn, let his stable companion, Kirriemuir, ridden by Willie Robinson, come up on his inside as we were going to the last hurdle and Kirriemuir was able to get a clean run through to win. I had to swing Spartan General around Dave Dick's horse, which caused me to be beaten by a length. Had I kicked on and taken the speed out of Kirriemuir I would have won because all Spartan General ever did was to gallop and jump; but to be fair, I was beaten on merit.

I felt badly about the Champion Hurdle until I won the George Duller Hurdle with Coral Cluster about an hour and a half later. This tough horse, trained by David Gandolfo at Burford, survived a rather hard ride from me to win from thirty-two starters.

After a disappointing Cheltenham, I rode The Fossa to win the Harry Isaacs Memorial Challenge Cup Chase at Hereford on 13 March. He was a grand little horse and a splendid jumper. When I first rode him, he was narrow, but he became stronger and more muscled up with age. He was a dark brown, with a high head carriage, and a very good Liverpool horse, winning the Grand Sefton Chase with Stan Mellor in October 1965. He was a very unsound horse, but won a lot of races. Later in his career he went to Fulke Walwyn's yard for Andrew Parker-Bowles to ride. He won several military steeplechases for his new owner who also completed the course on him in the 1969 Grand National.

I was steadily logging winners as the Grand National loomed up on the calendar. I rode Culleenhouse in the 1965 race on 27 March. This was the first time I had tried going round the Grand National course on the inside. When I jumped Becher's for the second time I was in front of the eventual winner, Jay Trump, and I landed a bit steeply. To my astonishment Jay Trump actually jumped clean over my left shoulder, clearing both Culleenhouse and me! It was an amazing feat, but Jay Trump, trained by Fred Winter, had an incredible pop in him and deserved to win that race.

Soon afterwards, Culleenhouse began to tire, and I let him come home in his own time. He was a gallant old horse, not quite a racehorse, but a bit more than a hunter, and I had had a lot of fun with him.

Tommy Smith, the American amateur who rode Jay Trump in that National, was a good guy. He was deep, and very American in his thinking, but he would listen to you.

Tim Durant was another American whom we all admired for his courage, for he was no youngster when he rode in the National; neither was the Duque de Albuquerque, who was totally fearless. He frequently asked us for advice and it was tragic when he broke his back at Liverpool in a bad fall.

Some visiting jockeys were not so likeable however. I recall an Australian who was riding a huge mare I had ridden myself, in a novice chase at Warwick. He cantered down to the start, very brash and knowing it all, and I suggested that he might do well to lengthen his leathers, as he was riding shorter than Lester Piggott. He did not want to know anything from a 'Pommie' jockey, retorting that he rode this way at home, so I wished him the best of luck, thinking what a cocksure little bastard he was. Sure enough, off he came. I was unkind enough to remark, as I passed him lying on the ground, 'I see you're down under again,' which was not very polite, but he deserved to fall.

One Australian for whom I had the highest regard was Laurie Morgan, who was not only a great rider over fences but a fine all-round horseman, winning many three-day events, including Badminton in 1961 on Salad Days, and taking the individual gold medal with the same horse at the 1960 Rome Olympic Games. He was an outstanding amateur, and not many people have won the Foxhunter Chases at both Cheltenham and Liverpool, which Laurie achieved with his super horse, Colledge Master.

I did not make a brilliant return to Cheltenham, although Nosey won the Stayers' Handicap Hurdle, on 1 April 1965, running bravely under top weight and just holding on at the post. I fell in the Gratwicke Blagrave Memorial Chase on Mrs Brotherton's Well Packed and was second on Vulmidas to Pat Taaffe in the Peter O'Sullevan Chase. The connections of Bronzino, my ride in the *Daily Express* Triumph Hurdle on the last day of the meeting, had high hopes of him in this race, and I know that a lot of money was lost when he could only manage third place.

On 20 April, I won my first Welsh Grand National at Chepstow with Norther, a horse belonging to Glanville Jones, father of Kingsley Jones, the international rugby player. Trained by Denzil Jenkins at Cowbridge, this nice dark bay horse should have been ridden by Ken White. Ken, however, was claimed by Jack Yeomans to partner Game Purston and so I came in for the ride.

Norther was my ninety-ninth winner of the season and it was not until I won the Bettisfield Handicap Chase at Bangor on 24 April 1965, riding Dundalk, that I made my century. I had won on him at Wolverhampton on 15 March for Doug Francis.

Dundalk had been trained by Fred Rimell before passing on to Doug Francis' yard where he began to win quite a few races. I had ridden several winners for Doug who was quite unlike his brother, Dick, in appearance, being heavily built. Seldom without a fag in his mouth, Doug was inclined to be tense, especially when you were beaten on one of his horses. Then his lips would twitch a bit and you could see that he wanted to kill you! If you won, he was laughing and cheerful. He was a close friend of Fred Rimell's, but his one delight was to beat him – he really got a kick out of doing that.

I felt so sorry for Fred Rimell that day. To ride my one hundredth winner on a horse that he had once trained, and which was now with another trainer, was ironic. To cap it all, I rode my next winner, Parkinson Minor, at the same meeting, and that *was* trained by Fred. I had been beaten in every ride for him since my win on Norther, only to win on Dundalk when it really mattered. It did not go down very well, but poor Fred did say wistfully, 'Well, I wish I could have trained that one for you,' which was quite understandable.

My win on Dundalk had made me the fourth National Hunt jockey to score 100 winners in a season. Fred Rees had done so in 1924; Fred Winter had achieved this with the then record total of 121 winners in the 1952–53 season; and Stan Mellor in 1960–61 with 118. The realization of this both humbled me and yet made me fiercely determined to try to beat Fred Winter's record, and there was not much of the season left in which to do it.

I went all over the country seeking winners, steadily creeping up on Fred Winter's total of 121. Included in my thousands of miles of travelling at the end of that season was a visit to France.

Madame Logut wanted Spartan General to run in the Prix La Barka Hurdle over 2 miles and 3 furlongs, run at Auteuil on 31 May. The owner was already in France, and I flew out with Mercy, Fred and Katie Gaze a few days before the race.

At the airport, Spartan General was loaded into the aircraft on a straight hoist, surrounded by packing cases but with nothing else to support him. Luckily he was a sensible horse and did not move. He could easily had panicked and fallen onto the tarmac. Fred was almost beside himself at the sight.

We stayed at Longchamp with Alec Head, a most charming host, and were able to school over the French hurdles for the first time and become familiar with them. The interesting part of the trip, for me, was riding on the gallops over there. It was so different from anything I had seen in England. The colts were ridden upsides like a group of hunt horses. The fillies, grouped likewise, followed behind, in bunches rather than in strings. We used the wide sand gallops and afterwards we went for long rides through the forests, with the fillies going one way and the colts another. You could ride for miles and I thoroughly enjoyed the whole experience.

I had to do a very light weight on Spartan General and Fred Rimell joined me, for the second time in all the years I rode for him, in a sauna bath near Longchamp.

Spartan General ran well in the race but he did not have the speed of the other horses and we were unplaced. Nevertheless, Madame Logut and everyone else seemed happy with his performance and the way he had adapted himself to his new surroundings; it was a very pleasant trip.

With the championship within my reach I rode Oblivious at the Stratford evening meeting to win the Farewell Handicap Chase on 11 June, and on the second day of the meeting and the last of the season, I rode my 114th winner when Joe's Girl, owned by Joe Tustin, won the Holbech Handicap Chase.

I had not beaten Fred Winter's record, but I was Champion National Hunt Jockey for the 1964–65 season. I had dreamed of this moment and travelled miles to achieve at least one of my major ambitions in life. It was such a wonderful feeling. I knew that I would be a permanent part of racing history by becoming champion jockey, which was a great thrill.

There was one typically individual message from Doc Wilson who, when Josh Gifford and I called round to see him that night, greeted us with a blast from his shotgun which he fired into the air from his bedroom window – a personal victory salute!

Having won the championship, my immediate resolve was to retain it at all costs. My appetite for winning was insatiable.

8

Champion Again, and a New Record

Although the National Hunt season was over in this country, I had to make a supreme effort to do the weight of 10 stone if I were to ride Spartan General again at Auteuil on 23 June. Stan Mellor was breathing down my neck for the ride, as he could do the weight easily, and while other National Hunt jockeys were lying in the sun getting fat, I was wasting myself to a shadow. The race was the Grande Course de Haies, the French equivalent of our Champion Hurdle, run over 3 miles 1 furlong, and the prize money of £15,919 was enticing.

Fred Rimell had flown to France with Spartan General and I was to follow him in time to school the horse a few days before the race. I still had to get off so much weight that it was almost unthinkable, but I said that I would do it. I stayed in the baths in Jermyn Street all night, knowing that I had to catch the plane to France at 5.30 the following evening.

When I arrived in France I went straight to the baths in the Champs-Elysées. I was still not light enough to ride without cheating, and the stewards are very strict about this in France. After a while I knew that I had made the weight. I came out weighing 9 stone 12 pounds which was fine. The speciality at those baths was the offer of a steak with a side salad, and a glass of white wine, when you had finished your session in the steam rooms. After the build-up and the hours of wasting it seemed too good to miss. I chewed the steak, but did not swallow the meat, and the side salad and wine were ambrosia and nectar to me at that moment. When I reached the racetrack I felt very fit, although I have never been so slender in my life.

I had arranged for my parents to fly to France with my valet to see the race, and when I arrived they were getting anxious, wondering what had held me up. They told me after the race that they did not recognize me as I had lost so much weight.

Going to post for the French Champion Hurdle there was a practice hurdle which Spartan General skimmed over. He was going so well in the race that I thought he would win by 100 yards. Turning into the straight I was lying about fourth and what happened then I will never understand. At every hurdle the other horses were gaining half a length over me. They were brushing through the top of the rather soft hurdles they have in France, while Spartan General was jumping cleanly as an English horse should do. Suddenly the rest of the field flashed past me and I finished sixth. It was as if I were standing still. Mercy Rimell said afterwards that she thought the ground was 'false' for Spartan General, but really, all he could ever do was to stay.

After the race I was so hungry that I started to eat a roll and could not swallow it, as I had no saliva. I could not drink either, and I felt ghastly. I would never go to such lengths again in order to lose weight. My bodily state in no way affected Spartan General's performance in that race, however. He was such a strong pulling horse that he just carried me, but he ran in company that was a bit too good for him.

At that time, the jumping game was not very healthy in Norway and the racing authorities over there asked if some good horses from England could be sent over. Willie Stephenson, who then had Michael Scudamore as his stable jockey, offered to provide nineteen of the twenty horses asked for, and sent Michael with them, both to train and ride them. It was a marvellous opportunity for Mike, and he, Mary and their children, Peter and Nicky, took a house at Oslo for eight weeks of the year.

I went out there several times to stay with them and ride schooling. It was through Michael that I met Tor Fossum, who organized most of the racing, and Leonard Sachs, his Swedish equivalent. I made many contacts who not only asked me to ride for them but who have remained my friends ever since. The Scandinavians are very pro-British and most hospitable. Their food was delicious and a great test of willpower for someone who loves it as much as I do. One of the nicest meals I had there was salmon, which had been wrapped in herbs and buried for about two weeks before being prepared for the table.

As well as riding schooling and racing once a week, we went fishing amongst some of the most magnificent scenery imaginable.

From the outset of the 1965–66 season I hit form, riding winners both for the Kinnersley stable and for John Barclay and Denys Smith.

One memento I have after riding four winners for John Barclay at the Newton Abbot meeting on 11 and 12 August is a bottle of Scotch with the signatures of the winning owners inscribed upon it.

Denys Smith asked me to ride two horses for him on 27 September at Hexham – Greek Scholar and Master Cop. The day before I travelled with Peter Jones to a celebrity show jumping event at Balsall Common.

After the competition there was a collection of jockeys and show jumpers, including Harvey Smith, Ted Edgar and David Broome, and we decided to play a ridiculous game of football on horseback. With five members of the team on horses and me on a donkey, we tried to push an enormous football into goal using our animals' shoulders. I had had a few jars with some of these jokers before the game and during the match I was knocked all over the place. The ball went over me, the donkey fell on me and apparently our antics greatly amused the onlookers. Afterwards we had a party and during the course of the evening Harvey Smith started doing some 'squat-ups' to show how fit he was. Then he said he could pick up a chair by one leg while doing a squat-up, which he did – and that takes some doing. I told him that I could also do it and managed, after a fashion. Harvey then said, truculently, 'Right then, Biddlecombe, try and follow this.'

Peter Jones, who must have weighed about 9 stone 10 pounds, was sitting in the chair and Harvey went down again on his haunches, caught hold of one chairleg and lifted it, with Peter still sitting there, high in the air. It was remarkable. I had no idea that Harvey possessed such formidable strength.

I vaguely remember Peter driving me home after the junketings, and the next day Dad took pity on me and drove me all the way to Hexham. It had rained buckets and the course was very slippery. After I had won the Langley Chase with Greek Scholar, I rode Master Cop, a good sort, in the Threepwood Novices' Chase. The race was a chapter of accidents with only one horse, Pallas Main, coming home. There were four runners, but they all slipped, ran out or fell, including Master Cop, who broke his back at the water, which made me more miserable. I was grateful to Dad for driving me home afterwards.

A rather eccentric owner who had her horses with Fred Rimell was Miss Barbara de Winton. She had been a great point-to-point rider and many people will remember her with affection. She was similar to Dorothy Paget in the way she dressed, usually in a frumpy old coat with a little beret on her head. She was very tough, did not give a damn what people thought of her and knew a great deal about horses.

I had ridden her little horse, Sharuk, to win over hurdles and fences; he was a versatile, consistent character who would do anything you asked of him. Miss de Winton also had another good horse, Mighty Element, which I rode in the Binfield Hurdle at Ascot on 8 October. There was a gamble on him that day and all went well until the last hurdle when he tried to duck out, then ran into it, half stumbled over it and picked himself up to go on and win by a short head.

Barbara de Winton, quite forgetting where she was, let out a 'view holloa' from the stands as I rode into the winner's enclosure. Everyone turned round to look at this strange lady with her big old coat and funny hat, but she did not turn a hair. She slapped me so hard on the back that she nearly knocked me over and, in doing so, infringed the rule that a jockey must not be touched until he has weighed in.

Lord Porchester came up to Fred and said, 'Rimell – tell your owner not to touch the jockey,' and Fred replied, 'My Lord, you tell her yourself – and mind she doesn't hit you with her bloody umbrella!'

Moonduster, an adaptable horse, won the Hugh Sumner Challenge Cup Chase with me at Ludlow that October. He was owned by Theodore West, who was a very natty dresser, usually decked out in a sporty suit with plus-fours, set off by a bow tie and an equally sporty hat with a feather in it, and carrying a thumbstick as the finishing touch.

Fred had passed the time of day with him at race meetings, but he happened to be sitting next to Theodore at the Ascot sales and it transpired that they were both going to bid for Moonduster. As the bidding passed Fred's limit, Theodore said, 'Well, you had better start bidding for me,' and when the horse was knocked down to Fred, Theodore said, 'That's fine, you'd better have him and train him for me.'

Fred had never trained for Theodore in his life, but that is how Moonduster came to Kinnersley, and he was to win a lot of races with me.

Soon after my success with Moonduster at Ludlow, I fell with

Wingeltange at Worcester on 27 October, and again on Mediterranean Blue at the same meeting. This second fall hurt me, and when I went to the clinic the X-rays suggested a possible fracture of my right shoulder blade. I could have aggravated an earlier break and I was advised not to ride until after the Liverpool meeting at the end of the month.

I saw my first wife at Stratford racecourse on 4 November 1965, soon after I had resumed riding. I had only one ride at the meeting on Sharuk, who won his race, and I then joined the throng watching the runners for the King Lear Handicap Chase circling the paddock. There were two young ladies talking earnestly to Pat Upton, trainer of one of the runners, Miss Surprise. Jack Cook, then the stable jockey, was also with them.

One of the girls riveted my attention. Dark-haired, slim and attractive, she made such an impression on me that I sought out Jack Cook after the race and asked who she was.

'Oh, that is Bridget Tyrwhitt-Drake – and the other one is her sister-in-law – she owns the mare.'

'Well,' I told Jack, laughingly, 'I could do with the little one!' which was Bridget, and then thought no more about her. At that time I was going out with a girl called Vivienne. She was a model whom I had met at a party and was strikingly pretty. I remember rushing up to Fred Rimell soon after meeting her and telling him that I had found the girl I intended to marry.

'That's nice, Terry,' he beamed. 'What's her name?'

'Vivienne,' I said.

'Vivienne what, though?' persisted Fred.

'I don't know her other name, but I am going to marry her.'

This amused Fred no end, but when he met Vivienne he liked her at once. I am afraid that Vivienne spoiled me too much. She was not a forceful girl and only wanted to please me, something of which I took shameless advantage, although I was very fond of her.

I was not to meet Bridget until the following year. I went on with my racing and continued my relationship with Vivienne as before.

Harry Collins, who farmed near Yeovil, had bred a colt foal from his mare, Woodlander. When Woodlander was sent to Domaha, he refused to cover her and Eastern Venture, standing at the same stud, sired her first offspring who was named Woodland Venture.

As a five-year-old, Woodland Venture had run disappointingly in

point-to-points and Harry Dufossee, who had acted as Harry Collins'
adviser throughout, suggested that the horse be sent to Fred Rimell to
be trained.

When Woodland Venture arrived at Kinnersley, Fred disliked him
on sight. Mercy thought he could be a nice horse but there is no doubt
that he was an awkward individual in those early days. There was one
person at Kinnersley who was prepared to take an interest in him and
that was Graham Nicholls. Graham had been with the late Peter
Cazalet before coming to Fred Rimell, riding Lochroe to win five
times, as well as other good horses, and he was a fine horseman. After
the rest of the lads had virtually said they did not want to know about
Woodland Venture, Fred asked Graham if he would ride him out.
Graham, who loved working with young, green horses, hacked
Woodland Venture around the roads, opening gates and popping over
a few hedges to keep him amused. He was, in Graham's view, 'just like
a big kid, green as grass and full of play. He took nothing very
seriously, which was the top and bottom of his behaviour. He had no
vice about him – but he could perform a bit!'

It was Graham who made Woodland Venture sweet with hours of
patient coaxing, scolding and not a few wild moments. The first time
he realized that here was a good horse was when he rode him work. At
that time, Graham had a pub near Kinnersley and was a little bit
heavier than the work jockeys. Even then, he found that when
Woodland Venture was right he could give weight away and still
gallop over the top of the other horses.

I rode Woodland Venture at Worcester on 10 November 1965, in
the 2-mile Felton Novices' Chase. He was not the prettiest of horses,
brown, standing about 16.3 hands, rather angular in conformation,
but there was something about him. He had the most lovely head and
a kind eye.

As soon as I got on his back in the paddock I felt the latent power of
this horse under me, waiting to be tapped. He ran raggedly in a
fast-run race, jumping three fences quite well before over-jumping at
the next. He did not fall, despite sliding along the ground on landing.
He was then out of the race and I pulled him up, but not before I had
felt him surge forward under me when I asked him, just as Graham
had sensed on the gallops.

I did not have time to think deeply about Woodland Venture
because I had the nerve-racking task of writing my speech for the
Jockeys' Dinner at Cheltenham on 12 November, at which I knew I

would be at the top table with some of the most powerful men in racing.

I was petrified. 'Ruby' Holland-Martin sat on one side of me, which was fine because I had been shooting with him at his Overbury estate and knew him well. I think Lord Willoughby de Broke was my other dinner table companion, but I was so nervous that my mind went blank. It was just like sitting between two headmasters at school! There was a lot of barracking from the other jockeys as I stood up to make my speech, but I got through it somehow. I have learned since to say as little as possible. Afterwards, everyone let their hair down, the bread rolls started to fly and we had a great evening.

I have been to many championship dinners in recent years and found that this atmosphere has tended to peter out. The stewards no longer join in the fun as they did in my day; there are too many people from the press around and the occasion has tended to become stuffy.

Later that year, I was awarded the Bollinger Trophy as Champion National Hunt Jockey for the 1964–65 season and was joined by Macer Gifford, who was leading amateur that year, for the presentation by Madame Bollinger of the perpetual silver salver, and a silver tankard as a memento.

At Newbury, on 26 November, I rode Noble Pierre for Edward Courage. This was the horse on which I had had my first ride for him at Cheltenham in 1961. Noble Pierre was galloping and jumping well in the Hopeful Novices' Chase until we came to the third from home, which was an open ditch. He stood off too far and turned over. I was catapulted out of the saddle. As I hit the ground I heard my horse's quarters thump on the turf beside me, just missing me. I was unhurt but he, unfortunately, broke his neck in one of the most spectacular falls ever photographed. It was a tragic incident and the premature loss of a fine steeplechaser.

Since I had pulled up Woodland Venture at Worcester, he had unseated Jack Lenehan, who sometimes rode for Fred Rimell, at Worcester on 20 November, and it was decided to put me up on the horse again for the Marle Hill Novices' Chase at Cheltenham on 17 December.

We set off and I had settled Woodland Venture in nicely to get him relaxed. He had crashed through one or two fences before going to the last open ditch, but I was delighted with him. I had taught him something which I had not had the chance to do before – I had got him jumping. He was back on his hocks and starting to race. After those initial mistakes, he was jumping well when, approaching the last open ditch, I saw Stan Mellor sitting on top of the fence where he had been deposited by his horse, aptly named Parting Gift.

Parting Gift was struggling to get out of the ditch and I thought to myself, 'Don't go on and jump this, your horse has done his job, pull out – don't lose his confidence.' I pulled Woodland Venture up for the second time in his racing career. Somebody riding alongside me said. 'You're taking the easy way out,' but he was wrong.

I did not pull up to avoid Stan – although I would have done my best not to hit him had I gone on! I did not want to destroy the confidence of a horse which I felt was destined for greater things in the future.

Christmas was the usual battle against the temptation of Mother's cooking. On 27 December, Spartan General found Kempton too sharp for him, and he could only come third in the Boxing Day Handicap Hurdle.

I loved riding for Fred Winter, although I did not produce many winners for him. I won on Indian Spice, which was trained by him, later that day at Kempton, and on 28 January I landed the 'Winter Double' at Windsor, when I deputised for Eddie Harty and won on both Austerity and Fools Delight.

The Kempton meeting was marred by the death of Colonel W. H. Whitbread's outstanding chaser, Dunkirk, in the King George VI Chase, which was won by Arkle. I watched the race from the stands and saw this super horse fall when in the lead. He was so bold that I marvelled that he had not had a fatal fall earlier in his career.

On 6 January 1966, at Cheltenham, I won the Malvern Novices' Hurdle on John Liley's Jupiter Boy, beating Paul Kelleway on Eros Boy, which was trained by Ryan Price at Findon. It was the kind of race that I revelled in – big stable racing against big stable. Jupiter Boy won a lot of races with me. He was a classy horse, bought off the Flat, and was a bold, clean jumper.

Then I had the leg up on Woodland Venture for the Western Novices' Chase over 3 miles 1 furlong. I still had such faith in this horse, even though he had not come anywhere near finishing a race since he had been at Kinnersley. Fred Rimell had no interest in him as a steeplechasing prospect.

In the paddock, Fred told me, 'When you come back, tell the owner that this horse should really go back to point-to-pointing.'

'I think he'll win,' I said, and I am sure Fred thought I was mad.

In the weighing room beforehand, Jimmy Morrissey had jokingly remarked, 'I see you're riding a "pup" today!' – referring to Woodland Venture's form on the racecard which read 'PUP'. Both Jimmy and Fred had to eat their words. Woodland Venture almost smashed the first fence and made a lot of mistakes during the race. He never once felt as if he was going to fall. He truly impressed me and ran on gamely to beat Willie Robinson on the talented Woodlawn by a head.

It was a different Fred Rimell who greeted me in the winner's enclosure. I had gone out on a point-to-pointer and come back, in his opinion, on a Gold Cup horse!

Woodland Venture came out again on 27 January to win the Lechlade Chase over 3 miles 1 furlong, again at Cheltenham. He was still making the occasional blunder. He did not just hit his fences, he practically parted them and he made a shocking mess of the last, again keeping his feet and going on to a six-lengths win.

I was to ride Woodland Venture again at the Newbury meeting on 19 February. I had had two crashing falls on the first day and was nursing my bruises at a party afterwards and chatting to Scudamore. He was riding Rutherfords against me on Woodland Venture in the Compton Chase the next day. He was quite confident that he would win, and I told him, very precisely, just how I was going to beat him.

Michael set up a fair old gallop in the race and I waited behind him, and then pulled out and passed him to win by a length. Michael was furious because the race had gone just as I had foretold. He has never forgotten it!

Woodland Venture could only finish fifth in the Totalisator Champion Novices' Chase at Cheltenham on 15 March. He did nothing wrong. He galloped and jumped well, but the race went to Different Class, owned by film star Gregory Peck. Woodland Venture was a difficult horse to train in that his form varied so quickly. He would be a good horse for a month, then he would go back a bit, and hit form again just as quickly. He needed a great deal of work and I never got to the bottom of him in a race – he stayed for ever.

Trelawny had returned to Kinnersley and I had won on him at Warwick on 5 March, which pleased his owner as her friends could see for themselves what a superb horse he was. He gave me another dream of a ride in the Spa Hurdle on 17 March 1966. That was something truly beautiful. I just sat on him for 3 miles, never changing hands as he jumped from hurdle to hurdle. It was the most fantastic feeling. If I lie awake at night thinking about the most memorable horses I have ever ridden, Trelawny immediately comes to mind.

He came out again to win the Coronation Hurdle with me at Liverpool on 25 March. He was so adaptable, so balanced, that 3 miles or 2 miles, whatever the distance, he literally took in his stride.

I did not have such a happy time in the Mildmay Chase when Magnus, owned by Fred's uncle, Will Rimell, became entangled with a bunch of horses, some falling, some jumping across him, and we were hit all over the place. How he did not fall I will never know, but he was strong and bold and managed to extricate himself. The photographs I have of this incident are remarkable.

My partner in the 1966 Grand National on 26 March was The Fossa, who was set to carry 10 stone 8 pounds. His owner's colours were the heaviest I ever rode in. They were nice and warm but they weighed about $2\frac{1}{2}$ pounds and I was nearly down to my limit where weight was concerned.

Vivienne was with me for the Liverpool meeting and, knowing that she was an excellent needlewoman, I asked her if it would be possible to make up a set of lightweight silks. She bought the material and sat up all night stitching my silks together. When she had finished, they weighed about $2\frac{1}{2}$ ounces. I did not deserve such devotion.

Apart from dropping his hind legs in the water The Fossa jumped immaculately in the National and I had a great ride round. He was one of those horses that would run his heart out and he finished a gallant fourth to the Fred Winter-trained Anglo, ridden by Tim Norman.

As Trelawny had displayed such brilliance over hurdles, Mrs Carver was keen to find out whether he would be as good over fences. Although Fred agreed over the telephone to give him a school, I could tell that he was not happy about the suggestion, and neither was I. We both thought so much of Trelawny that we did not want anything to happen to him.

We said nothing to each other beforehand. Fred went in the Land-Rover to the park where the schooling fences were and I took Trelawny to meet him there. Nobody else was present. I turned Trelawny in, let him have a look at the first fence, turned him back and then away he went. He was foot perfect – like a Gold Cup horse – magic.

'How was that?' Fred asked as I pulled up.

'Great.'

'Do you want to jump him again?'

'No – I didn't particularly want to jump him anyway.'

To my relief Fred agreed with me.

'Neither did I,' he said.

We went back to breakfast and Fred telephoned Mrs Carver.

'The old horse tried to stop at the jump – diabolical. It's no use, he'll break his bloody neck and that would be rather sad, don't you think?'

I am sure that this was the first time in all the years Mrs Carver had had horses with Fred that he had overridden her wishes. That was one of the nicest incidents I remember concerning Fred Rimell, and it revealed the softer side of the man that I always suspected was there. Racing is a business in which nobody can afford to be soft, or to be seen to be soft. Nevertheless, Trelawny finished his racing career honourably, as he deserved to do, and then retired to end his days with his owner.

During the 1965–66 season I travelled some 80,000 miles. Unlike the flat-race jockeys, my travelling was mostly by road and rail, but I was so keen to be champion again that it did not seem to affect me.

However, I flew to the Ayr Meeting on 16 May, winning with Pretentious for Denys Smith before going on to Perth on 18 May and scoring again on another of his horses, Wifes Choice.

The Turkish baths in Edinburgh were excellent. At the Darlington baths, they wrapped you in sacks of salt which made the sweat pour out of you, and Newcastle, also, was very good.

In those days, I often encountered Chris Collins in most of the northern baths where I would find him sweating his guts out. He had twice as much to lose as I had. He was riding for Arthur Stephenson at the time and was a dedicated waster and a great amateur rider.

Major Guy Cunard was the hardest waster I have ever seen. He was well into his fifties when I first knew him and used to ride mainly at Sandown. He rode sixty-one winners under National Hunt Rules, and 251 point-to-point winners. He had an incessant battle with his weight. Many a time when we younger jockeys went to the baths in London, there would be the old major, sweating away in a pair of longjohns. He would waste for hours, and the next morning he would still be at it when we woke up. Major Cunard invariably won his races after these all-night sessions. We used to see him in the weighing room afterwards when he was changing and he had lost so much weight that his skin was loose; it almost looked as if he were still wearing his longjohns! He was a great character and a superb horseman.

Steve Davenport, riding Beautiful Boy, beat me by a short head at

Southwell on 28 May, when I was riding Guy's Choice for Albert Bacon, an appropriately named butcher for whom I had ridden successfully earlier that season. Steve used to annoy me intensely because he beat me in more photo-finishes than any other jockey. He was a good little horseman but he used just to sit there and seemed to be doing absolutely nothing.

On 30 May, nothing could go wrong for me at Uttoxeter. Quick Approach, Honey End, Buchan Loon and Stars and Bars all won their races for me.

At Uttoxeter again on 11 June, I rode Honey End to win the Midsummer Chase over 3 miles. This was not only my 100th winner of the season, breaking the record as the first National Hunt jockey to ride over 100 winners two years running, which, as I write, has yet to be beaten, but I was a certainty for the championship for the second year in succession.

From Uttoxeter I went with Scudamore and Josh Gifford to the evening meeting at Market Rasen. After racing, plans were made for a celebration. Four of us, Michael, Josh, Roy Blandford and I, decided to go into Lincoln. We drove all round the city trying to find somewhere to eat and finished up in a Chinese restaurant which did not serve any alcohol! We had Coca-Cola instead. The next drink we had was at Stratford railway station, and that was cocoa which we obtained from a slot machine. It was an unbelievable situation in which to find ourselves.

I was so thrilled to be champion jockey again, especially as this time the honour had not come my way with some of my chief protagonists laid up with injury, which had been the case with Josh Gifford and David Mould the year before.

I made absolutely sure of my position by winning on Lieutenant Colonel D. Kirkness' Buckaroo at Southwell on 13 June and finishing up with a win on Michel Andrew, owned and trained by Guy Harwood at Pulborough, which brought my total for the season to 102 winners.

That summer, Vivienne and I went to Sardinia with Mercy and Fred and Martin and Edna Tate; Lord and Lady Chelsea were also staying there. We had a day in Rome en route, which was beautiful. We had a marvellous time in Sardinia. The food was good and so was the weather. It was an expensive holiday and it could have been even more so for me because one night we started playing 'Farmers' Glory'. I was getting good cards but could not win. I kept writing IOUs and at the end of the day I owed a bit more than I could afford to lose. Mercifully both Fred Rimell and Charlie Chelsea refused to allow me to honour my debts.

Charlie Chelsea owned one of the most fabulous jumpers I ever rode, Roman Holiday, which was trained by Major C. Bewicke at Didcot. He was a beautifully balanced horse; he did not pull but seemed to float when he jumped. Of all the horses I have ridden, Roman Holiday ranks in the top five as a great jumper, an opinion shared by Jeff King, who also won many races on him.

9
Gold Cup Year

One of the most enjoyable events of the year for all of us in National Hunt racing was the Finmere Jumping Show, held every August in aid of paraplegics.

Top show jumpers from all over the country supported this show, which also staged the Grand National Jockeys' Jumping Competition, and the Jockeys' Donkey Derby. The jumping events attracted volunteers from so many jockeys that it was impossible to find enough horses for them.

The donkey derbies and 'Grand Nationals' were great sport. We went all over the country to take part in these, including Finmere. They inevitably provided riotous scenes with jockeys being pushed off, falling off, being trampled on, or running in pursuit of rebellious donkeys. In the Grand Nationals we had straw bales for fences and these events provided some good laughs, as did the sulky races. I remember Richard Pitman beating me in one of these after a great battle.

We had a smashing donkey at home for years, called Joey, who would go like the wind left-handed, and refused to budge if you asked him to go to the right. He won endless donkey derbies and raised a lot of money for charity before he retired. After a while, I became tired of these events. There were too many of them, and people wrote to the RSPCA complaining that some of the jockeys were too heavy to ride donkeys. Nevertheless, we raised quite a bit of money while these races lasted.

Despite having won the championship for two years running, I knew that I would have to go all out to retain it. There were too many very good jockeys riding against me and hungry for the spoils.

Michael Scudamore was still commuting between this country and

Oslo during the late summer of 1966, leaving his family to enjoy themselves in Scandinavia. He had a bad fall at Market Rasen at the beginning of the season, spraining his knee, and Vivienne, Mike and I went to Heathrow the following morning so that I could fly to Oslo; I was to ride Acrobat in the Swedish Champion Hurdle at Malmo, on 15 August.

Acrobat was owned by E. Tiedman Johannessen, and was a big, dark bay. I was going very easily, tracking Leonard Sachs, when about two hurdles from home I slipped up on the bend. I was not at all pleased.

To ride in the Swedish Grand National I had to do a light weight to ride a small but good horse, and I took full advantage of the Turkish baths out there. I lost a lot of weight and was feeling quite sharp as I went to post. Following a mistake at the first fence I could not get back into the race. Every time we came to a bend I was shut out. Finally, my horse made a mistake again right in front of the stands, and I fell off. Having started favourite, this debacle only added to my humiliation.

I made some influential contacts during my visits which were to lead to many invitations to ride at the Scandinavian Sunday race meetings.

Early on in my racing life, I had become friendly with John Bebbington when, as an amateur, he rode in point-to-points and came to some of our parties after race meetings. His family were farmers and lived near Ludlow racecourse. They also bred several good-class racehorses, among them The Laird.

I had done quite a bit of shooting with John, and before the Ludlow meeting on 21 and 22 September 1966 he invited Josh Gifford and me to stay with him and have some duck shooting after the first day's racing.

On the first day at Ludlow I won the Downton Chase on The Fossa; then I won on Spanish Dictator, one of my few rides for Roy Whiston, and again on Fulminato, trained by Fred Rimell. It was a good start to the meeting and we went back to John's home for an evening's duck shooting as arranged. Mr and Mrs Bebbington were away, and after some fine sport, we decided to throw a party which developed into a pretty heavy evening. There were plenty of attractive females present and I had about an hour's sleep at the most.

Early in the morning I got up, knowing that I had to lose 6 pounds in order to ride that day. The bathroom was large and a bit draughty, so I collected all the electric fires I could find and switched them on to heat the room up before running a bath so hot that I could hardly bear it, to make me sweat. Feeling quite terrible, I drove with Josh to the racecourse where he proceeded to beat me by three quarters of a length on Mr Fizz, trained locally by Stan Wright.

I rode Royal Emblem for Peter Ransom in that race, one of three horses I was to ride for him that day. Peter trained at Leominster, in Herefordshire, and he was a volatile but good-hearted man. When he discovered that I was carrying 3 pounds overweight he exploded.

'If you hadn't been living it up all night and got your weight off, you would have won that,' he raged. Which was uncomfortably close to the truth.

However, I won the Salop Hurdle on his Cat's Cradle, which made Peter a little happier, as he had backed it at 6–1, and then I drove Mon Bon Homme up to beat an infuriated Scudamore in the Bettisfield Chase, before winning the Ashford Novices' Chase on another of Ransom's horses, Mintop. It was not over then, because I had a great ride on Jack Peacock's Delapre Lad to win the second division of the Salop Hurdle, before rounding off the day by taking the second division of the Ashford Novices' Chase with Dumpy, for Fred Rimell. I was feeling very pleased with myself – three winners on the first day, a hectic night, and five winners on the second day – it was a lovely feeling – when up came Peter Ransom again and he said to me, somewhat sourly, 'Of course, if you had gone to bed early you would have won on all of them!'

I was steadily riding winners when I had a crashing fall on Oak Beam in the Bleasby Hurdle at Southwell on 17 October. I injured my left elbow and split a muscle in my arm. The pain was severe but a quick X-ray showed that nothing was broken.

I was not so lucky at Newbury on 21 October when I rode Sheridan in the Wyld Court Hurdle for Derrick Robins, who was manager for Coventry City Football Club. Sheridan went well until two out when he fell. I knew that I had done something more serious this time as my right wrist was throbbing. An X-ray at Bill Tucker's clinic revealed a fracture. I had to have my wrist in plaster and I missed the Doncaster and Chepstow meetings as a result.

Subsequently, as advised by Bill Tucker, I wore a moulded leather gauntlet fastened with a zip on my left wrist, and a similar support on my right wrist, which I buckled on. I wore these for every race until I retired.

In the meantime I had paid a visit to the Horse of the Year Show and it was there that I met Bridget Tyrwhitt-Drake for the first time after seeing her at Stratford racecourse almost a year earlier. She was descended from Sir Francis Drake, and her family had been associated with horses and racing for generations, especially the Grand National. Bridget loved her show jumping, although she was never in the top flight, and her father, who had horses in training for his second wife, was a keen horseman.

I had gone to Tom Brake's caravan to have a chat – and probably to remind him that I had taught Lizawake to jump – when I saw Bridget sitting apart from the others in the party, having a quiet smoke. I went over to talk to her and found her just as attractive as before. She seemed to be quite interested in me, which was encouraging. She was sharing a caravan with Althea Roger-Smith, a super girl and a well-known name in show jumping, who was later to marry Josh Gifford. I made sure of a future meeting with Bridget before returning to the Ascot meeting to ride Spartan General on 27 October.

My wrist was still in plaster when I had the leg up on him for the National Hunt Centenary Cup Hurdle, and the horse was full of running when he hit the third hurdle really hard and fell. That was the only time he fell in his life. I was unhurt, but Spartan General broke his jaw. He was unable to eat anything for some time and lived on gruel which he managed to suck into his mouth.

Spartan General recovered remarkably quickly. He was such a robust, gutsy horse, both on and off the racecourse. When he went to John Thorne's Chesterton Stud in 1970 he proved to be an outstanding sire. He died in 1979 but his son, Spartan Missile, carried John Thorne, then no youngster, into second place behind Aldaniti in the 1981 Grand National.

I was meant to ride Cecil Haynes' Snakestone in the Rock Handicap Hurdle at Wolverhampton on 1 November. I could not do the weight, so Fred asked Michael Scudamore to take my place.

I watched the race from the stands and Snakestone was going well until he slipped up on the bend past the stands, bringing down three other horses. Michael was kicked several times by the thrashing hooves of the horses getting to their feet and I saw the ambulance racing down the track. When I went to the ambulance room Michael was sitting up with blood pouring out of him. Luckily he had not been knocked unconscious because he could have choked to death. His face was smashed to pieces and he could not talk. I visited him in hospital a couple of days later and found him with his face swollen and his jaw wired up where it had been fractured in six or seven places. He had split his palate, broken his nose, cracked both cheekbones, suffered bad cuts to the head and broken some ribs. One lung had collapsed but, worst of all, he had lost 90 per cent of the sight in one eye. I looked at Mike, bravely sucking soup through a straw into what was left of his mouth and felt terrible at seeing one of my best friends smashed up on a horse that I should have ridden.

It was a close call for Mike, and the end of his riding career. At that time he was at the very peak of his ability, riding like a man possessed. He was in hospital for about three weeks and when he recovered, he started training at his farm, Prothither, near Hereford, in 1967.

My wrist was giving me a lot of pain and after riding Magnus to win at Warwick on 5 November, I was advised to rest for a week, which meant that I had to miss a number of important meetings, including Cheltenham. Eddie Harty deputised for me on Woodland Venture in the Cheltenham Chase Stakes to beat a good-class field. I did not have a ride in the Mackeson Gold Cup which was won by Paddy Broderick riding Pawnbroker for Arthur Stephenson.

Paddy Broderick was one of the most popular National Hunt jockeys. It is the Brods of this world who make English racing. He was a very hard man who squeezed his horses, picked them up and got them jumping. He looked untidy when he rode but he knew what he was doing.

In his later years when, occasionally, he was beaten on Night Nurse, people who should have known better muttered, 'Oh, put a decent jockey on that horse and he would have done a better job.' In my own mind another jockey would not have won the race if Brod had not done so. He was a fearless, no-nonsense man, and when he was at Arthur Stephenson's he followed the tradition of most of Arthur's jockeys which was to drive the horsebox to the races, take charge of the colours and saddle up the horses. If you handed him a roll of £1 notes and told him there were 100 in all he would feel these carefully and tell you immediately if there was one short! He was one of the magic men of racing.

I do not remember the 1966 Mackeson Gold Cup very well because the night before I had attended the dinner held in my honour as champion jockey for the 1965–66 season, at the Queen's Hotel, Cheltenham.

Josh was riding at Cheltenham and staying with us as usual. After racing he dragged me out of the Cellar Bar, where I had been drowning my sorrows, having no rides at my favourite course. As soon as I got home I went to bed, to sleep it off, only to be woken by Josh shaking me frantically and saying, 'Wake up, get out of bed – you've got to get a speech ready for tonight.'

I was horrified, I had forgotten all about it.

'What on earth shall I say this time?' I asked Josh.

We gave it some thought. I knew that I was to be presented with a print or painting, and between us we drew up an outline speech. When we had finished, Josh said, 'Now, just thank everybody for the picture, and leave it at that, because you are daft enough to say that it would look lovely hanging in the cowshed.'

I thought this was uproarious and fell about laughing.

At the hotel I sat through dinner, trying to collect my thoughts. I had just managed to clear my head by the time the presentation was made. Major W. D. Gibson, the Senior Steward of the National Hunt Committee, proposed the toast to me, and many of the great patrons of racing were at my table, including Lord Willoughby de Broke, Colonel Whitbread and Earl Cadogan.

I still thought the addition to my speech dreamt up by Josh was very witty and when my turn came to reply I stood up and said, 'My Lords, gentlemen, thank you very much for these two lovely "Snaffles" prints, which I am sure will look splendid hanging up in the cowshed,' and paused, waiting for the laughter. There was a dreadful silence, broken only by a loud guffaw from Josh somewhere in the sea of faces. It was terrible. I was so embarrassed it was not true. I managed to fluff my way through the remainder of my speech and sat down thankfully. I will never forget it. It was rude and stupid of me to say such a thing. I can only say that everybody there made nothing of it afterwards, and we had a terrific evening.

I came back to the racecourse to ride Knockaphrumpa at Leicester on 14 November. He had been bought from Ireland by Fred for Katie Gaze and must have been one of the biggest horses I ever rode. This giant of a horse with his gangly legs and huge jump ran an exciting race with me until we reached the fourteenth fence when we crumpled. I hurt my wrist again and my leg was in agony from my knee to my ankle. I could barely hobble.

At that time I was going out with Vivienne and also Bridget, with neither of them knowing anything about the other. Bridget was staying with Douglas Bunn at Hickstead and expecting to meet me there, so I persuaded the unsuspecting Vivienne to take me to Coventry station on the pretext that I was going straight to Bill Tucker in London to have my leg X-rayed. It was a rotten trick but, grand girl that she was, she believed me and I was soon on the train to London, where I caught another heading towards Brighton.

I had already telephoned Douglas Bunn to tell him I was on my way. On the way I downed about half a bottle of brandy to try and kill the pain, with little effect, and I got to Duggie's place absolutely done for.

'I've got just the thing for you,' he said, regarding me with pity, and fetched two pills from his medicine cupboard.

'Take these,' he said, 'they'll ease the pain.'

I swallowed them, with a champagne chaser, and then began to feel very light-headed.

'What on earth is in those pills?' I asked,

'Oh,' replied Duggie, 'only Butazolidin that I give the horses!'

I did not feel a thing after that until the tablets wore off. The next day I went to London for an X-ray. I had a badly bruised right ankle and a fractured bone in the lower part of my right leg. I was advised not to ride for three weeks.

In fact, I was riding a fortnight later at Chepstow on 3 December, to finish fourth on Norther in the Rhymney Breweries Chase to Bobby Beasley riding Kilburn.

I then had a period of riding horses into second place and below before winning with K. F. Alder's good horse, Saucy Kit, at Kempton on 27 December 1966. Trained by Mick Easterby, Saucy Kit was a chance ride for me that day, and afterwards I was asked to ride him in the Champion Hurdle the following spring. As it turned out, I was 'jocked off' but the horse won the big race with his usual partner, Roy Edwards, beating the Queen Mother's Makaldar.

Reunited with Woodland Venture once more, I set out afterwards to ride in the King George VI Chase, in which Arkle was also a runner. It was a small field and I could sense that Woodland Venture was at his peak that day, while Arkle was, by virtue of his engagements in Ireland and this country, bound to be travel weary. I was upsides Arkle and Pat Taaffe, absolutely cruising going to the second last. I felt sure that I had the race in my pocket when Woodland Venture over-jumped and fell. I could have wept with frustration because I would have won so easily. The race was doubly sad because the great Arkle finished second to Dormant, ridden by Jeff King, and pulled up lame, having broken a bone in his foot during the race. As is well known, Arkle never raced again, but was nursed back to health and enjoyed a happy retirement with his owner, Anne, Duchess of Westminster.

A happy occasion early in December was the presentation to me, for the second time, of the Bollinger Trophy. The amateur champion that year was Chris Collins, who had ridden twenty-four winners, and was to be champion the following season with a total of thirty-three.

I hated riding over fences at Doncaster. The going was always fast over the moor and the fences loomed black and menacing as you raced towards them. They reminded me of the fences at Manchester, which were also black and stiff, but although the Doncaster fences had more gorse in front of them to make them appear less formidable, one or two had nasty drops to them. The Doncaster track is also perpetually on the turn and when you eventually hit the straight, especially on a novice, the fences come rather too fast.

I rode Mrs Maxwell Joseph's Glenn in his first novice chase at Doncaster on 26 January 1967, and he went well to win easily. On the same day, unknown to me, a little bay horse called Gay Trip won a hurdle race at Gowran Park in Ireland, and what a part he was to play in my life!

It was very wet that year, with many fixtures cancelled as the courses were waterlogged. I went wherever there was a meeting, taking every ride I could, trying to keep my championship for the third year, with Josh Gifford hot on my heels.

The Cheltenham meeting went ahead with the going officially 'soft'. I rode Mrs Jackie Brutton's Ten Pins in the Totalisator Champion Novices' Chase on 14 March and thought I would have a fair chance on this athletic seven-year-old who had given me two good wins at Leicester and Cheltenham the year before.

It was a good-class race with nineteen runners. I was going so well on Ten Pins approaching the last open ditch. I saw my stride and started kicking. Going into the fence my stirrup leather broke and I nearly fell into the ditch in mid air. As Ten Pins landed I just slipped down his shoulder and the race, for me, was over. They were brand new leathers but the right one had snapped clean through, and I can only think that there must have been a fault in the grain. It was not a happy start to the first day's racing at Cheltenham.

The next day I rode Glenn in the Cotswold Chase. We were all bunching up together and my horse was simply flying down the hill when he hit the third fence from home and fell, bringing down Josh Gifford on Flandre II, and L. McLoughlin on Stonehaven. It was quite a pile-up and Glenn kicked me hard above my knee, ripping my breeches and almost castrating me. I rode Autobiography unplaced in the Champion Hurdle for Denys Smith afterwards and it was not until I reached home that evening that I found I could barely walk.

I was desperately worried that I might not be able to ride Woodland Venture in the Gold Cup the following afternoon, and in despair I went round to see Doc Wilson. He examined my knee and diagnosed torn ligaments. I told him that I would never pass the course doctor, but that I could ride provided I felt no pain. He knew how badly I wanted to ride in the Gold Cup and agreed to come to the weighing room before racing and give me a pain-killing injection. I had two other rides before the big race and I had to be sure in my mind that I was capable of riding well. It would not have been fair to Harry Collins, Fred or, indeed, Woodland Venture, if I had been in too much agony to ride a good race.

Doc Wilson was as good as his word. He sneaked into the weighing room and gave me a shot of local anaesthetic straight into my leg, which numbed it almost immediately. I managed to get round, unplaced, on Northern Challenger in the Spa Hurdle, and survived a fall on Katie Gaze's Even Break in the County Hurdle without experiencing pain or injury. I knew then that I could ride in the Gold Cup with confidence.

As I recall, it was a warmish day, with the odd shafts of sunlight breaking through onto the course. The going was good with just enough bite to provide good jumping ground.

There were eight runners in the Gold Cup. We were called over, came into line and were off. Woodland Venture hit the first fence quite hard and smashed through the second before settling down and starting to jump quite well. Coming down the hill on the first circuit, we were not going much of a gallop and David Nicholson joined me on the great Mill House. Going to the fence which would be the last the second time round, he said to me, 'If we jump this well, Biddles, we'll be on the Christmas cards next year.'

We were upsides and on an even stride. I thought I saw a good stride, and David thought he saw one too. We let our horses' heads go and there was an almighty crash as we both hit the fence. As we landed in a flurry of birch I shouted across, 'That's cocked up the Christmas cards!'

Having gathered up our horses again, David and I set out once more into the country, having a little chat, until we came to the last ditch where I pulled out and challenged. Woodland Venture simply flew the fence, and I thought that David had come with me but Mill House had failed to get the reach he needed. The next thing I saw was David down by my knees somewhere, getting lower and lower before finally rolling out of the saddle. I was delighted to see one of my chief dangers out of the way, but conversely it meant that I was left in front on my own. Woodland Venture was not a horse to do much by himself and he started to look about him. There had been a few showers and the course management had erected little shelters for the first-aid men to sit in. The shelters were too close to the track and Woodland Venture shied away from one of these which displeased me. I wound him up coming into the straight, quickening as I sensed that there could be something poised to challenge me. I was right. The grey form of Stalbridge Colonist, with Stan Mellor in the saddle, was steadily narrowing the gap. It put the fear of God in me because Stan was the last man I ever wanted to see taking me on in any race, let alone the Gold Cup – he was so good from the last fence. He was drawing nearer and nearer and, as we jumped the last fence practically together, I dropped my nearside rein. The crowd could not see this as it was on their blind side, but I was trying to ride a finish while frantically gathering up my loose rein at the same time.

On the run in, Stan headed me for a few strides. I remember thinking, 'He's going to beat me,' then, 'He has beaten me,' when, within a stride, Woodland Venture was fighting back at him and I thought fiercely, 'No way is he going to beat me!' I think that is the longest run in I have ever experienced. I could hear Stan shouting, but Woodland Venture lengthened his stride and I was holding Stan, I was going to hold him – and suddenly I had held him, to win. That feeling of holding him during those last few strides was so intense that I will always remember it.

I had won the Gold Cup, the Blue Riband of National Hunt racing, and achieved my greatest ambition. As I pulled up I could feel the tears streaming down my face.

The wind, blowing down the course, dried my cheeks and I

managed to get a grip on myself as I rode into the winner's enclosure. The ovation we received was unbelievable. I have never known any racecourse like Cheltenham for genuine warmth. The atmosphere there is unique and the cheers that day were deafening. I cannot describe how I felt. I imagine it would be the same for a cricketer reaching his first century, or a footballer scoring the winning goal at Wembley, but for me it transcended even that. I dismounted and unsaddled, standing by the horse and hearing the acclaim, knowing but not quite believing what I had done. I think that the Gold Cup being won by an English-trained horse helped to sustain the cheering too!

Fred Rimell was overjoyed. From where he had been standing at the end of the paddock, the angle of vision had convinced him that Stalbridge Colonist had just got up to win. It was only when my number was announced over the tannoy that he knew we had won the Gold Cup.

Harry Collins was so pleased with his horse's performance, and with me, that it was overwhelming. I learned afterwards that in order to put more money on Woodland Venture he had taken an old barren cow to market, without telling his wife, and increased his stake by £100.

It was ironic that Harry Dufossee, who had bred Stalbridge Colonist, should have recommended to Harry Collins that he put Woodland Venture with Fred Rimell, only to be beaten by him in this race of races.

After some of the tumult had died down and I was making my way back to the weighing room, I was confronted, to my horror, by the sight of Doc Wilson, his blue eyes alight with triumph, waving the hypodermic needle ecstatically in the air and shouting, 'This is what won him the race – this got him round!'

'Shut up, shut up!' I kept saying to him, but it was to no avail. The upshot of it was that the course doctor came to hear of it and we were reported to the Stewards. We were let off with a severe caution – delivered in a light-hearted spirit!

After racing, Fred came into the weighing room and told me that Harry Collins was giving a party at the Queen's Hotel, Cheltenham for about twenty people, and could I be there, with Bridget, for about 8 o'clock. I thought this would be great, and went off to have a few glasses of champagne with some of the other jockeys in the Cellar Bar, known only to those of us in racing and situated under the grandstand.

You could buy drinks there at cost price and over the years it became rather overcrowded.

When I came out, I bumped into David Coleman, the television commentator, and he and I with several others went to a little pub in Prestbury. As a result of these celebrations we arrived at the dinner late. The other guests were sitting down to the first course. Harry Collins did not seem to mind one bit, and the smile of welcome that he gave me was terrific. The look I received from Mercy Rimell could have killed!

We had a very good party, and afterwards Josh Gifford, Bridget and I went to Charlie Hornby's flat to play poker. He had been an assistant trainer to Fred some years before and I had won several races on his horse, Stormtrooper.

My luck was still holding, because I stood to lose nearly £90 and I got out on the last hand with two terrible cards. I did not know what the others had and I kept raising them and raising them, not taking another card and eventually I called. They put down their cards and I collected the pool. I do not think I even had a pair!

On the way home, with Bridget driving, I fell asleep after a day that will remain bright in my memory for the rest of my life.

After Cheltenham, I managed to keep bringing the winners home, including some for Jack Holt who trained at Basingstoke. I was to ride quite a few horses for Jack, perhaps eighteen in a season, of which I might win on fourteen or so. He was a good trainer and his horses were fit and beautifully turned out.

John Oaksey riding Brumby Hill beat me on Glenn in the Schilizzi Challenge Bowl Chase at Towcester on 25 March. John was not the best of losers – like me – but he was a character. If any of us took the mickey out of him he would rise very quickly and get really annoyed. I have often told him that is one of the reasons for him losing his hair. He was not much of a stylist but he had a tremendous way with horses. He rode with a good length of rein and horses would run and jump for him – what else can you say about a horseman? His knowledge of speed and judgement brought out the best in him. When he went for his stick, however, he was so untidy! He would flap about and his legs would go faster than those of his horse. One of the best amateurs ever to put a leg over a horse, John Oaksey is a brilliant racing journalist and I have a very high regard for him. He has been exceedingly nice to me in his racing coverage and if I pull his leg a little here it is perhaps to even the score when he described my attributes as a footballer in 1968, saying that I was 'a master of sophisticated ball control' – the point did not escape me.

I have been, in some people's view, outrageous in my time, but I must make it clear that my actions have not sprung from any cocky conceit. Predicaments in which I have found myself have usually stemmed from my love of life and the manner in which I have savoured it to the full.

One dreadful social gaffe occurred when I rode Penharbour in the Territorial Army Handicap Hurdle at Ascot on 31 March 1967. The night before, Bridget and I had been to the *Horse and Hound* Ball in London, where we had thoroughly enjoyed ourselves and I had indulged in more than a few jars. I arrived at the racecourse feeling very carefree, had the leg up on Penharbour and won on the bridle.

Afterwards I was told that the Queen was to make the presentations and I rushed off to the weighing room to brush my hair and tidy up before returning to the enclosure.

Percy King was there, and George Todd, and I stood on one side like an idiot not knowing what to do because nobody had briefed me.

The owner was presented to the Queen, and then the trainer, who both received their trophies, and then it was my turn. Nobody moved, so I thought, 'Oh, well – here goes,' and walked up to Her Majesty and introduced myself. She looked a little taken aback as I told her how great it was to ride such a good horse as Penharbour to win, to which she made an appropriate polite comment; then I gabbled on about how much I had enjoyed the *Horse and Hound* Ball, to which I believe she said something like, 'How nice.' I was then presented with a solid silver tumbler cup.

The Queen had been so kind; I knew that I was in for a present from the owner, and I was so happy with life that I completely forgot myself and threw the trophy in the air and caught it again as I left the enclosure. God knows what would have happened had I dropped it.

The old Duke of Norfolk drew me aside afterwards and, looking very severe, said, 'Er, now, Biddlecombe, you should never talk to the Queen unless you have been formally introduced to her' – which was quite correct. I received a good telling off which I deserved, but I hope that I caused no real offence, for certainly none was intended.

After that little incident my thoughts were concentrated on Liverpool, where, on 7 April, I rode Boy Wonder for D. H. Dick, a little permit holder from Northallerton, in the first division of the Coronation Hurdle. I was tracking Josh Gifford on Impact and as we turned into the straight, I said to him. 'How many more times have we got to go round?' as I had completely lost my way.

'Just once,' he replied. I relaxed and just cantered round on Boy Wonder, barely able to hold him, when I saw Josh go for his whip.

'You lying bastard!' I yelled at him, and kicked on for all I was worth to win by four lengths, with Josh way down the field.

I had my revenge when I rode Glenn in the Mildmay Chase afterwards. I waited and waited on him in front, knowing that I had 2 stone in hand, whilst behind me Paddy Broderick on Dusky Don and Josh Gifford on Sheridan were really struggling. I kept on looking back at them and shouting, 'Come on Paddy, come on Gifford – you've done this to me before!' This was after the last fence and they were doing their nuts because they had no more to draw upon. I eased back and still kept baiting them, 'Come on Gifford, Brod – what's the matter with you?' before letting out half a reef and winning by three quarters of a length.

Mercy Rimell went mad afterwards.

'Don't you ever do that – you let him win by as much as he likes – how dare you give me such a fright?'

I thought it was great, and would not have missed such fun for the world.

I rode Greek Scholar in the disastrous Grand National of 1967. As usual, he gave me a lovely ride and I was really enjoying the race. I had just cleared Becher's for the second time and was galloping on, nicely tucked in on the inside, when I saw a loose horse running up and down the length of the next fence and not knowing where to go. I was right on the inside rails as this horse charged towards me and there was nothing I could do about it. It all happened so quickly that instead of getting knocked over at the fence, Greek Scholar landed on top of it with his forelegs stuck fast in the middle of the birch and brush. I was unable to back out as other horses crashed in all directions – there were loose horses everywhere with jockeys shouting at each other to get out of the way and it was absolute pandemonium. The twenty-eight horses still left in the race fell, refused or were baulked at that fence, except Foinavon.

When some of the uproar had subsided, I managed to extricate Greek Scholar and was backing out when I saw Foinavon with Johnny Buckingham, and Josh Gifford on Honey End, coming towards the fence. I must have been at least twenty lengths in front of them.

Foinavon came on and popped through a gap in the fence, and Josh's horse, Honey End, which had been my 100th winner in 1966, refused. Josh turned him round and jumped the fence at the second attempt by which time I was able to follow his lead. Greek Scholar jumped the fence well and after that it was just a race to see who could catch Foinavon. Josh thinks to this day that he was unlucky not to win, and I maintain that had I been knocked over I would have remounted, I think, as quickly as anyone else, and gone on to win. But that is the lottery of the Grand National. I make no excuses whatsoever for finishing fourth, and I recall racing with Josh and Brian Fletcher to reach a nice hole in the fourth fence from home and colliding in mid air! Brian on Red Alligator just beat me on the run in and was to win the following year for Denys Smith. No one was more surprised to win the National than was Johnny Buckingham on Foinavon, and his horse was thought to have such a slim chance in the race that neither his owner nor his trainer was there to see his victory.

My relationship with Bridget had deepened into something stronger than friendship and we decided to get engaged. I had come to know her family and was extremely fond of them, especially Bridget's brother, Bill, who loved shooting as much as I did.

Bridget's father, Captain Francis Tyrwhitt-Drake, was a star man to me. I knew I would have to ask his permission before we could become officially engaged and I seized the opportunity when I was staying with Bridget's family at her home near East Meon, Hampshire.

I went into the kitchen and found the captain getting his dog's tea together and I must admit I felt a bit nervous as this was something I had never done before. He asked me if he could get anything for me and I said, 'No, thank you – yes – can I marry your daughter?'

He looked at me for a moment and I thought he was going to say, 'No,' but instead he answered, 'I hope you know what you are taking on.'

'I think I do,' I replied.

'Well, then,' he said, 'let's go and have a bottle.' Which I thought was very sporting of him.

We announced our engagement at the end of May 1967, and went up to London where I attended an all-male function which lasted until the small hours, before meeting Bridget for lunch the following

Above: Early days at Hartpury. (left to right) Mother, Tony, myself and Dad

Below: Tony falls on Jungle Beach (left), bringing me down on Icanopit in the Ansells Brewery Chase at Worcester, November 1962

Opposite top: An early holiday in
Majorca with (left to right) Johnny
Lehane, our 'physiotherapist' and Josh
Gifford – at the end of a hard season!

Opposite bottom: On the way to beat
Josh Gifford at Kempton, 1963

Above left: Honour Bound winning the Martin
Mahony Champion Hurdle at Punchestown,
April 1963
Above right: With brother Tony at Sandown, 1964
Below: Red Thorn on his way to win the Grand
Sefton Chase at Liverpool, 1964, and giving me one
of my greatest thrills

Facing page
Top left: Spartan General winning the
November Handicap Hurdle at Liverpool,
1964

Top right: Percy King's Nosey taking the last
flight to win at Newbury, January 1965

Bottom: Josh Gifford being asked to open
the bowling at Ascot Cricket Club!

Above left: A free lift back for Brough
Scott at Uttoxeter

Above right: Mrs L. Carver's
Trelawny winning the Spa Hurdle at
the Cheltenham Festival Meeting,
March 1966

Below: Mr W. Rimell's Magnus
survives a typical Aintree hazard

Facing page
Top left: A dream come true. Harry Collins leads in his Gold Cup winner, Woodland Venture, followed by a jubilant Fred Rimell

Top right: Show jumping, for a change, at the National Equestrian Centre, Stoneleigh

Bottom: Stalbridge Colonist and Woodland Venture at the last fence in the 1967 Cheltenham Gold Cup

Above: Gay Trip beating Andy Turnell on Mayfair Bill in the Heinz Chase, Ascot, 1968

True to form, Fearless Fred uproots the last before winning at Haydock

Bryan Jenks' Normandy cantering to post before winning the Gloucestershire Hurdle at Cheltenham, 1969

Dark Jet recovered from this bad blunder to win the Bookham Chase at Sandown, 1968

Above: Shedding a few pounds, and enjoying a bottle at the Southport baths with (left to right) Ron Barry, Graham Thorner, Richard Pitman, Bill Shoemark and Pat Buckley

Below: Coral Diver going out to win the *Daily Express* Triumph Hurdle at Cheltenham, 1969

Opposite top: HM the Queen Mother presents me with the trophy for the Mackeson Gold Cup after Gay Trip's first victory in this race in 1969

Opposite bottom: Glenn, making nothing of the last before going on to win at Newbury in November 1969

Below: The 'Biddlecombe' style

Above: A line-up of champions. (Left to right)
B.R. Davies (1968-69, 1969-70, 1971-72);
T.W. Biddlecombe (1964-65, 1965-66, 1968-69);
S. Mellor (1959-60, 1960-61, 1961-62);
T.F. Rimell (1938-39, 1939-40, 1944-45, 1945-46);
B. Marshall (1947-48); G. Thorner (1970-71);
J. Dowdeswell (1946-47);
F. Winter (1952-53, 1955-56, 1956-57, 1957-58);
J. Francome (1975-76, 1978-79, 1980-81);
T. Brookshaw (1958-59)

Facing page
Top: My last meeting, the
Cheltenham National Hunt Festival,
1974. I exchange a few words with the
Queen Mother after finishing third
on her Game Spirit in the Gold Cup,
with Cath and Fulke Walwyn
looking on

Bottom: A happy occasion —
returning to the winner's enclosure at
Newbury after winning the Weyhill
Handicap Chase on HM the Queen
Mother's Game Spirit, December
1973

This page
Left: Unseated in the Finmere 'Donkey
Grand National' by 'Darkie' White's
famous performer, Jasper

Below: And for my next trick. . . !

Opposite top: 'This Is Your Life' –
Eamonn Andrews and fellow
conspirators (left to right), Michael
Scudamore, Tim Brookshaw and
Macer Gifford, surprise me in the
Savoy Baths, Jermyn Street

Opposite bottom: Back at the studios
I find, among many others, Mother and Dad . . .

Above: Bob and Sue . . .

Below: And my ally for nearly forty
years, Doctor Bill Wilson

Best man, Josh Gifford, tries to steal my
bride, Ann, at our wedding in 1981

morning. We were going to buy the engagement ring, but Bridget decided that I was in no fit state to help her choose one and insisted on making a separate trip to London for the purpose later on. I knew then that I was going to have a most independent lady for a wife!

Tony retired from racing in 1967 and devoted his time to running the farm at Upleadon and helping Dad with the horses. Not only did he renew his interest in show jumping, one which he shares with Dad to this day, but they also bred, over the years, some very nice bloodstock, many of their youngsters being sired by horses I had ridden.

In the summer of 1971, Tony married a local girl who had worked with Bert Chugg's horses near Severn Stoke, Worcester. Sandra has proved a grand wife to Tony and shares his love of horses.

The season ended with Josh Gifford becoming champion jockey for the third time with 122 winners, beating Fred Winter's record by one and thereby achieving one of my own ambitions. I was thrilled for him, because injuries had put him out of the hunt previously, and he thoroughly deserved the title.

I was second in the list with eighty-three winners, and I was then determined not only to regain my championship but also to break the new record that Josh had set up. I had quite a task ahead of me.

10
Bryan Jenks, Gay Trip
and Marriage

The 1967–68 season was important to me in that Bryan Jenks, a most astute businessman, with interests in both industry and farming, decided to place his National Hunt horses with Fred Rimell.

A quiet, thoughtful man, with a huge sense of humour, he sought the best advice from the top men in racing and invested large sums of money in his horses which repaid him handsomely over the years. His best flat-race horse, Song, was second in the 1968 Gimcrack Stakes and was sold afterwards to Jim Joel for an undisclosed price. Bryan Jenks bought his jumpers wisely, treating the racing game as a business first and as a hobby second. I do not think he ever had a large bet on any of his horses, but they gave him tremendous pleasure. Some of them were to prove the finest hurdlers and chasers of their day. At one time he had eighteen horses in training at Kinnersley.

I had won on his mare, Necklet, at Bangor-on-Dee, on 28 April 1962, but it was not until now that I had the chance to ride his first-class horses.

On 6 September at the Devon and Exeter meeting I rode Jungle Beach into sixth place behind Roddy B, in the Duchy of Cornwall Handicap Chase. Roddy B, trained by Les Kennard, was ridden by a young man who had just turned professional and was to give me one hell of a lot of trouble in the future, Bob Davies, who had drawn attention to his ability as a jockey as an amateur. I had been aware of his skill but did not realize at that point just how good he really was. I was not to remain in ignorance for long.

The rider of the third horse in that race was Ted Fisher, a friend who was a jockey-cum-trainer near Bath. Whenever I went racing in Devon I spent quite a lot of time in the Turkish baths at Torquay.

On one of my visits there with Ted Fisher, I was sitting in the hot room waiting for Ted, who had vanished into the steam room for a few minutes, when in came a good-looking, dark-haired man whose face seemed familiar. I thought that, given a top hat and a cane, he could be Frankie Vaughan, and that is just who it turned out to be. We got talking, and he expressed a deep interest in racing before asking me to suggest a good person to train his horses for him. At that moment, out stepped Ted Fisher and I said to Frankie, 'There's just the man for you.'

They were friends immediately. We shared a bottle of champagne and Ted and I were given tickets for Frankie's show then running in Torquay. Not only did Frankie send his horses to Ted to train but I was to ride several winners for him later.

Fred Rimell had been asked to find a good horse by Tony Chambers, a businessman from Worcester. At the time of the request, Fred had been talking to Pat Taaffe in London and told him that he was looking for a nice animal for an owner. Not long afterwards, Pat rang up and recommended Gay Trip, then in Ireland, and Fred went to see the horse on his own. Gay Trip had been blistered and Fred told Pat that he would return a few weeks later. This time he took Tony Chambers with him, they both liked the horse and bought him.

I never knew how much money changed hands for Gay Trip, but it was considerable. When I schooled him soon after his arrival at Kinnersley, he was outstanding. He was by Vulgan, that great sire of steeplechasers whose progeny were usually large, like The Dikler, or relatively small, compact and neat, as was Gay Trip.

I was to ride Gay Trip in the Halloween Novices' Chase at Newbury on 27 October 1967, and the starting price was 20–1.

In the paddock, Tony Chambers and Fred came up to me and Fred said, 'Listen, Biddles – we've had a little tickle. We're a good thing.'

Gay Trip felt marvellous under me as we went to post. He jumped the first two fences like a buck. It was fantastic. Then, at the water jump in front of the stands he took off perfectly, only to slip up on landing. I walked, downcast, back to the weighing room. Fred came to meet me.

'Bad luck, matey,' he said. 'That's racing.'

Tony Chambers was also very understanding but Gay Trip would have streaked up that day.

However, Andy Turnell rode him the next time out to win the Sheffield Novices' Chase at Doncaster, on 25 November 1967 and although he started at much shorter odds, I think that Fred and Tony Chambers got their money back.

After Glenrowan had fallen with me at Wolverhampton on 30 October, I went to London for an X-ray because my right hand was painful, but no bones were broken. After four days out of the saddle I fell again at Cheltenham in the Mickleton Chase on 3 November and was slightly concussed.

I went to post the following afternoon aboard Glenn for the Mackeson Gold Cup. I had walked the course with Josh the day before, testing the ground, and we had bet a suit on whichever of us won the race, something we often did in our riding days. I told Josh I would win, and he said I had no chance against his horse, Charlie Worcester.

When the starter let us go we went close up on the stands side, tight against the wings of the fences, and I went a right purler. I hit the ground right in front of the stands. I was in such pain, and it was a terribly cold wet day, which made it worse. I was near enough to the racecourse buildings not to bother with the ambulance and I walked back across the course feeling awful. Bridget took me to Cheltenham hospital for an X-ray, where a doctor told me that I could have strained the muscles of my shoulder, or possibly have cracked a bone. I went to Bill Tucker's on the Monday where a further X-ray confirmed that I had fractured my right shoulder and also the outer end of my collarbone.

I was annoyed with the doctor at Cheltenham, not because I wanted preferential treatment, and not because he had incorrectly diagnosed my X-ray plates. Had I been a little boy with a broken arm or collarbone, however, and my X-ray been poorly read, I could have ended up with a bone deformity, which, to me, would have been very wrong.

Josh won the Mackeson Gold Cup with Charlie Worcester and I had to pay up!

This was the year when the foot and mouth epidemic struck much of the country and halted racing for several weeks. As I was out of action with my shoulder anyway, it did not affect me, but I felt very sorry for the farmers who were forced to slaughter their stock. The disease stopped just short of the farm, with the Ministry of Agriculture containing it within the outskirts of Tewkesbury.

After the foot and mouth outbreak came the frost and snow which again delayed racing for a while. I loved a bit of frost as a rule because

I could relax with my gun, but this came too soon after the foot and mouth epidemic and I needed to ride for my living.

As Andy Turnell had won on Gay Trip at Doncaster, and my first ride on this horse had ended disastrously, I was worried that I might not partner him at Lingfield on 19 January 1968 in the Godstone Handicap Chase.

However, Fred put me up for the second time on this athletic horse which gave me a flawless ride, taking the lead from the ninth fence to win comfortably.

In the January Novices' Hurdle later in the day, I had a ride which was as different from the one I had had on Gay Trip as it is possible to imagine.

Fred Rimell had bought Grock II from Newmarket for Bryan Jenks. When he arrived at the stables his mouth was sore so Fred decided to run him in a hackamore – a bitless bridle – and I had never ridden a horse in one of these before, let alone raced with one. Fred thought the horse was a certainty in the race and I managed to get down to the start without much difficulty.

Once we were running, though, Grock II tried to run out with me passing the stands. It was a frightening experience because I had no steering whatsoever. I had both hands on one rein trying to pull him back into the race and eventually I picked my whip up and gave him a crack across the jaw, just in time to miss one of the steeplechase fences. I dodged the wing and managed to jump the correct hurdle by which time I had dropped right out of the race.

Stan Mellor on Cool Hand had gone some twenty lengths ahead and I sent Grock II scalding after him up the hill, knowing this would steady him. I dared not take my hands off him going to the last so I just picked him up and hit him. He simply flew and I hit him again to get up to win by a head from Stan, who had counted me out of the race. Without wishing to sound big-headed, I think I was pretty good that day. Nine times out of ten I would have let a horse like that go, but if I had done so on that occasion I think I would have ended up in the brook flanking the racecourse.

After that, I decided that bitless bridles are useless for racing purposes.

I had ridden a big, black, leggy horse called Domacorn, trained by Harry Dufossee, in the Powderham Castle Hurdle on 10 August 1967 at the Devon and Exeter meeting. He had been point-to-pointed and subsequently had not proved successful over fences. The ground was exceptionally hard and although I finished way down the field on this horse I felt he would perform much better on soft going. I mentioned the possibility of offering him to Bryan Jenks through Harry Dufossee and Fred Rimell.

By the early part of 1968, Domacorn, bought by Bryan Jenks on Fred's advice, had been in training at Kinnersley for several weeks, and I rode him at Ascot on 7 February in the Heatherwood Novices' Chase. The ground was soft and Domacorn jumped extremely well. He could make some awful mistakes and he was a horse that had to have his mind made up for him. He really did get to the bottom of me, both physically and psychologically, but this day he was outstanding. He did his job well that day to win from the 1981 Grand National hero-to-be, Mr Bob Champion, then an amateur, on Glide Scope.

When Domacorn won the Compton Chase by eight lengths at Newbury on 17 February, we realized that he was a really good horse. Bryan Jenks' Pick Me Up, which won the Great Metropolitan that year with Lester Piggott, put up a sparkling performance to win the Ashford Novices' Hurdle at Kempton on 1 March, and this was followed by another success for the Jenks–Rimell combination when St Cuthbert won the KP Hurdle with me the next day.

I was looking forward to Cheltenham. I had some good horses to ride and was anticipating some exhilarating racing when Fred decided to take all the Cheltenham runners down to Tim Holland-Martin's home at Bredon where there was a 1½-mile straight gallop.

We galloped the horses over about three days before the Cheltenham meeting which I felt was madness. As a result, I suspected that this fast work had taken the edge off the horses, but jockeys never question the actions of their trainers. Fred and Mercy, for their part, thought they had done the right thing.

Nevertheless, Jackie Brutton's Arctic Feast was unplaced in the Gloucestershire Hurdle at Cheltenham on 19 March. Gay Trip, up against a good horse in Herring Gull in the Totalisator Champion Novices' Chase, could only keep galloping and jumping to finish second.

When I came in, Fred was getting on his high horse.

'Right,' he ordered, 'out of that gate, you'll win on this one.'

I thought I would win Division II of the Gloucestershire Hurdle on Pick Me Up, and did not worry unduly when L'Escargot made the running from the start. I had never seen L'Escargot before, nor even heard of him. He was just a horse that had come over from Ireland with very little known about him. I was used to waiting with Pick Me Up and I let L'Escargot and Tommy Carberry bowl along in front to establish a good twenty lengths' lead. I was the first jockey to go after him because he showed little sign of coming back to the rest of the field, and as I raced down past the water he was still twenty lengths in front.

Going down the hill I drove Pick Me Up on to get within five lengths of L'Escargot when the Irish horse set off again up the hill to beat me by six lengths.

Fred was incensed.

'You let him slip you – this bloody Irish thing coming over here and beating you! You should have won a minute!'

I felt a bit crestfallen but, as history was to prove, we were beaten by a horse that was to win two Gold Cups, a Grand National and a host of other races. Some snail!

In the Cheltenham Gold Cup on 21 March I had the ride on Stalbridge Colonist, on whom I had won a 2-mile chase at Ascot on 1 April 1966.

I lost this race coming out of the dip and over the last two fences when the saddle slipped up his neck and I was unable to set him about his job when he needed really strong handling. This stalwart little grey was such a battler from the last, as I knew from the way he had kept coming at me on Woodland Venture in the race the year before. He hit the third last and the second last, but he was not beaten very far – a neck and a length, by two good horses in Fort Leney and The Laird.

Had I been able to get after Stalbridge Colonist at the finish I am certain he would have gone on to win. It was one of those days and one of those meetings.

I was so fed up that I went all the way down to Lingfield the next day to ride Young Davy for Patrick Burr. Not only did I win but Patrick, good man, gave me £50. The miseries of Cheltenham were forgotten, which just goes to show what an unpredictable game is racing.

Liverpool came hard on the heels of Cheltenham and after winning Division II of the Coronation Hurdle on 29 March on Pick Me Up, I rode Vultrix, trained by Frank Cundell, in the Grand National the next day.

He went well in the race but he suddenly tired and put his brakes on going to the last ditch. I shot over his shoulder and landed in the gorse, with sharp pieces of birch piercing the joint of my elbow. I had to have masses of splinters removed and my arm was bruised and sore for days.

After Liverpool I had no rides until the Ascot Meeting, where I was to ride Gay Trip in the Heinz Chase on 6 April 1968.

Gay Trip was most people's epitome of the ideal steeplechaser. He was elegant, close-coupled, athletic, with a neat, intelligent head that could not fail to draw the eye. He pulled hard but loved his galloping and jumping. He could not carry too much weight but if he was allowed to relax in a race he would invariably win. His one weakness was his tendency to run himself into the ground but, like all the Vulgan horses, he was a great ride.

At the start of the Heinz Chase, nobody set up much of a gallop. I was up with the leaders and Gay Trip was jumping beautifully. As I had been forced to lie up with the rest and push on, I was unable to let Gay Trip get his second wind. Jumping down the back stretch he had not made any mistakes but, turning into the straight, four horses swept past me and I thought that I had lost the race. I decided to give Gay Trip his 'little blow' and was just sitting there when he filled his bellows up and was ready to race again. The rest of the field had gone on too soon, so I thought to myself, 'Right, come on old man,' and pulled him out going to the second last. He simply flew it. I was now back in the race with a vengeance and the thought then flashed across my mind, 'God, I'll win, now!' I went to the last and gave Gay Trip a reminder going into it, one in mid air and another on landing, before winning on the run in by one and a half lengths from Andy Turnell on the favourite, Mayfair Bill.

I was so delighted with Gay Trip that when I dismounted I said to Tony Chambers, 'This horse will win the National.'

Whether he took me seriously or not I do not know, but Gay Trip went on to win the big race without me. That is another story.

Josh Gifford was again champion jockey with eighty-two winners, and I finished the season with sixty-eight. There were more pressing things on my mind that year because Bridget and I had been looking for months for a place to live. We searched everywhere and I was getting increasingly fed up with house-hunting. After a most frustrating day looking at property in the Cotswolds, we called in at David Nicholson's home. Di Nicholson had the local paper handy and showed us details of a cottage with five acres of land which was for sale at Corse Lawn, near Gloucester. We went to look at it and although it needed extensive renovation, we decided to buy it.

I was most grateful to Di for her help, especially as she tended to view me with some suspicion. After an evening out with David and some other jockeys, in London, some time before, we had driven round the city in a very happy mood and found ourselves in a quiet square where some pigeons were strutting about. Without any warning, David leapt from the car, grabbed one of these unsuspecting birds and got back into the car with it. He nursed this pigeon all the way home, cooing to it and stroking its feathers until we eventually tumbled him out of the car outside his house. It was only then that we saw that his dinner jacket was smothered with pigeon muck. Quite oblivious to anything, he swayed indoors while we drove off before the storm broke! Di Nicholson swore that I had spiked his drinks, which I had not, but that was one of the funniest sights I have ever seen.

Bridget and I were married at the 800-year-old church of All Saints at East Meon, her Hampshire home, on 26 July 1968.

My brother, Tony, was best man and everything went according to plan until Bridget and I, leaving the church as man and wife, came out into the sunshine expecting to be greeted by a guard of honour composed of fellow jockeys who had been drilled by Tony to form an archway of hunting crops for us to pass beneath. There was nobody in sight! Luckily, David Mould spotted us standing there, surrounded by bridesmaids and looking bewildered, and shouted, 'We're over here!'

They had formed their archway outside another door. I might have expected it. We went back into the church, with the bridesmaids giggling, and made a second exit. This time the boys had taken the right course and all was well.

After a grand reception at Bridget's home, we set off on our honeymoon in Majorca.

When we returned, Bridget and I lived with my family at Upleadon until our new home was ready for us to move into.

Cecil Haynes, whose horses I had ridden for some time, was a builder from Malvern, and he worked for several months renovating our cottage and extending the living space. There was still a great deal to be done to The Woodlands but we were anxious to have our own home and were in residence within the year.

When the new season started Josh Gifford was uppermost in my mind as the man to beat in the championship table. I had reckoned without Bob Davies, who had signed up with David Barons, that excellent farmer–trainer at Kingsbridge, to ride for him as first jockey.

Bob had fairly set the racing press alight with his spectacular run of winners the season before, but some people thought that this could be a flash in the pan and that Bob's successes would be confined to the West Country tracks where most of his triumphs had occurred. How wrong they were.

He had a flying start at the beginning of the season with a spate of winners at the Devon meetings. I dealt my first blow at Josh Gifford at Southwell on 10 August when I rode Moon Shot for 'Taffy' Williams to beat him on Slave Driver by two lengths.

My step-mother-in-law, who had horses in training with Pat Upton at Wantage, asked me to ride her horse, Just a Gamble, at the Devon and Exeter Meeting on 21 August where he won the City of Exeter Challenge Cup Chase. Later in the month I rode him in the Malvern Chase at Hereford on 31 August and nobody wanted to go on when the tapes went up. Just a Gamble was unenthusiastic until he was warmed up and we came to the second ditch without much impulsion, where he propped, slipped, and fell through the fence, bringing down four other horses – it was lovely! Roy Edwards went ahead unscathed on Bluecoat to finish alone and it was a glorious mix up with nobody getting hurt.

I had been asked by Leonard Sachs if I would ride his horse, Sorrento, in the Norwegian Grand National that autumn. This horse was a prolific winner in that country and I jumped at the chance. I flew to Norway straight from the Hereford meeting on 31 August, to ride in the big race the next day.

I carried a few pounds extra. Sorrento was a light-framed chestnut horse with a good jump in him. The orders were given to me from the trainer through an interpreter, and I set off round the undulating, figure-of-eight track, which reminded me of Fontwell. The fences resembled those on a cross-country course, with bullfinches, water jumps and banks, but Sorrento made nothing of them.

John Oaksey was also in the race and actually headed me at the last fence. I remember thinking to myself that it was a long way to come for an amateur to beat me. However, Sorrento pulled his way to the front and although Terje Dahl, the leading trainer out there who also rode in races, tried to 'screw me up' once or twice, I managed to win.

On 5 September I had a cracker of a race at Fontwell on Clareman to win the Aldingbourne Chase by two lengths from Paul Kelleway on Jenken. Clareman was owned by Mrs R. Henriques and trained by Bryan Marshall at Newbury.

Bryan was a tremendously tough jockey in his heyday, being champion in the 1947–48 season and breaking almost every bone in his body several times over. An example of his resilient courage occurred when Bobby Beasley was asked to ride a colt for him at Newbury. This horse had come off the flat and was rather a handful. At the start Bobby was in the saddle looking a bit tense, as Bryan led the colt round, trying to calm him down without much success. Eventually, Bryan offered the colt a sugar lump and, like lightning, the horse snatched at his hand, bit off the end of one of his fingers and spat it out onto the grass. Without any fuss, Bryan picked up his finger, put it in his pocket, pulled out his hand again and offered the colt some more sugar before going off to hospital to have the finger sewn back into place.

Jack Doyle, the bloodstock agent based at Dublin, had telephoned Fred Rimell about a horse he wanted him to see at the beginning of the season. Fred asked what the horse was called and Jack hesitated and said he would rather not say. Fred replied that if Jack did not tell him the horse's name, he was not going over to look at him. Finally, Jack gave in.

'His name is Fearless Fred,' he said, waiting for the reaction.

'That's done it!' exclaimed Fred Rimell, 'I'm not coming!'

He did go to Ireland, however, saw the horse run and win there and bought him from Pat Hogan, who succumbed to a little pressure from Pat Taaffe.

Fearless Fred, which was bought on behalf of Bryan Jenks, was the most ignorant old devil I ever sat on. God, he could hit a fence. You could get him jumping and he would be pinging his fences; then all of a sudden he would meet one spot on as you thought, and for no reason at all just keep galloping. He literally hit fences with his chest and always took every inch of rein out of my hands. I rode him for the first time at Warwick on 15 October in the Extel House Beginners' Chase, one of many races he was to win with me, but I never enjoyed riding him. It was hair-raising.

When Fearless Fred won the Badger Brewery Chase at Wincanton on 31 October, he had one of his good days. He jumped brilliantly, in fact, and cantered in. I thought that I had found the key to this horse, but I was mistaken.

The trophy which went to the winning owner was a solid silver badger. It was magnificent and Rose Jenks used it as a centrepiece on her dining-room table.

It was entirely my fault that Gay Trip did not win the Mackeson Gold Cup at Cheltenham on 16 November. Nobody went at much of a gallop and after jumping three fences I had settled Gay Trip nicely, tucked in behind but on the rails, with everybody tightly bunched up beside and in front of me. I was used to this brilliant jumper picking up and jumping a fence without actually seeing it, but this time he did not make it. He took off at the right place, completely unsighted by the horses in front, and fell. It was all over. I should never have allowed myself to become trapped on the rails and I take full responsibility for that fall. The only consolation for the Kinnersley stable was that the first and third places were taken by John Liley's Jupiter Boy, ridden by Eddie Harty, and Moonduster, with Willie Robinson up.

11

The Battle for the Championship

Among the flat-race horses that Bryan Jenks had in training with Pat Rohan at Malton in Yorkshire was a brown colt with a large white star on his forehead. His name was Coral Diver and he had won a few races on the flat, showing considerable promise. He had been due to run at the Ascot meeting in October 1968, and Bryan had said to Pat Rohan that if he won with this horse at Ascot, he could keep him in his yard.

As if by destiny, the course at Ascot was waterlogged following torrential rainstorms and the meeting was cancelled. Bryan Jenks decided to call in at the Kinnersley stables to see if Fred and Mercy would like to take charge of Coral Diver. When Bryan asked Mercy about this horse afterwards she said, 'If Pat Rohan has got any more like him in his stable, tell him to send them down.'

As soon as I saw this three-year-old colt I loved him. He looked at me from his box with his head on one side, knowingly, and I could tell immediately that he was a character. He stood about 16.3 hands high and was not much to look at. He was all legs and did not have much depth to him. He was basically a lazy, good-tempered individual who schooled to the point of brilliance at home. He was a natural jumper and I cannot remember him making many bad mistakes. He stood well off at his hurdles and jumped very flat, never bending his back, but he always got there – with his old ears flapping!

I rode him in Division II of the Plant Novices' Hurdle at Doncaster on 22 November in which he ran a trifle erratically, clouting the second last but managing to win nicely by four lengths. I noted that *Chaseform* had described him extremely accurately as a 'good sort'. That is exactly how he felt to me.

Bob Davies was still bringing in winners, not only from David Barons' stable but also from that of Colin Davies at Chepstow. Brough Scott, Colin's stable jockey, had suffered a bad fall on Atalanta Queen at Worcester in October and Colin, quick to spot riding talent, not only had asked Bob to deputize for Brough but later secured first claim on his services when they were not required by David Barons.

The press were beginning to recognize that Bob was a fine jockey who might well run me close for the championship, a feeling which I was inclined to share with the racing journalists.

I had come to know Bob well since his arrival on the racing scene. He was quite brainy, graduating in agriculture from Wye College. He had a fantastic temperament and I got on well with him. The one thing I dared not do was to ask him how his horse had gone in a race. All I wanted to hear was, 'Great — hung a bit — hit the last — a bit unlucky,' but oh, no! I would be told every detail from when he jumped off until he cleared the last fence — he would even tell me when his horse changed legs. It was very amusing and if we were in the car I would just sit there with my eyes closed and let him ramble on. He was never a great talker in a race, however. I would shout across to him 'How are you doing?' and he would only grunt in reply!

We often drove to meetings together and Bob would argue his point of view on anything, whether he was right or wrong, until I gave up the fight. In a fit of exasperation one day I told him he was like Hitler as he was so impervious to other opinions and I have called him by this name ever since.

It was a good day for me at Chepstow on 14 December when Domacorn won the Rhymney Breweries Handicap Chase easily, making light work of his race and galloping and jumping faultlessly. It was quite a high-class field, with Vulgan's Pleasure and Highland Wedding in second and third place.

Bob Davies in that race fell on Hurricane Lord, but he came back at me in the next to win with Colin Davies' cracking horse, Oberon, leaving me trailing down the course on Cecil Haynes' Tudor Times.

In the Poacher Handicap Chase I rode one of Colin's horses, Commodore, into fourth place and although Bob did not win the race he was still two lengths in front of me to come third on Flandre II for David Barons, and my blood was up. We both weighed out for the second division of the Brewmaster Hurdle and it was a right battle. We rose at the last hurdle together but I had Bryan Jenks' King Candy under me and he ran on to win by three quarters of a length. But Bob had the last laugh. He went out, quite unruffled, on yet another consistent horse from the Chepstow stable, Colditz Story, to win the second division of the Gold Label Hurdle by two lengths. Where was I? Unplaced on Vulgan Flipper and wondering what I was going to do about this Welshman who was getting in my way.

Then the big freeze up of 1969 set in. During this cold spell Bridget and I went to stay with Arthur Freeman at Newmarket, as Thomson Jones had asked me to go shooting the following day, before going on to a dinner party. When we arrived we went with Arthur to have lunch with one of his owners at Colchester, who intrigued me by wearing shorts in the biting cold weather. When we returned to Arthur's house after lunch to clean up and change to go to the dinner party, Arthur said to me, 'Have you got your smoking jacket?'

'No,' I said, 'what's a bloody smoking jacket?' I had never heard of one in my life. Arthur gave me a pained look and fetched his own jacket from his room. I put it on and it was about six sizes too big. Bridget said I could not possibly wear it, which only made me more determined to do so, and then Arthur said as an afterthought, 'You must wear my smoking shoes to go with it.'

It was now all or nothing, so I donned these embroidered smoking slippers and set off, with a most disapproving wife, to the dinner party. Of course, I was late, and when I walked into the room the other guests were well into their pre-dinner drinks. In those days, Newmarket was a very tight society with solid traditions and this was quite a powerful gathering, with Humphrey Cottrill, Thomson Jones and several other trainers present. I did not exactly feel right in this huge smoking jacket, plus the embroidered shoes and the looks on the various faces ranged from the outraged to the convulsed. Bridget was terribly embarrassed and I tried not to laugh. I thought it would be better when we sat down to dinner but, to my horror, it was not a sit-down affair at all – we had Newmarket sausages and mash, standing up to eat it.

The whole evening, in retrospect, was one of the funniest I can remember, but Bridget did not share my feelings for some time.

The next day I went shooting just outside Newmarket. I took up my stand just around the corner from Thomson Jones, who was standing in a piggery with an old sow and her piglets all round him. He was having a grand day and had shot three and a half to four brace of pheasant. I had a couple of shots at woodcock and missed; as I was walking back through the wood I saw old Tom Jones clambering through the fence absolutely fuming. He had been shooting and killing pheasants so thick and fast that he had laid them at his feet, quite forgetting the sow and her young, who had eaten the lot.

A new arrival at Kinnersley that year was Normandy, a four-year-old colt bought through Jack Doyle for Bryan Jenks. Normandy was a small, light bay with beautiful markings. He stood about 16 hands but he was all horse: short on the legs, plenty of depth, with a good hind leg and strong quarters. He had an intelligent head with a blaze tapering into a race on his face. His temperament left a lot to be desired as far as people were concerned. He was reputed to have savaged a stable lad in Ireland and when he came to Kinnersley he was nasty in the box. He would not allow a vet to come anywhere near him and he was very quick with his teeth. He could also cow-kick brilliantly, but he was a tough little horse.

Tommy Burns had trained him in Ireland and as a three-year-old he had won on the flat over there. He had never been ridden over a hurdle in his life. At Kinnersley he had only jumped a hurdle in the loose school but had never jumped anything with anyone on his back, let alone on a racecourse. Mercy was devoted to him and thought he was better than Coral Diver, which annoyed me.

I had never sat on Normandy until I rode him at Kempton on 28 February 1969 in Division III of the Ashford Novices' Hurdle, which was his first run over hurdles.

In the paddock, Fred told me, 'This will win.'

'What does he jump like?' I asked.

'Brilliant,' came the reply. 'He's a natural.'

When Fred gave me that sort of information, whether I had ridden the horse or not beforehand, I knew that I could go out and give it a good ride. Some trainers will tell a jockey all manner of little untruths about a horse, but Fred never did that to me.

Normandy was every bit as good as Fred had intimated. He streaked over every hurdle with impressive agility and I found that he would do anything I asked of him, bend, stand off – he was exceptional. I just kept hold of his head and sat there. He led from the fifth from home to run in on the flat to win by three lengths, on the bridle.

We were all inspired by his performance and I looked forward to riding him at Cheltenham in March.

My main objective at Haydock on 8 March was the Victor Ludorum Hurdle over 2 miles in which I was to ride Coral Diver. Earlier in the meeting I rode Great War for Bobby McAlpine, trained by Doug Francis, a horse in which Bryan Jenks had a share. As I left the paddock, Bryan said, 'If you win on Great War and on Coral Diver, I will give you the Victor Ludorum trophy.'

This was a beautiful silver pheasant which I had secretly coveted. Mrs Rose Jenks was a bit taken aback when Bryan said this to me because she too fancied the pheasant.

I gave Great War quite a hard ride, just getting up to win, and I thought, 'All I have to do now is win on Coral Diver and the pheasant's mine.'

I had a dream of a ride on him. He never touched a hurdle and cantered in to beat the Queen Mother's Escalus by four lengths.

Coral Diver was a grand horse. All I had to do was to steer him and talk to him. I would talk to him all the time in a race – 'Come on boy, come on – here comes the next one – don't you bloody miss – right, one, two – go on!' He used to listen to me all right, with his old ears going this way and that way. If he got a bit close to a hurdle, which was not often, I would say, 'Come on, you lazy old bastard!' and he would stand off so far at the next one that he scared me to death. I swear that horse knew every word I said to him. I adored him.

I will never forget that race or the way Coral Diver went for me to win it. As Bryan Jenks remarked afterwards, 'I don't call that a race – it was a theft!'

Bryan honoured his promise and gave me the silver pheasant. It was a day to remember always.

Cheltenham again provided me with some unforgettable moments at the March meeting.

Normandy gave me a scintillating ride in the Gloucestershire Hurdle on 18 March. He was a remorseless battler. Coming out of the last bend I was flat out and although Normandy was receiving a bit of weight from the other twenty-seven runners, his performance in getting up to win from Ron Atkins on Grand Erg by a short head was all the more remarkable because of his age. Not many four-year-olds beat five- and six-year-olds in a race of that class, but he had done so and in heavy going as well.

In the Arkle Challenge Trophy Chase, on 19 March, Chatham, owned by Charlie Knott, ran the race of his life. I had previously won the Birchfield Novices' Hurdle on him at Haydock on 3 January and he was another horse that needed time to develop. He had already won a lot of races but I felt that if he had been given less to do in his early days he would have been a great horse. He was very green when he ran at Haydock, but game. He was not sure what to do but when he hit the front he just kept going.

The ground was on the heavy side for him at Cheltenham and when the other horses started to drift out, taking me with them, I switched Chatham to the inner and he flew the last to win by two lengths. He was exhausted when I brought him in. It was a great achievement on his part and I did not think that he would come back to race again, but he did. He was brave and very consistent.

I sometimes said to Fred when we had a horse like this in the yard, 'He'll make a lovely horse, don't do too much with him, will you?'

He would agree at the time, but racing is a business and owners need winners if they are to be kept happy. For me, though, a really good trainer is one who never runs the guts out of green, brave and promising horses, even if they win in the process. There are plenty of trainers who churn out the winners, but I know of others who produce good horses to last for years because they have given them plenty of time to develop their full potential.

French Excuse had been bought by John Jennings from Paddy Sleator in Ireland, and he was fully expected to run well in Division I of the George Duller Hurdle that afternoon. Unfortunately, the horse had not travelled well and sweated up in the paddock. He ran a disappointing race and there were some long faces when we came in to the enclosure. He had not acclimatized to his new surroundings but he was a good horse as he was to prove, despite his tendency to break blood vessels.

One of my memorable races with Coral Diver was the *Daily Express* Triumph Hurdle on 20 March at Cheltenham. There were twenty-six runners and it was a race in which I knew I had to be up with the leaders because they were going to go a right gallop. I also knew that Coral Diver would get the trip, but as we jumped out of the gate I was in difficulties. I could not hold my position and going down by the water jump I was in real trouble. He had not made a mistake but he was just not making progress, so I picked up my stick and gave him one. He surged ahead and passed one horse and, encouraged by this, I gave him another smack and then another to get myself into position at the top of the hill. I had been riding absolutely all out and was tiring by this time, so going down the hill I really chased Coral

Diver to keep in touch with Willie Robinson on Shawcross, who was belting on. I pulled Coral Diver out going to the second last, which he almost disdained and I gave him another reminder on landing. Going away from the hurdle he began to travel and I was going so well that I pulled my goggles down, thinking that I had everything under control, when Coral Diver started to labour under me again. Once more I drove him on with my body, and not a few reminders and he ran on to skim the last like a bird. On the run in he caught hold of his bridle, pricked his ears and won in a canter. I could have killed him! He had been making a fool out of me throughout the race – if horses can laugh, Coral Diver was laughing.

I think that is one of the reasons I loved him because he enjoyed taking me on, never mind other horses.

When I came in the reception was terrific. I had beaten everything, including Shawcross which was owned by the *Daily Express* and was four lengths behind in second place. They thought he was a certainty, but had reckoned without me and my old pal.

By this time, Bryan Jenks had had two winners at the meeting in Normandy and Coral Diver, which was not bad going, and I went to post on Domacorn for the Gold Cup.

I knew I would have to hold him together to get him round but he did everything right that day. He stuck his head in the air a bit but I felt sure I was going to win with only What a Myth in front of me as I came to the second last fence, a mean-looking obstacle with a bit of a dip on the take-off side. Domacorn, with most of his weight on his forehand going into it, missed it completely. How he did not fall and how I managed to stay with him was a miracle but in those bundling split seconds I lost my whip. It shot straight up into the air, I tried to catch it and missed.

There have been occasions when I have had this happen and caught my whip before it hit the ground, but no such luck this time. I was helpless. Domacorn really needed a belt to send him on and I went to the last fence hitting him with my hand and slapping the reins down his shoulder, making no impression whatsoever. I had perhaps four lengths to make up after jumping the last fence and I could see that I was not going to get there. If only I had had my whip I would have won my second Gold Cup. As it was, What a Myth and Paul Kelleway beat me by one and a half lengths. It was so tantalizing and I could not pinch anybody else's whip because there was nobody near me!

When I came back and explained my predicament, Fred was

philosophical and Bryan Jenks said, 'Well, that was bad luck – it would have been nice to have had three!'

They had not seen my disaster and could not understand why I was just sitting there and not riding Domacorn out.

I must say, Bryan Jenks was a good loser. Whenever I had the leg up on one of his horses he would say, 'Have a good ride, look after yourself,' or, 'Come back in one piece.' He always felt concern for both horse and rider and he was a wonderful owner to me, win or lose.

On 24 March I went to Folkestone to ride Wawel, trained by 'Ginger' Dennistoun at Wantage. I had not ridden for him many times and certainly not for some while, but Ginger was one of those marvellous characters one never forgets.

When John Oaksey married Ginger's daughter, Victoria, he gained an absolute star of a father-in-law who not only was an excellent trainer but a man who enjoyed life in many different ways. He was a keen shot, loved sailing and anything which on the face of it was a bargain he found irresistible.

Wawel was an easy winner of the Deal Novices' Hurdle and Ginger was very happy as he had had a nice little gamble on this horse. After racing we took a taxi to the station. On the way, Ginger gave me £75, which I thought was most generous of him and as the taxi wound its way through the back streets of London he suddenly said, 'Quick, Biddlecombe – tell the cabman to stop here.'

We came to a halt outside a shabby shop with pipes and smoking accessories in the window. Ginger got out of the cab, went into the shop, came back out again and said to me, 'Lend me a tenner,' which I did, and he vanished into the shop again, only to reappear with a dozen pipes, all seconds, all unpolished, which he regarded with immense satisfaction before announcing, 'By the time I've finished with these, nobody will ever know they were "seconds",' and stuffed them into his pockets!

I never had my tenner back and I ended up paying for the taxi, but I did not mind one bit, he was such a character and he was so proud of his 'bargain'.

I used to shoot with him quite often and there was one occasion I will remember for as long as I live. We had both been invited to a shoot near Abingdon and I was drawn next to Ginger who, at that time, I had never officially met. I can see him now, standing there in a long, old mackintosh and battered trilby hat, with his pipe going full blast and his yapping spaniel at his heels. The pheasants were streaming over him flying very low, and Ginger was banging away and not hitting a thing. I would think he had about twenty birds over him and he never touched a feather.

All of a sudden he started to stamp on the ground before he let out a fearsome scream of rage and yelled, 'Well – fuck my tits and whiskers!' throwing his pipe on the ground and jumping on it. It was so funny – God, I did laugh, but he was an amazing man.

Ginger loved a practical joke. He was following a car with a small boat on its roof rack one day and he shot in front, flagged the driver down and asked him, in all seriousness, 'Excuse me, sir, but did you know there's a boat on top of your car?' before beating a quick retreat to his own vehicle and tearing off to the races.

When he retired from racing, he messed about in boats himself quite a bit. He and his crew had won a good race one afternoon and in the evening they threw a celebration party. The man who had his boat moored next to Ginger's started up his engine and kept it running in order to charge the batteries. This went on for some time, and the noise, coupled with the fumes, was beginning to affect the merry goings-on aboard Ginger's boat, and he complained to his neighbouring boat-owner several times, asking him to stop his engines as he was spoiling the party. His requests went unheeded, so Ginger then went aboard the other boat and told the man that unless he stopped disturbing the peace he was going to report him to the police. When this failed, Ginger, madder than ever, got into his car and drove to the local police station.

'I'm filing a complaint against my neighbouring boat because they are making too much noise and ruining my party,' he told the sharp-eyed constable on night duty.

'Oh, yes, sir,' replied the constable, following the irate Ginger to his car. 'By the way, sir, have you been drinking?'

'I've come to make a complaint,' Ginger insisted, exasperated. It was no use. He was breathalysed, and had his licence taken away!

He was a fantastic, colourful character and his death robbed his family and the racing world of a great personality.

I was looking forward, as usual, to the Liverpool meeting, apart from my ride on Fearless Fred in the Grand National.

I had some good rides to come before that and the first of them was on Mrs Maxwell Joseph's Table Mountain in the Lancashire Hurdle on 27 March. I had ridden him to win or be placed over 2-mile hurdle races earlier that season. He was a relentless galloper and would stick his head out and just keep going.

At Liverpool I fully expected him to win but two hurdles out he fell heavily, and I was momentarily knocked out. The racecourse doctor diagnosed concussion and I went for a routine X-ray, but there was nothing broken. However, I was advised not to ride that day, or the following one.

On the same day, at Wincanton, Bob Davies had a bad fall from Ashiq which put him out of action until 12 April.

Meanwhile, I had plenty of time to think about my ride on Fearless Fred in the Grand National. As he was such a frighteningly unpredictable jumper I was not looking forward to riding him in the race; Bridget thought it was terrible that I was riding him; Fred knew that I did not want to ride him and I have since learned that Bryan Jenks was not happy about it either.

The night before the race I did not go to bed very early and played pontoon and poker. When I eventually went to bed I could not sleep and had visions of Fearless Fred going to the first fence with his old head low on the ground – I always said he ate grass going to the first fence anyway – and then turning arse over tip. The very thought hurt!

In the race itself he jumped the first fence cleanly. I thought to myself, 'My God, that's not bad.' We came to the second, saw a good stride – and Fearless Fred really could stand off – and he jumped it like a cat, never nodded. I thought, 'Well, you've really adapted yourself to these fences,' because he had been successful round the park tracks. We then went to the first ditch, the biggest on the course, for me, and it stood up like a mountain. I then thought, 'If I'm going to ride you round thirty fences, mate, I'm going to see if you can fiddle a bit.' So I asked him to stand off a long way and he did fiddle it. He popped over it like a little fairy and then I thought, 'Great, unbelievable, I will now win,' because he was really going like a good Grand National horse. I went to the next fence full of confidence, met it spot on, kicked, squeezed and did all the things in the book that one should do. He never touched a twig but he landed on his head. I could not believe it. I picked myself up, swearing at the horse because I had done nothing wrong and walked back to the weighing room.

Fearless Fred by this time had been caught and returned to the care of Jack Kidd, Fred's travelling head lad. As I came within earshot I heard him say to Fred, 'Jesus, Guv'nor, there's not a mark on the bridle or the saddle – that fucking Biddlecombe's fallen off again!'

I think I had done about ten somersaults.

The most important ride I had at that time was Jimmy Scot in the Charlecote Chase at Stratford on 17 April. This was the first winner I ever rode for Fulke Walwyn, then trainer to the Queen Mother, following the death of Peter Cazalet.

I had been friendly with Fulke and his wife, Cath, since my early Kinnersley days, meeting them at various racecourses all over the country, and sometimes socially. As first jockey to the Kinnersley stable my loyalty lay there, but I enjoyed riding for Fulke and Cath when the opportunity arose, and they were to play a vital role in my life. But I was not to know it then.

On 19 April, Fearless Fred was entered for the Scottish Grand National at Ayr. Bryan and Rose Jenks, Fred, Bridget and I climbed into a private aeroplane and sat tightly packed together for the flight north. Mercy held the fort at home.

The going was on top and everyone went a tremendous gallop. Fearless Fred was getting lower and lower over his fences as the pace stretched him to the utmost. He fell so heavily at the fifteenth that I was amazed he was unhurt. Past experience told me that I had broken my left shoulder somewhere, as the pain intensified in the ambulance. I went to the local hospital for an X-ray, where I had another dissertation 'with the doctor there who wanted me to return the following day – from Gloucester! The journey back was hell. We were so cramped in the plane and I had to crawl along the wing to get inside. I was in so much pain that I felt faint. The X-rays in London revealed a fractured shoulder blade and so I was side-lined.

Bob Davies was steadily totting up winners and it was not until 22 May 1969, at Wolverhampton, that I was able to get back into the hunt when I won with Bryan Jenks' Sugar Apple in the Wrekin Handicap Hurdle.

The day before, Josh Gifford married Bridget's chief bridesmaid and long-time friend, Althea Roger-Smith. Bridget and I played a prominent part in bringing this pair together. We arranged for them to meet at the Three Counties Show the year before and it was, as they say, love at first sight.

I went to Uttoxeter on 27 May to ride Normandy in a small race Mercy Rimell had found for him to finish his season and he trotted up. I added another win to my tally at Newton Abbot on 28 May on Quick Polish, trained by David Gandolfo. Bob Davies won on

Ombrello and Bull Run at that meeting, but Sugar Apple and Arctic Feast put me back on form when they won their respective races at Stratford on 30 and 31 May.

At Plumpton on 3 June, I could only come second on Navy Lark in the Findon Handicap Chase; Bob won the Balcombe Chase on Mustardflower, and I slipped up on the bend before the last hurdle on Hans Andersen in the Bob Butcher's Challenge Trophy Handicap Hurdle.

By the time we clashed again at the Devon and Exeter meeting on 11 June, I was two winners ahead of Bob and the situation was becoming more and more tense. He was the first to score with Anac Cuan, then I rode Prince Babu to win the next race. Bob fought back to win the Fairmile Chase on Mustardflower again, which annoyed me because he did not usually ride for Bill Marshall, and I must confess to a feeling of glee when his next mount, Right and Left, ran out in the Upottery Novices' Hurdle.

It all rested now on the evening meeting at Uttoxeter on 12 June. I was just one winner ahead of Bob and the pressure was immense.

Bob levelled the score when he won on Swing Along in the Season's End Novices' Hurdle and I was unplaced on King's Temple in the same race; on Parasang in the June Handicap Hurdle; and also on Sharuk in the Lido Handicap Chase.

Again, Bob had a winner with Little Handsel in the second division of the Season's End Hurdle. This was a chance ride for him and one I was convinced he had cadged by telephone, which made me mad! – even more so when I trailed in unplaced on Pinacinth, which had started favourite.

We both drew a blank in the June Handicap Hurdle, Bob finishing ahead of me on Great Khan, and I followed him up the course on Rusty Robert, absolutely determined not to let him take the championship. Despite all my urgings, Tamally was second in the Replacement Novices' Chase, and I came third on Bernini in the Summer Handicap Chase.

Bob was now one winner ahead of me and this called for desperate measures. Jack Cook had had a nasty fall on Sir Nulli in the Yarcombe Handicap Hurdle at the Devon and Exeter meeting the day before, cutting his face quite badly. I had seen him in the ambulance room and he told me that although he had rides at Uttoxeter he did not feel much like taking them and, if I needed a winner, he would forgo his ride on Mrs Brotherton's Golden Berry in the last race, if she was agreeable.

Having asked permission from Mrs Brotherton and Bobby Renton, who wished me luck, I weighed out on Golden Berry all the more determined to win because I had caught sight of Bob's smug face grinning at me. I do not remember many occasions when I have ridden so hard but I drove Golden Berry with everything I had from about two out in the third division of the Season's End Hurdle to win by threequarters of a length from Michael Dickinson on Kilpatrick.

It was the last race of the season and we were joint champions with seventy-seven winners apiece. To add to this triumph, Fred Rimell and Bryan Jenks were the leading trainer and owner for the 1968–69 season which was a terrific thrill for everyone connected with Kinnersley.

Fred Rimell was to become leading National Hunt trainer the following season, and again in 1975–76, which was no mean achievement.

I had ridden 19¾ miles to draw level with Bob and I have never felt so tired. I drove back with Sue, Bridget and Doc Wilson, dying for a celebration bottle, but everywhere was closed. We eventually stopped at a service station where they offered us some fried eggs swimming in grease, which none of us could face, so we went straight home.

Even then, Bob was the victor. My sister, Sue, had set out with us that evening, determined to see 'this jockey who has been such a nuisance to Terry'. She can look very fierce when she wants to but the moment she clapped eyes on Bob her expression changed; she found him, as she put it afterwards, 'quite a nice fellow'.

Something told me that this likeable rival would somehow end up as my brother-in-law.

He did.

12
Triumphs and Tragedy

Bridget and I returned fresh and fit from our holiday in Elba where we had spent several weeks with Richard and Myrtle Tate, and Bob Davies.

From the outset, Bob and I chased round the meetings, both riding winners, and the fight was in progress once more.

My best race at Newbury on 25 October 1969 was when Moonduster won the Sports Medicine Chase, making all and virtually running away with me. Unfortunately he broke down in the ICI Nitram Chase on 1 November at Teesside, where we started favourite.

It was not the end for Moonduster as he went to Eric Cousins the following season to win more races, before breaking down with me for the second and last time in his career at Uttoxeter in 1971.

On the day that Moonduster came to grief at Teesside, Bob Davies rode Indian Yeldah to victory at Cheltenham, and just pipped me for the 19-Vat-69 Sportsman of the Year Award. With sixty-eight winners to my credit, I was given six bottles of Vat-69 Scotch whisky as a consolation prize.

Fearless Fred gave me a heavy fall at Cheltenham on 14 November. I was bruised but unhurt, which was fortunate as I was to ride Gay Trip in the 1969 Mackeson Gold Cup the next day.

I knew he would win as soon as I sat on him. He felt like a lion under me, all bounce and muscle. In the race they all went a decent gallop and I went round on the inside. Gay Trip took hold as usual and jumped immaculately. The race got under way coming down the hill and I was in a fairly good position when I saw David Mould, on the Queen Mother's Makaldar, coming to challenge. David Mould was a hard man to beat, but Gay Trip kept quickening. Makaldar was a tough individual but had given his all going to the last fence and Gay Trip jumped it like a deer. When he touched down on landing he was away and into his stride very quickly, an ability which was to win him many of his races. He was not like some horses who land in a heap and take a few strides to get going again.

Ron Barry, on Titus Oates, and carrying more weight than I was, challenged me at the second last. He screwed in the air, and it was lovely to hear the crash as he hit the fence. He did not fall, but it took all the stuffing out of him, and one of my 'dangers' was out of the way. From then on it was Gay Trip's race and he scampered up the straight to win by two and a half lengths from Titus Oates, with Makaldar a further two lengths behind in third place.

This was the first time I had been presented with a trophy by the Queen Mother. As soon as I had unsaddled and weighed in I rushed into the weighing room to spruce myself up before returning to the enclosure. There she was, with that lovely warm smile, happy for me, and not minding one bit about her horse being beaten. It was one of those moments I will always remember, not only having ridden a great steeplechaser to victory, but receiving the trophy from the Queen Mother.

It was a wonderful day altogether, for Normandy, having run an inexplicably bad race at Wolverhampton on 10 November, came to himself at this Cheltenham meeting to run brilliantly to win the Lansdown Hurdle.

Tony Dillon, a newspaper magnate from Birmingham, placed a nice horse called Inishmaan in training with Fred this season. He was not very big, nor up to much weight, but he was classy, and when I rode him to win the Merit Hurdle at Nottingham on 17 November, I found him to be an outstanding performer.

A rather reserved man, Tony Dillon always looked worried about life. He was a great philanthropist, contributing a lot of money to the Injured Jockeys' Fund as well as instigating the Dillon Awards at Wolverhampton. He gave a dinner every year and presented Midland jockeys and trainers with his personal awards for their achievements, which were either in the form of a silver horseshoe set into an ashtray, or a silver salver – trophies of that nature – and his generosity was much appreciated by us all.

Tony Dillon had another good sort in The Pantheon who, after winning the Tom Coulthwaite Chase brilliantly with me at Haydock on 3 January 1970, broke down in The Great Yorkshire Chase at

Doncaster, later that month, when we were three fences from home.

Fearless Fred ran a reckless race at Haydock in the Sundew Handicap Chase on 3 December 1969. He pulled for his head, and smashed through one or two fences, to win on the bridle. An additional hazard whenever I rode this horse, discounting his erratic jumping, was that however far forward I managed to sit on landing, he frequently caught me in the backside with his own.

I had previously experienced some pain in my back when French Excuse made a couple of blunders before winning the Woolavington Chase at Ascot on 22 November; then at Newbury, on 29 November, I won the North Street Handicap Chase on Glenn, but he too had twisted awkwardly over a fence, which hurt me. Fearless Fred's enthusiastic efforts at Haydock must have been the final straw. It did not take effect immediately, but when I was lowering some hay bales from the barn to feed the cattle at home, I jumped down from the loft and collapsed in agony.

I could not move, and Doc Wilson was puzzled as to what the injury could be. There was nothing broken and he could only presume that the nerves at the base of my spine had been damaged when riding.

At that time I had ridden forty-nine winners, seven more than Bob Davies, and I was worried in case I had incurred the kind of injury that would mean a long lay off, especially as I was to ride Gay Trip in the King George VI Chase at Kempton on Boxing Day, and had the prospect of partnering Normandy in the first-ever running of the Irish Sweeps Hurdle on 27 December 1969.

A trip to the London Clinic revealed no serious damage but I was advised to rest and to wear a spinal corset when I resumed riding. The pain disappeared as suddenly as it had come. I had been out of action for twenty-two days, during which time Ken White was not only deputising for me, and had ridden Normandy to win at Cheltenham on 6 December, but was standing by to ride him in Ireland should I be still unfit. Johnny Haine had also ridden Gay Trip in the Massey-Ferguson Gold Cup at Cheltenham and gone under by a length to Titus Oates, thus reversing the placings in the Mackeson Gold Cup.

I was fit to ride Gay Trip at Kempton on Boxing Day where he could only manage to come fourth, again to Titus Oates, ridden this time by Stan Mellor. Coral Diver ran a great race in the Christmas Hurdle afterwards to beat the Queen Mother's Escalus; then Inishmaan won the Charlton Hurdle very sweetly indeed to round off a super day for me.

Immediately after racing, Fred Rimell and I caught a plane to Ireland in readiness for the Irish Sweeps Hurdle to be run at Fairyhouse the next day. It was as well that we went when we did as thick, swirling fog clamped down over most of the British Isles, except Ireland, which meant that Bryan and Rose Jenks and Mercy were marooned at Wolverhampton. Instead they had to gather round a portable television set in the airport lounge, which was very frustrating for them.

The inaugural running of this race was at Fairyhouse as Leopardstown was in the course of being reconstructed.

When I walked the course it was like a rough point-to-point track. I can picture it now, with huge hurdles which to me resembled gates, and I looked long and hard at these, working out my strategy. I had found out earlier, on Scottish Memories, that Irish jockeys do not like you to come creeping up on the inside, so I thought the best thing to do was still to keep on the inside but not be near enough to the others to be interfered with. That way I would save ground without getting trapped on the rails.

We lined up for the 'off' and I jumped out of the gate in about fifth position, keeping right on the inside as I had planned. I never really saw a hurdle clearly because the others did not give me any light, but Normandy kept on picking up and jumping. If he had made one mistake it would have been a disaster. He saw just enough to know when to take off and he was so brave it was unbelievable. The other riders saw me poised behind them and they tried to thwart me a couple of times, but I just held my place. They had not realized that their tactic of easing away before a hurdle and closing in immediately afterwards was helping me no end! Whenever they spread themselves, even a little bit, I was just able to ping the hurdle before they closed up again to stop me, but I was still there. I must have saved ten lengths by going round on the inside.

As we came to the second last, I was still on the rails and Persian War looked set to win unless I made a move. I eased out before the second last and I had a tremendous run, with Orient War on the inside of me. Jimmy Uttley tried to push Persian War through the middle and I think that if he had given his horse a little more room he may still have won. As it was, he got in the way of my whip which caught Persian War on the head as he should not have been there in the first place. We rose to the last hurdle together and after we landed it was one long drive to the line. We were riding like flat-race jockeys, with all the skill we possessed, all three with a chance.

I could see the winning post drawing close and I was lying up Normandy's neck, knowing that he was just going to get there in front. It was a deep, deep thrill and I even thought to myself, 'God – I'm going to win – what's ten per cent of £10,000?'

We won by a neck from Orient War, who ran a fine race, with Persian War a length and a half behind him in third place. The reception when we came in was tremendous, with Waterford crystal being presented to owner, trainer and jockey, Fred accepting Bryan Jenks' prize as he was unable to share our victory in person.

Not only was it a great win for the Kinnersley stable and everyone connected with it, but it was also a masterly piece of racing strategy on the part of Fred and Mercy Rimell. As Normandy would not have been a five-year-old until 1 January, the traditional birthday of all thoroughbreds, he was still a four-year-old and entitled to receive 12 pounds from the other runners.

In Fred Rimell's view, that was one of the best races I ever rode for him. There were celebrations afterwards and when Fred telephoned Bryan Jenks with, as he said, 'whisky running out of his shoes', Bryan asked him to throw a party in his absence. People came from everywhere. The champagne was flowing freely and the only people who were thoroughly miserable were Henry Alper and his wife. When Persian War had finished third, Henry Alper simply could not take it in, and actually objected to Normandy and Orient War, to no avail.

What a race Coral Diver ran in the National Spirit Hurdle at Fontwell on 11 February 1970! I only spoke to him once after he had galloped straight on at the first hurdle and made a mess of it; then he gave me the most fantastic ride to win by five lengths.

After a period of frost and snow in many parts of the country, my next important engagement was at the Chepstow meeting on 21 February 1970, where I was to ride French Excuse in the Welsh Grand National. He had been given 10 stone 9 pounds including an 8-pound penalty, and I said that I would do the weight.

I went to the baths at Gloucester that morning to get as much weight off as possible. It was a humid morning and extremely hot in the baths. Peter, Buck Jones' brother, was in the baths with me, and the sweat simply poured out of me. I think I lost almost 9 pounds in just over two hours. When I came out, I foolishly had nothing to drink. When I got to Chepstow I weighed 10 stone stripped.

Before the Welsh Grand National, I rode Chatham in the Tote Investors' Trophy Chase, to win from Nigel Wakley on Hardyglass Lad by four lengths. When I came in I felt a bit weak, and had a heavy nosebleed in the weighing room. I plugged my nostrils with cotton wool before weighing out for the Welsh Grand National over 3 miles 6 furlongs.

French Excuse went well until we came to the water on the second circuit and he lost his hind legs in it, coming almost to a standstill. I nearly pulled him up, thinking that he might have hurt his back and then he started to go on again. I kept persevering and turning into the straight he really started to run. I gradually overhauled a few runners to get a little closer to the leaders and then the race was between me and Jimmy Bourke, who was riding Bryan Jenks' horse, Astbury. I thought to myself, 'Do I keep on the rails or move to the outside?' I decided to keep to the rails and, getting the last ounce of effort from French Excuse, managed to get up on the inside of Jimmy and win by half a length.

As I passed the winning post, all my energy drained away. When I pulled up I felt dizzy and almost fell off. My nose began to bleed again and somehow I rode back to the enclosure, dismounted, weighed in and sat down in the weighing room, feeling really rough. My head was pounding and I could hardly see. I walked to the ambulance room where the air felt freezing cold. The course doctor told me that I was suffering from exhaustion and dehydration, and prescribed a glass of Guinness – with salt in it. It was horrible. I drank it because I was so thirsty, but the sudden rush of fluid to my insides brought on an attack of colic and I had to have an injection to counteract the spasms. I have never felt so sick in all my life, and I did not ride again that day.

French Excuse gave more of himself than I did and never really got over that Welsh National. He ran a wonderfully brave race, not only to recover from his mishap at the water but also to battle on so resolutely to overhaul Astbury at the finish.

The 700th winner of my career, discounting any that I had ridden outside England, came when I rode Specify to win the Fairlawne Chase at Windsor on 25 February. He ran well to beat Richard Pitman on Freddie Boy and Jeff King on The Laird. After this race, Specify was sold by his owner, Paul Rackham, to Fred Pontin, later 'Sir Fred', the holiday camp magnate. He was to have a lot of fun with this horse which went on to win the 1971 Grand National ridden by Jack Cook.

I was now well ahead in the jockeys' table.

How could I have known, when I set out for Kempton with Bridget on 27 February 1970 that I would nearly kill myself? It was no different from any of the hundreds of times I had left home, gone to the baths and to one of any of the racecourses with which I was so familiar.

I had only two rides at Kempton. The first was on Gypsy Boy. The second was on King's Dream, a chestnut colt belonging to David Robbins, who was connected with Kempton Park racecourse and also the Radio Rentals empire.

I finished unplaced on Gypsy Boy in Division II of the Ashford Novices' Hurdle. Then I weighed out to ride King's Dream in Division III of the same hurdle race.

I was slowly away at the start and not going at all well in the heavy ground, which had become very cut up by this time. I was at the rear of the field, without a chance, and galloping alongside Paul Kelleway on Nerko between the third last and the second last hurdle when, for no obvious reason, my horse went down onto his knees. He shot me over his head and, being a colt, he did not want to fall and tried to save himself. In doing so, he bowled me along with his knees as he struggled to keep on his feet. Then he knelt on me with his full weight, and I can remember crying out with the excruciating pain. Instinctively I scrambled under the rails, still conscious, thinking there could be more horses behind me, and the next thing I remember is lying on the grass groaning. I longed to pass out. Instead, I tried to be brave and get up, only to fall down again. I hurt inside everywhere. It was the last race of the day and it was getting colder with the dew coming through the ground.

The ambulance arrived very quickly and the journey back to the ambulance room seemed endless as I was semiconscious and the vehicle went all round the outside of the track. In the ambulance room I was laid very gently on a bed and the pain was really bad.

Bridget came in and from the look on her face I could see that she was very worried. Fred came in and asked me how I was. I told him that I was fine and tried to sit up and make nothing of it. All at once I went giddy and the sweat started to run off my body. I remembered the symptoms of earlier accidents and thought, 'Oh – ribs again,' but when they took my blood pressure it was soaring. The next thing I heard was another ambulance coming with its siren blaring and I thought, 'Oh, God, a hospital job.' I wanted to cough, or at least to clear my throat and, to my dismay, I found that I was bringing up blood. I asked to lie down and after that I do not remember a great deal.

In no time at all I was in the Ashford hospital, near London. It must have been rather dramatic, looking back, because I had a police escort with the sirens going – the lot! Once in hospital I was given a shot of pethidine and I was away. I did not feel a thing.

The next morning I was still full of pethidine and they asked me to pass water. It was full of blood and they told me then that I had split my kidney and that it might be necessary to remove it. The very idea petrified me and I asked the specialist in charge of me not to perform the operation if it could be avoided. He was marvellous but he did say that I was a very lucky man to have survived.

'The state you were in when you got here, you could have been pushing up daisies by now,' he told me.

'Thanks very much,' I replied, but I was very grateful to him, and to all the staff who looked after me during the three weeks I was there. Bridget was terrific. She sat up with me for three nights and never missed a day when visiting time came round. She stayed with Nick and Judy Gaselee at Ascot and their hospitality made it possible for her to come as often as she did. I often marvel at how kind friends are when things are going badly, and they really came up trumps. I had lots of friends visiting me in hospital. Most of them brought dirty books for me to read, but it was lovely to see so many people who cared about me. Others sent letters, and I was marvellously looked after all round.

The X-rays showed multiple injuries, including three broken ribs, but the worst damage was to the lower pole of my right kidney, which had been ruptured. It never crossed my mind that I might be prevented from riding again, especially as my water gradually became clear while I was in hospital. One or two of the doctors were a bit doubtful, but I told myself that there were plenty of people managing normally with one kidney, so that I was that much better off with one and a half. To tell the truth, I was very frightened. On one of my wanders round the hospital I nipped into a lavatory and was relieved to find that all was normal. When I reported my findings to the specialist he soon brought me down to earth and told me that my right kidney was totally blocked and that the left one was doing all the work.

Nevertheless, the time came for me to go home and rest up. Josh Gifford came to collect me and when we reached Oxford I felt poorly.

I went into the toilets and, to my terror, I passed bright red water. I stood there, sweating with fright, and Josh said, 'Are you all right?' and I said, 'Yes, I'm OK,' because I did not want to go back to hospital again. I never told a soul. When I got home I went straight to bed and lay there for three days, too scared to go to the toilet. At the end of that time things were normal again, and it must have been the vibration of the car during the journey home which had aggravated the bleeding.

Several people have asked me if I am religious or have had any serious thoughts about dying, usually when this bad fall I sustained crops up in conversation. The answer is that, yes, I am religious in so far as I believe in God. Now and again I think of 'that little man upstairs' and think at the same time, 'Please let me win here, or let me win there' – and that does not always work!

I only go to church for weddings, christenings and funerals, but I have always loved the Harvest Festival, with the sheaves of wheat, corn dollies and the produce from the farms and gardens in the church. For me, that is beautiful. I think that religion is a matter for the individual, but I do believe in God.

As far as dying is concerned, that did not cross my mind after my fall at Kempton. When I was in hospital, I was there and yet not there, due to the drugs I had to kill the pain; and if I was going to die I was going to die.

What does bring death home to me is the loss of good friends on the racecourse, which has happened, and which is a fearful blow. But if that had happened to me, so what? I would have been killed doing the very thing I enjoyed most – what better way to go?

Before my accident at Kempton I had ridden seventy-seven winners and was well ahead of everybody else in the championship table. Now I had to sit at home, willing myself to mend and trying to ignore some of the medical warnings that if I rode again that season I would regret it. Most of the doctors, with the exception of Doc Wilson, thought I was mad even to consider doing so. I just listened and concentrated on getting fit while Ken White, able jockey that he was, took over most of my rides.

I missed my favourite Cheltenham National Hunt Festival, in March, where Ken came second on Inishmaan in the *Daily Express* Triumph Hurdle and sixth on Gay Trip in the Gold Cup, which was won by L'Escargot, my earlier adversary from Ireland whom I had so vastly underestimated.

When it came to finding a jockey for Gay Trip in the Grand National on 4 April, Fred Rimell sought out Pat Taaffe, with Ken White riding French Excuse, carrying the lighter weight of 10 stone 2 pounds against Gay Trip's 11 stone 5 pounds.

The night before the race I had a long chat to Pat Taaffe and told him everything I knew about Gay Trip which could be of help to him. I watched the race at home on television in the sole company of Doc Wilson. We nearly put £50 each on Gay Trip and I had actually picked up the telephone when we both got cold feet. We did not back him. We drank champagne all afternoon, watching the build-up to the race. Then came the great moment when the riders were called over, moved into line and were running. I saw Gay Trip fumble the first but Pat picked him up in a flash. From then on he gave him a terrific ride to win, twenty lengths ahead of the second horse, Vulture.

My emotions were very mixed. I was jubilant that Gay Trip had won and had jumped so well; I knew that, but for my fall at Kempton, I would probably be standing there in front of the cameras being interviewed as the winning jockey. But there again, I have never had a deep ambition to win the Grand National. Of course I would have loved to have won it, but never in this world has any achievement of mine exceeded the thrill of winning the Cheltenham Gold Cup. Not even when I became champion jockey. When I was champion jockey I was over the moon. When I won the Cheltenham Gold Cup I had a few tears. Perhaps the answer lies in those reactions.

Immediately after the 1970 Liverpool meeting, Josh Gifford began his new career as a trainer, taking over Captain Ryan Price's jumpers at Findon. He was splendidly equipped to become, as indeed he did, as good a trainer as he had been a jockey. He had learned all his disciplines under the kind but firm eye of Sam Armstrong; knew how to ride a race better than anyone and had a thorough knowledge of bloodstock through being associated with Ryan Price for so long. I wished him well with all my heart.

About a week later my sister, Sue, announced her engagement to Bob Davies, then in the lead for the jockeys' championship. I could not have been more pleased and felt that it would be even more fun to beat him as a brother-in-law than as just another jockey.

Early in April, Fred and Mercy invited Bridget and me to join them for a week's holiday in Portugal as their guests. Although my accident at Kempton was not in any way their fault, I knew that they were upset because I had not ridden Gay Trip in the National. It was a most generous gesture which we greatly appreciated.

I was feeling stronger all the time and ready to ride in public at the end of April. On 29 April I rode Pipplepen, owned by Harry Collins, unplaced at Worcester in the Spinners' Hurdle. I did not mind about not winning. I was riding in races once more and the championship was still within reach.

It was Coral Diver who really restored my confidence in my fitness when he came out on 2 May to run in the Lord Protector Hurdle at Huntingdon. Ken White had found that he could manage him better if the horse wore blinkers. Going to Huntingdon, Fred informed me that he had again put blinkers on Coral Diver and I was horrified. I had never ridden the horse in blinkers and did not want to do so now, but Fred was adamant that I was not yet 100 per cent fit and told me that the blinkers would remain.

Coral Diver ran away with me and made all to win easily from Willy Robinson on Lucky Match and Stan Mellor on Hully Gully, the only two other runners in the race. It was marvellous to be on my old favourite again and especially to win on him within a few days of returning to racing – but I felt sad about the blinkers!

Everyone seemed to rally round to give me rides which would put me up with the leaders in the jockeys' table. Denys Smith sent Auckland Girl down to Nottingham on 18 May, and Geordie Lad to Market Rasen the next day, and both horses won; Arthur Stephenson put me up on Dun Oir at Uttoxeter, on 26 May, Mid Day and Huperade at Market Rasen, on 30 May, and they all came in first. Fred's horses were giving me a few wins at the tail end of a hard season and the championship rested, as it had the year before, on the last meeting of all, this time at Stratford on 6 June.

Bob Davies, with ninety winners to his credit, was just ahead of Stan Mellor and me, who had eighty-nine winners apiece

At a little after 3.30 that afternoon, Bob had made sure of the championship for the second time when he won the Summer Selling Handicap Hurdle on Kalikrug, beating me on Mrs Wentworth. Stan then won the Falkland Islands Hurdle on Mugatpura, which put him into second place and I was forced to pull up both Arctic Count and Tipperty, which left me in third place with eighty-nine winners from a total of 347 mounts.

It was a terrific finish to the season and Bob Davies was a worthy champion with ninety-one winners.

The news of the death of Fred Dixon, a young and promising rider, following a fall at Chepstow in May, had shaken us all. Injury may have robbed me of my fourth championship but at least I had my life and my health. I had a great deal for which to be thankful.

13

The Bend in the Road

I suppose the most outstanding feature of the 1970–71 season was the emergence of Graham Thorner who, although I had always liked him and regarded him as a good jockey, had never been so close up in the jockeys' table as to present a threat. He was retained by Tim Forster at Wantage and remained loyal to him to the end of his racing career.

Graham was one of the younger generation of jockeys. He was always friendly and a great talker. He did not drink much and he kept his head in that he looked after himself, saved his money and had a great sense of purpose. He did not mix very often with the hard clique of jockeys with whom I associated, but when he was at a party he had a lovely, dry sense of humour which was a great asset. For me, he had all the qualities of a good jockey, tough, rather hard on his horses, and a difficult man to beat.

He began the season as he meant to go on by riding Zermatt at Newton Abbot on 13 August to beat me on Clear Wood, which started favourite. It was not until things got well under way that I and others realized Graham was a force to be reckoned with.

It was at this time that I formed a successful relationship with Ken Wheldon, who had horses in training with the late Vernon Cross at Stockbridge, and I rode a string of winners for this partnership at the beginning of the season.

Bermondsey belonged to Des O'Connor, ex-Redcoat and well-known television personality. I rode this horse to win at Hereford on 29 August and Des not only gave me a handsome present afterwards but we shared a bottle of champagne. I found him a rather quiet man, but full of fun, and he liked to have a good gamble.

After I was unplaced on Bermondsey at Cheltenham on 16 September, however, and had been beaten into second place on him in the Hugh Sumner Cup at Ludlow on 7 October, I was never asked to ride the horse again!

When I fell with Fulke Walwyn's Jimmy Scot in the Bagshot Chase at Ascot on 8 October, I had severe concussion afterwards. I was due to go to Norway to ride Robert Sangster's Sunny Lad in the Norwegian Grand National on 11 October, and I persuaded Doc Wilson to declare me fit to ride.

I had ridden my first winner for Robert Sangster on Sunny Lad in the Clanfield Chase at Newbury on 28 November 1969, and had won on him subsequently. Robert Sangster was a friend of Bryan Jenks' and I thought a lot of him. He was never too busy to have a chat and was an enthusiastic supporter of racing.

When I had retirement in mind, he offered to help me with the stud side of my business. To my subsequent regret I never followed up this offer. I was so intent on riding winners, and wasting in order to do so, that I took less interest in the other aspects of racing than I should have done. It was a criticism that Mercy Rimell levelled at me and she was right. But everyone can be wise in hindsight.

Robert and Christine Sangster, Fred and Mercy Rimell, Bridget and I flew to Norway in Robert Sangster's private plane two days before the race. The night before I was to ride, Fred was determined that I should not leave my room and live it up, so he and Robert Sangster wedged a chair under the door handle, believing that they had me trapped inside. They had not noticed another door which led to the room adjacent to mine and which enabled me to escape into the corridor and out of the hotel. When everyone else came to bed, Fred and Robert tiptoed to my room, removed the chair quietly and peered inside to make sure that I was asleep. The bird had flown! They never did find me, and I had a great evening, returning the next morning to find that everyone had taken it in good spirit.

That year, David Nicholson had the ride on Sorrento, who won the race in great style, whilst I was third on Sunny Lad, beaten a head by the German rider, F. Possberg, riding Colton. Later on, Fred Rimell had Sorrento in his yard to train and we found that the horse could not perform over English fences at all, but he certainly excelled in Norway.

Racing has its compensations but I had not expected to have a walkover in the Koko Chase at Kempton on 16 October, especially on Fearless Fred. I had only to go past the post and canter back again. It was the best race he ever ran! I felt that I thoroughly deserved that victory.

Following our meeting in the baths at Torquay, Frankie Vaughan had put his horse Aldium in training with Ted Fisher at Chewton Mendip. I won with Aldium at Chepstow on 20 October, and was pleased as I had suggested the arrangement in the first place. I was to win several races with Aldium, and Frankie Vaughan had an added bonus through his association with Ted in that he could indulge his passion for fishing on the lakes and reservoirs close to Ted's establishment.

Meanwhile, I had been anticipating a good ride on Inishmaan in the Fighting Fifth Hurdle at Newcastle on 28 October, with its prize of £3973.

Fred had been away from Kinnersley for a while, leaving Ron Peachey in charge of the training. Ron was a genius at giving the horses enough work to keep them fit and fresh without a lot of galloping.

I spoke to Ron the day before the race and he told me that Inishmaan should win because the horse was so well in himself. On the morning of the race a thick fog came down and we could not get a flight from any of the major airports to Newcastle. We eventually had the offer of a flight from Bristol. Fred, Tony Dillon and I raced over there, by which time the fog was a peasouper and all flights were cancelled. Fred then tried to charter a plane and finally found a pilot who would fly us to Newcastle but who had to be roused from his home in Bristol. When he arrived, he told us that there would be a further delay because somebody had locked the aircraft, leaving the keys inside, which meant taking the door off the aeroplane. We had a few brandies and ginger ales while this was being done and the fog thickened steadily.

The pilot was quite an elderly fellow and by the time we were all in the plane he demurred a little, saying that he did not think we would be able to take off after all.

Fred talked him into taxiing the plane onto the runway. Tony Dillon sat behind the pilot, and I sat behind Fred, with Tony Dillon looking extremely nervous. When we reached the runway the pilot said, 'I can only see the first red light,' and Fred, livened by a few brandies and not wanting to miss the race at all costs replied, 'When you get to that bugger you will see the next – go on, kick it in the belly – have a go!'

We took off and flew above the fog. I was not feeling very happy and Tony Dillon was sitting there, very tense and white, but at least we were airborne. Suddenly I felt cold, and said so. A few seconds later I could smell burning and saw some faint smoke coming up from somewhere in front. I tapped Fred on the shoulder.

'I think the bloody thing's on fire,' I said, urgently, 'I can smell it.'

Tony Dillon went a paler shade of pale and got lower and lower under his seat. Fred laughed to cover, I suspect, his own concern, and the pilot turned round and said, 'It's all right, it's only the dust from the heater drying off.' Oh, the relief!

We had an uneventful journey after that and when we landed at Newcastle the weather was glorious. I was to ride in the first race on a novice chaser and Fred was adamant that I should not ride this horse and risk injury before the Fighting Fifth with Inishmaan. We took our time at the airport and arrived at the course too late for the first race, with the perfectly reasonable excuse that our delay had been due to the fog.

Inishmaan looked and felt tremendously fit under me when we went to post. The ground had come right and although we were up against class horses such as the Queen Mother's Escalus, Persian War, Big Valley, Even Keel and others which could spring a surprise, I felt I was going to win.

I sat in behind and waited in about fourth or fifth position. Two hurdles from home Richard Dennard on Escalus was going a great gallop just in front of me. Approaching the last I thought, 'There's only one way to go and that's through the inner. If I pull out I will be beaten.' I sent Inishmaan up on the inside and he jumped the hurdle superbly. I should not have been there really but it was one of those situations where you win or lose a race. Inishmaan touched down, was into his stride and just got up to win by a head from Escalus, with Even Keel four lengths behind. Persian War, which had started favourite, was in fourth place with Jimmy Uttley. I thought that he had been run off his legs in the race but a Stewards' Inquiry afterwards revealed that Persian War had swallowed his tongue three hurdles from home and lost his place.

After the race there was a bit of a celebration in the stewards' room, with the sponsors and their guests, and somebody shouted, 'Right, bring in the jockey.' To my amazement, Fred then told everybody the true story of how he had delayed me intentionally at the airport so that I would be unable to ride in the first race, and that the fog was not entirely to blame. I was aghast, having stood up in front of the stewards earlier and told them such a lame lie, but everybody up north is very sporting, and the whole thing was lost in the laughter and good will.

On 5 November, at Newbury, I rode Mount Mills in the Wood Speen Novices' Hurdle. He was a green, gawky chestnut and although I tried to settle him in behind he scrambled over the first hurdle and turned over at the second, sending me flying. I landed on my back and knew that I had done more damage to myself than mere bruising. I passed out in the ambulance and was sweating all over when I came in, but I said that I was all right, and was allowed to go home.

Not only was I going to a boxing gala that evening with Fred Rimell but at the back of my mind lurked the awful possibility that I might be declared unfit to ride Coral Diver in the Nuneaton Hurdle at Wolverhampton on 9 November. I washed and changed to drive to London with Fred and throughout the journey the pain in the lower part of my back got worse. During dinner, Fred asked me if I was all right, and I assured him that I was, trying to kill the pain with a large port and brandy, which did not do any good at all.

The next morning I went to the Park Street Clinic where my back was X-rayed. The plates revealed compression and fracture of my lumbar vertebrae with the associated tearing of muscles and surrounding ligaments. Bill Tucker said I was mad to ride, and that if I did, I risked never riding again should I have another fall with my back in that state. I went home, took no rides and went to see Doc Wilson. I did not tell him that I had, in effect, broken my back, but he knew that I was in awful pain and also that I dearly wanted to ride Coral Diver at Wolverhampton. He gave me some painkillers and told me to rest for a few days.

Looking back, I think that had I gone straight home to bed after my fall I would not have realized what damage I had actually done to myself. By keeping moving, I had been driven to seek help from Bill Tucker, even though the knowledge of what was wrong with me did not stop me moving heaven and earth to ride Coral Diver. I often wonder what it was about that horse that made me want to ride him against all odds.

In the Nuneaton Hurdle on 9 November 1970 Coral Diver went to post and proceeded to pull my arms out and, although I had dulled all feeling in my back with painkillers, I think he may have wrenched it even more during the race, which he won extremely easily.

Afterwards I was in agony. I did not ride again until Boxing Day and Ken White, once again, deputised for me at Kinnersley.

I was well enough to attend Sue's wedding when she married Bob Davies on 21 December at St Mary's Church, Newent. That was a super day and although Bob was ahead of me in the winners' list and had had the nerve to carry off my sister as well, I joined with everyone in welcoming him into the family.

At the end of 1970, the Horserace Writers' Association honoured me with the Derby Award for my services to National Hunt racing and I was presented with a solid silver horseshoe as a memento.

Vincent O'Brien, who also received an award for his contribution to flat racing, sat next to me during dinner. I had the highest regard for him as a trainer, as had everyone else. What did surprise me was his knowledge of what I had done. In the course of conversation he invited me to visit him in Ireland. The fact that I did not take him up on this has been a source of regret to me ever since. I met him a couple of years later and he said, 'You never came to stay with me.' I wish that I had gone for I am sure I would have treasured the memory.

The meeting at Kempton on Boxing Day was abandoned due to snow and just as I was looking forward to a few more days' holiday Mercy Rimell telephoned and said, 'Guess where we're going?'

I thought quickly. 'I suppose we'll be going to Newton Abbot?'

'That's right,' she replied, 'and don't tell anybody because there is going to be a little coup.'

I was hopping mad. It had started to snow and I let Mercy drive all the way to the racecourse. I did not speak to her throughout the journey and I think I went to sleep for some of the time. When we went into the paddock, Mercy asked, 'Are you cross with me?'

I said that I was, and she said, 'Well, this horse, Charlie Lad, will win, and you must not be beaten as there has been a big gamble on him in Ireland.'

I did not know a thing about the horse but he won the South West Novices' Hurdle by seven lengths.

My second ride was Cecil Haynes' Instep in the second division of the same hurdle race, and before I went to post, Mercy said, 'This horse will win even further,' and it did, coming in eight lengths clear of Richard Pitman on Katie Gaze's Cold Day.

It was a very different journey going home. The snow came down like goosefeathers and I decided to drive, nearly skidding into a bank in the blizzard, and stopping here and there to celebrate. I enjoyed

Mercy's company hugely – when she had had a few tots she was great fun – and how we got home I do not know as the snow was so bad.

Afterwards, I had a nice present from the Hayneses and, to be truthful, I was glad that I had ridden at Newton Abbot.

I flew to Ireland to ride Inishmaan in the Irish Sweeps Hurdle at Fairyhouse on 28 December 1970. Once again, we were up against the great Persian War, ridden as usual by Jimmy Uttley. The ground was very heavy and Inishmaan ran well to finish third in going which did not suit him. Little Jimmy Uttley won comfortably on Persian War, beating the second horse, Lockyersleigh, by eight lengths, which in turn finished five lengths in front of me.

After the race, Jimmy only laughed at me in the nicest possible way. He never held anything against anybody and was a great hurdle race jockey. A quiet, rather deep man, I liked him.

Although I was riding winners and keeping fit I was having trouble keeping my weight down. Ken White was taking more of my rides and the old routine of going to the Turkish baths did not come as easily to me as it had when I was younger. I usually managed to do the required weights, with a struggle, and at worst carried a few pounds extra.

Since my accident at Kempton, Bridget had wanted me to retire from racing and it had been discussed between us rather vaguely at intervals. I made half-hearted promises to give up, but I did not want to retire. I was in love with racing and felt that I had many more years ahead of me as a jockey. Nevertheless, I travelled about the country with Bridget when I had time, looking at possible training establishments, but the prospect did not excite me at that time. I did not want to leave my native Gloucestershire but Bridget was quite anxious to rejoin her circle of family and friends in the Home Counties. It was a factor in my life which was beginning to pressurize me, but I tried to dismiss it and rode as hard as ever.

Clem Magnier, the well-known Irish trainer and stud owner from County Meath, sent over a small, liver chestnut colt called Deep Run to Kinnersley with the intention of letting him win a few races before retiring him to stud. I rode him in the Knottingley Novices' Hurdle at Doncaster on 22 January 1971, which was his first run. He was classy, with a good shoulder, bags of presence and immense courage. He won his race easily but at the time it never entered my head that he would make a good stallion. He must have had some deep breeding somewhere in his pedigree as he is now throwing top 2-mile hurdlers and 3-mile chasers, including Bright Highway. Deep Run has subsequently taken the place of Vulgan as a sire of outstanding jumpers.

I then had a spell when I could not get into the winner's enclosure, try as I may, especially with the Kinnersley horses. I had one winner for Josh Gifford with Sable Tang at Nottingham on 2 February, and one for Fred with Tudor Times at Haydock the following day, but when I was unplaced in all my rides at Sandown on 5 and 6 February, I decided to go down and stay with Douglas Bunn at Hickstead to get away from some of the irritation which I felt was building up as far as I was concerned.

I won with Coriolanus at Plumpton on 8 February and again with Sable Tang at Newbury on 12 February, for Josh, but I did not ride a winner for Fred Rimell until 15 February, when Inishmaan won the Wolverhampton Champion Hurdle Trial.

I rode my first winner for Douglas Bunn on Manicou Bay at Ascot in the Earley Novices' Hurdle on 18 February 1971 and he was delighted, as he had done most of the basic work on this horse himself.

Division III of the Earley Hurdle was the last race of the day and resulted in an unpleasant atmosphere between Fred Rimell and myself. Le Mydoc was owned by John Liley and I thought the horse had considerable potential. As we cantered to post he coughed at intervals. I knew that Le Mydoc's connections had backed him heavily and I said to the starter, 'This horse is coughing,' and Le Mydoc obligingly coughed once more. On hearing this the starter asked me if I wanted to withdraw the horse. I was not sure what to do, so he said, 'We'll give him another minute, and if he coughs again we'll take him out.'

Le Mydoc did not cough again and, as the starter usually acts on his own judgement and not that of a jockey, we came under orders. At Swinley Bottom I picked him up off the bridle, giving him a reminder, knowing I had no chance but at least showing that I was trying. The rest of the field was going a fair gallop and as I approached the second last I had dropped my hands for all to see. The other horses, having run out of steam, then came back to me and my horse suddenly ran on again. I was still beaten some twenty lengths, to be fourth.

Quite rightly, the stewards called Fred Rimell and myself in to know why I had dropped my hands on Le Mydoc when I did. As we went to the stewards' room Fred was fuming because he had expected me to win and knew that the owner was upset. We stood in front of the stewards who asked Fred, 'Were you satisfied with Biddlecombe's riding?'

'Yes,' he replied.

Then they turned to me and I said, 'As you probably saw, I was off the bridle at Swinley Bottom and then going up the hill I came under pressure.'

'We saw what happened,' they said. 'This is just a routine inquiry to confirm our opinion.'

There was considerable ill feeling afterwards as a lot of money had been lost. Nevertheless the horse should not have run because there is little doubt that the race damaged his lungs and he never ran well again. Suffice it to say that at Chepstow later, John Liley apologized to me for any hard things that had been said and agreed that I was in no way to blame for his horse not winning at Ascot. On reflection, I should have pulled Le Mydoc out of the race immediately I heard him cough, but I did not and the outcome was unfortunate.

Josh Gifford was fierce in my defence at Kempton on 27 February 1971. He had booked me to ride Melody Rock, owned by Bob Woods, who had horses in training with both Josh and Captain Ryan Price. Bob had asked Ryan Price about me when he knew I was going to ride his horse and Ryan had said that I was over the top and should retire. Josh was outraged. He informed Bob Woods that I was riding his horses and that if I was good enough for him I was good enough for Ryan, so Bob agreed that I should ride Melody Rock. The horse cruised in. I dismounted, went over to the owner and thanked him and walked away from Ryan Price, feeling that I had justified myself, even if I was being discourteous. Until then, Ryan had been one of the men in National Hunt racing whom I respected. He was an exceptional trainer, very down to earth, and nothing seemed to defeat him. He went down in my estimation after this incident.

At that time there was a bit of talk going on behind my back about my battle with my weight, my ability as a jockey and all the rest of it. In my view, when this happens to anybody they must resolve to keep coming back and never be beaten by anyone or anything. I felt more determined than ever to prove to those members of the racing fraternity who were out to upset me that I did not give a damn.

The Pantheon, fully sound again, was exceptional in the Mandarin Chase at Newbury on 6 March 1971. He was always a good horse and he made no mistakes in the race to beat 'Buck' Jones on The Otter by a head. Tony Dillon, once again, was very happy, as was Fred Rimell. I must admit that that was one of my better races. I rounded off a splendid day by winning the Highclere Hurdle with Persian Majesty, an attractive horse that Ken Wheldon had in training with Ryan Price. Ken had not forgotten the good run I had had with his horses at the beginning of the season and his loyalty was repaid by this win on which I know he had his usual nice touch!

Persian Majesty beat Fred Winter's promising horse, Killiney, in the Gloucestershire Hurdle at Cheltenham on 16 March 1971. This was a great achievement but Ryan Price did not even go to see Persian Majesty run as he thought he had no chance. Ken Wheldon wanted his horse to run, however, and he was as thrilled as I was to win that race.

Disregarding the Grand National, the Champion Hurdle was a race which consistently eluded me. There were times when I thought it was within my grasp, and lost it through no fault of my own, and times when I know I should have won. The 1971 Champion Hurdle came in the latter category.

I rode Major Rose for Ken Wheldon and his wife and it was on this horse that Josh had come second for them in the 1970 race to Persian War.

Major Rose ran well with me down the hill. I was a bit over-anxious and I should have sat still on him longer than I did, especially when he ploughed through the second last, dragging his legs through the flattened hurdle and losing his momentum. I was able to get him running again, but that mistake cost us the Champion Hurdle, which went to Bula, from Fred Winter's stable, with Persian War second and Major Rose in third place.

There was nothing in the yard that year for me to ride in the Cheltenham Gold Cup. If I was not riding at Cheltenham for any reason, I liked to stand by the rails to have a brief exchange with my fellow jockeys as they paraded before any 2- or 3-mile race there. I loved the parades when I was riding. Old friends would call out to me, 'Are you trying today?' or, 'Will it win?', which was entertaining, and at the top of the parade, just where the horses turned to go to post, was a jellied eel stand. Whenever I saw this I longed to get off my horse and have a dishful of eels!

I never enjoyed watching the Gold Cup from the stands. I longed to be out there and canter down to post, with the wind in my face, and to see the great backcloth of Cleeve Hill which had become so familiar to me over the years. Watching the race was frustrating. I could see where I would have picked a horse up; where the dangers were; where I would have kicked on or crept behind, letting the rest run themselves into the ground so that I could shoot ahead and win! I would do this at any track if I was not riding, but I felt especially miserable when I had no ride in a race at Cheltenham. It was an unhappy Biddlecombe who watched the Irish take first and second places with L'Escargot and Leapfrog, with Gay Trip's close relation, The Dikler, in third place.

It was a disappointing Cheltenham for me overall, and I finished the festival without another winning ride.

If ever I was confident that I would win the Grand National it was in the 1971 race, when, at last, I was to partner Gay Trip. The newspapers were full of praise for him; everyone, including me, remembered the fluent race he had run the year before to win with Pat Taaffe and I thought to myself that even if I still regarded the National as a lottery, I had drawn a marvellous ticket.

As the favourite, he was given 12 stone to carry, with only The Laird, with 11 stone 12 pounds and Charter Flight, carrying 11 stone 8 pounds, anywhere near him in the weights. I think that everyone felt that, barring bad luck, we would win, and even I gave some confident interviews to the racing press, knowing what a fine, game horse I was to ride and one that I knew so well.

We weighed out for the Grand National on 3 April, with the old familiar tensions in the weighing room, the silences, the secret thoughts and strategies occupying everyone's mind.

Once I was astride Gay Trip I felt brimful of confidence. We led the parade, and then cantered down to the start. He felt super under me. We were called over, each jockey selected his place and we were off towards the first fence at quite a good gallop.

Gay Trip jumped it, landed and then another horse, which I later found to be Battledore, landed almost on top of him, hitting him in the hindquarters. The next thing I knew I was on the deck. I had fallen or, more accurately, I had been knocked over at the first fence, bringing down Bob Champion on Country Wedding. I remember swearing loud and long and glanced along the fence after the cavalry charge had passed to see another figure whose language would have been stronger had it been anyone other than Eddie Harty. His horse, Twigairy, had also been brought down at the first fence, having tried in vain to dodge the two other fallers there, Craigbrock and Brian's Best. I think Eddie thought it was my fault entirely, and called me a 'bucking fool', but apologized almost immediately. That was Eddie Harty.

My own feelings were surprisingly philosophical. I felt sorry for Tony Chambers and Fred, who had such high hopes of Gay Trip, but it had happened and there was nothing I could do about it. A lot of people, including Fred, thought that Gay Trip had over-jumped, sprawled and then been bumped as he was collecting himself together to go on, but that was not the case. He jumped that first fence well but he was knocked over from behind. I should know – I was the man on top!

I did not receive a bollocking. There was no point. I related what had happened and reminded myself for the umpteenth time that the Grand National is an unknown quantity, however certain you may feel beforehand that you are going to win.

At Chepstow on 13 April 1971 I rode Cecil Haynes' True Luck in the Welsh Champion Hurdle. This was a grand horse which had won the Lancashire Hurdle at Liverpool on 1 April with me in great style. As usual, Cecil had worked out his horse's form to the last pound and inch, and estimated that I could beat Bula by a head. I kicked True Luck into the lead two hurdles out but Bula rejoined me approaching the last. I drove for home but True Luck started to hang left-handed, away from the whip, on the run in. I thought briefly of putting my whip down and straightening my horse up but Paul Kelleway was upsides me on Bula and I knew that I would be beaten if I changed my rhythm. As it was I was drifting away from Bula and he beat me – by a short head. Champion hurdles, somehow, did not seem to be my scene.

It is mentally exhausting when a horse hangs badly as True Luck did that day. I often think that tooth trouble can be one of the main causes of this habit. Abscesses under a horse's teeth, rough tartar building up on the tooth making the cheek sore, even poor dental conformation, can, I think, make a tremendous difference to the way a horse runs and these factors play a vital part in the way a horse should be bridled.

I then had a long period without success. The Cheltenham meeting in April proved fruitless, with my horses either being placed or falling; on 17 April 1971 I travelled up to Ayr to ride Pick Me Up in the London and Northern Securities Future Champions Chase where he knocked himself early in the race and finished third, but lame. Gay Trip was favourite in the Scottish Grand National which followed and again I pulled him up before the twenty-first fence. The ground was too fast for him and I felt he should not have run. I had the same problem with

Major Rose which finished fifth in the Scottish Champion Hurdle. I pulled up Even Delight at Bangor on 23 April and also pulled up Stalbridge Colonist at Worcester on 28 April.

The truth was that these horses had had a long, hard season and although they looked a picture, they were tired and feeling their legs.

I was still well in with a chance for the championship, due mainly to the run of winners I had had at the beginning of that season. I went all over the country trying to find good horses to ride.

The winners eluded me until I rode Assad, a gallant partner of several seasons, to win at Wye on 10 May. Trained by Guy Harwood, Assad had at one time been 'shared' by Josh Gifford and me with consistent success.

I had been feeling off colour and dizzy at intervals, the symptoms of high blood pressure following the injury to my kidney at Kempton.

Bill Tucker had been joined at the Park Street Clinic by Alun Thomas, a young but brilliant consultant whose premature death in 1981 was a savage blow not only to me but to his other patients and devoted staff. Alun had been keeping an eye on my blood pressure and was in constant touch with Doc Wilson. After a visit to the clinic that April it was discovered that my blood pressure had risen considerably since it had been checked in the November of 1970 after my fall on Mount Mills when I cracked my vertebrae.

This meant that I had to rely on drugs to stabilize my condition and I was fortunate in having a doctor who was so conscientiously devoted to my welfare.

Many of the good horses had finished their racing for that season and I was struggling for rides. Graham Thorner was in similar trouble, with most of Tim Forster's horses having been roughed off for the summer. When I rode Colonel Harris for Josh at Wye on 10 May my total number of winners was sixty-six to Graham's sixty-eight. With seven jumping days to go we were level with sixty-nine winners apiece. There was the added incentive of the new £2,000 prize awarded to the champion jockey by the Sportsman Club, which sent us both scurrying all over the country seeking winners.

Graham scored at Stratford on 5 June with Red Hugh in the first race and I countered in the next with a win on Regal Jump. Graham was one winner ahead of me and we tore up to Market Rasen for the evening meeting where we both had a ride in the Summer Handicap Chase at 7.30 p.m. I went by helicopter, accompanied by John Oaksey, who needed one winner to take the Amateur Riders' Championship at the grand old age, in a jockey's world, of forty-two. I had agreed with John that, should Graham win the championship by winning the earlier race, then he could have my ride on Arrow Trout, trained by Barbara Lockhart-Smith, in the Final Fling Novices' Chase at 8 p.m.

Graham beat me soundly in the Summer Chase on Tam Kiss to take the championship with seventy-four winners, while I had seventy-two. After congratulating him, I went to Barbara Lockhart-Smith to arrange for John Oaksey to ride Arrow Trout. She was not at all keen about this but was persuaded to change her mind. John rode a fine race to take the amateur championship by one win from Graham Macmillan. The following day the racing press were rather hot under the collar about this, saying that amateur riders, however good, are not as likely to win on a horse as professional jockeys; and in this particular race Arrow Trout was joint favourite with Graham Thorner's mount, Misty Dell.

The only thing, in my view, which was not quite the done thing was that we had gone against the wishes of the horse's trainer but, as John Oaksey remarked afterwards, he had not exactly been offered a chance ride on Arkle!

Graham Thorner, at twenty-two years of age, had taken the title outright on merit. He had come from the ranks of the relatively successful to beat the best, which certainly put everyone on their mettle for the season to come.

14

I Turn Freelance

That summer, Bridget and I spent the first of three holidays we were to enjoy with Fulke and Cath Walwyn as members of their house party at Lady Aitken's villa in the South of France, just outside Monte Carlo.

It was a glorious place, owned at one time by Lord Beaverbrook who was sometimes joined there by Sir Winston Churchill. Subsequently it was run by the Beaverbrook Trust, based in Canada, but Lady Aitken and her friends spent a lot of time there. She had a few horses in training with Fulke, and I rode for her several times. She and her family usually came with us on these holidays, as did Charlie Toller and his wife Sammy.

The villa was set in about five acres of gardens and walks with its own swimming pool. We spent our time sunbathing and swimming and every day after lunch I would set off up the hill to fetch the papers before anybody else could get their hands on them, and also to treat myself to a cold beer and a brandy. Charlie Toller, Clerk of the Course at Newbury, Bath and Chester, when in England, had the job when in France of toiling up the hill at about tea time to fetch me and, of more importance, the newspapers, because everybody was tired of waiting for them. I would see his perspiring figure struggling towards me, and have a brandy in readiness for him when he arrived. This became an enjoyable ritual.

In the evenings we went to some fine restaurants before going on to the casino to play the fruit machines or have a few francs at the roulette table. Fulke gambled more heavily at roulette than most of us and he was pretty successful. The most I ever won on fruit machines was £10, or the equivalent of a round of drinks for the whole party.

These were thoroughly enjoyable holidays spent in the most fantastic surroundings.

All through the summer, however, I had felt restless. I had not been very successful for Fred, and Ken White was not only riding well for other owners, but he was standing out in his own right as a first-class jockey. I was also having a battle with my weight and I would dream up any excuse not to sweat it off unless I had to. Some of my old zest had faded and I needed a fresh stimulus in my life.

With Josh Gifford getting into his stride as a trainer at Findon, I made an arrangement with him whereby I would ride for him if Fred Rimell did not need me. This was the first step I made officially to divide my services. I had also, quite unknowingly, set the pattern for my future as far back as November 1969, when Fred asked me to suggest a jockey to ride Cecil Haynes' Palm Beach in a 'claiming' race at Newbury, on 6 November.

I had noticed Bill Smith riding winners for Bill Marshall, and he had impressed me. Bill had previously worked at Kinnersley for about a month, almost unnoticed, and had returned to his previous position as a salesman with Messrs Moss Bros., feeling rather disillusioned. He lived near Stuart Matthews at Southampton and began to ride out for him, which rekindled his interest in racing. He rode a few winners for Stuart, and Les Kennard, before riding with great competence for Bill Marshall.

I told Fred that I thought Bill would ride Palm Beach very capably, and the arrangement was made. Bill rode a fine race to win the Chequers Handicap Hurdle, and I felt a little proud that I had 'rediscovered' him.

Bill and I are firm friends and the fact that he eventually became stable jockey at Kinnersley before moving on to Fulke Walwyn to carry, among others, the royal colours of HM the Queen Mother, only proved my judgement to be correct. The subsequent pattern of events had nothing to do with our personal relationship. The direction my life was to take had been determined long before and the outcome was inevitable.

When the season started off, I accepted as many rides from outside trainers as I could. I rode for Ken Wheldon and Vernon Cross to bring off a marvellous double with Ryan's Choice, winning at Newton Abbot on 30 August, and at Devon and Exeter on 1 September, which was a great feat of training. He came out again to win at Ludlow on 16 September and yet again at Cheltenham on 22 September.

That was a heartening Cheltenham for me because I won on Stepherion for Stuart Matthews; then Burns, for Thomson Jones, before having a good laugh at Macer Gifford on the second day's racing in the Marle Hill Chase. Macer had partnered Larbawn to win a lot of good-class races, including the 1968 Whitbread Gold Cup, but the horse invariably ran away with him. As we cantered past the stands at Cheltenham, Macer called out, 'Oh, dear – I'm going!' – and away went Larbawn, who was a terrifically strong puller, with Macer helpless on his back with no chance of holding him. Once Larbawn took it into his head to go, that was that. I was delighted, because I knew that Macer would be all right, but Larbawn, who was joint favourite with me and Fearless Fred, would now be out of contention. The only thought that crossed my mind as we waited for Larbawn to come back was that, by now, the race could have been over, and with Fearless Fred as my partner the alarming possibilities were still confronting me. As it was, he ran a good race, crashing through the tenth but making most of the running to win from Richard Pitman on Vintage, with a tired Larbawn being pulled up after the sixteenth.

I had always regarded Fearless Fred with some misgivings. He had given me some crashing falls and many hair-raising rides but he gave of his very best, even if he tried to go through or even under fences to get round. I once described him as 'a bloody old hunter – with a big heart!', and he was as honest as the day is long.

I went to post on him for the umpteenth time in the Koko Chase at Kempton on 15 October, knowing that he was in form as he had won all his races so far. This was the first time that Fearless Fred had raced at Kempton, having walked-over in this race the year before. It is a right-handed track and a sharp one. He was jumping from fence to fence and really getting things together. The reason he was jumping well was that he was leading with his off foreleg and landing on it, and as he cleared the thirteenth fence, I felt him break down. I pulled him up and he was hopping lame. After all the things I had said about him, there he stood, with the off foreleg gone. It was so sad. That was the only time I felt really sorry for him. I did not think that he would ever race again. He did, but that was the last time I rode him. He had won over twenty races with me and he was one of the most ignorant but smashing horses one could wish to ride. I could never forget a horse like Fearless Fred. He was a character.

At Haydock on 29 October I had a crushing fall on Karacola in the Blackpool Chase. I was due to ride Royal Mark at Cheltenham the next day but Fred did not think I was fit to ride. Jeff King substituted for me and won his race easily. I felt perfectly fit, but if Fred felt otherwise there was nothing I could do about it except to ride winners for other trainers. I did just that at Lingfield when I rode Rabble Rouser owned by Frank Pullen and trained by Josh Gifford to take the Crowborough Hurdle. I had first met Frank and his son at Plumpton in the January of 1971 when I had won on Larvotto, also owned by them and trained by Josh. They were colourful characters. Every time Frank Pullen went racing he bought himself a new, really fancy hat, the spivvy sort with feathers on the hatband. It became quite the thing to look out for him and see what he was wearing at each meeting.

I went to the Cheltenham meeting on 13 November 1971 full of confidence, anticipating an exhilarating ride on Gay Trip in the Mackeson Gold Cup.

When I rode him out of the paddock he was bouncing like a little rubber ball, holding his head high and showing himself off to the crowd. He was a great exhibitionist, Gay Trip. By now I knew him so well that I felt sure he had a good chance in the race. He was supremely fit, and although they all went a right gallop, he was always there with them. The ground was just to his liking and he gained ground at every fence. I was able to give him his 'breather' coming down the hill. As we came out of the bend I felt him change gear. I gave him a bit of a reminder and he lengthened his stride, hanging right-handed as he always did but going beautifully. Coming to the last fence I saw the most perfect stride and I gave him a slap going into it, one in mid air and one on landing. I had two or three good horses with me going to the last, with Chesapeake Bay and Brian Fletcher, Straight Fort with Eddie Wright, and Lucky Streak ridden by Bob Davies, all in with a chance.

As Gay Trip bounded over the fence, I saw Bob's horse falling to my left and from then on it was Gay Trip's race. He sped away from the last like a little fox and sprinted up the run-in to win from Chesapeake Bay by four lengths, with Straight Fort another length away in third place.

For the second time with Gay Trip, I received the lovely trophy of a horse's head in bronze, mounted on a marble base, this time from Mrs Bill Whitbread. It was a wonderful moment and I felt so proud of Gay Trip. God, he was a good horse and he jumped fantastically to win that race. Fred Rimell was so thrilled because this was the fourth time he had won the Mackeson Gold Cup.

John Liley's Notification had run well for me at Newbury on 26 November but at Sandown on 4 December he missed the open ditch completely in the Sovereign Chase. We had gone quite a strong gallop throughout and Notification just galloped straight through the fence. He should have turned over and I was just starting to bale out when somehow he found a leg and shot me back into the saddle again. There was no way in which I could have stayed there by this time and I turned over in mid air with a fleeting glimpse of the backsides of the two horses in front of me before I hit the ground hard. When I came back to the weighing room, Fred said, 'You fell off!' which annoyed me. Nobody falls off for fun, but the photographs of that incident are amazing and won a place for the photographer, Gerry Cranham, in the 1973 *British Journal of Photography Annual*. Over the years, Gerry has established himself as a racing photographer with a difference. His eye for the spectacular has resulted in a stream of pictures which reflect steeplechasing and hurdle racing in a way that no other photographer has managed to achieve. The speed, power, colour and grace of horses and riders in action leap out of his photographs, which sometimes verge on the surrealistic. He is a great artist with his camera.

I rode Coral Diver in the Christmas Hurdle at Kempton Park on 27 December. He must have got himself fit in two earlier races at Sandown and Cheltenham that month in which he had run moderately, because he absolutely cruised in. It was the old Coral Diver under me once more and nothing was going to beat us that day. It was a great feeling.

When I had the leg up on Gay Trip at Wincanton on 13 January 1972 for the John Bull Chase, he was full of himself. It was a four-horse race, with Kinloch Brae, The Laird and East Bound as my opponents. Gay Trip started favourite. He jumped like a stag and going to the last fence I was about twenty lengths clear of the field with the crowd cheering us home. Gay Trip had been standing off at every other fence and why I *asked* him to do so at this one I will never know because all I had to do was to sit there. Anyway, I really kicked him and, to my dismay, he did not come up – he was looking at the crowd! I just sat tight and let him hit the fence. If he had fallen or galloped straight through it, or even stood on his head, I might have been forgiven. Instead, he just 'put down' and I was all over the place. I was clinging on to his head around his ears; I was underneath him, then I was between his hind legs. I was determined not to let him go but he got away from me and dragged me halfway to the winning post. It was awful. I thought, 'Christ – I've never been so humiliated!'

My horses had it in for me that afternoon. Riding Viroy, for Josh Gifford, I set off in the Jamboree Handicap Hurdle, cleared the first, cleared the second and was preparing to settle down to race when Viroy decided he had had enough and came to a stop. He was inclined to be a bit windy and nothing on earth would make him go on. I did feel stupid. Looking back, I had an entertaining day with Gay Trip and Viroy.

Frost and snow caused several meetings to be abandoned at the end of January and the beginning of February, but I had the ride on Maniphe at Sandown on 4 February 1972 in the Park Handicap Chase. I had put on a lot of weight during those few days when there was no racing and I am afraid that I cheated the Clerk of the Scales and the trainer, P. Blackburn, because I had promised that I would not be more than 2–3 pounds overweight. When I got to the races I would have been about 10 stone 10 pounds stripped. I went through the scales at 10 stone 12 pounds, carrying 5 pounds overweight; then there was a chammy, which was added, a cloth, my irons and 'cheating boots' – little paper-thin boots which some jockeys use to pass the scales but which are not really permitted. I must have carried a total of 9 pounds extra.

Maniphe made nothing of the elephant on his back and beat the favourite, Some Jest, ridden by Paul Kelleway, by half a length. When I weighed in, the Clerk of the Scales said to me, 'You've done it again, haven't you?' and I had to confess that I had. He did not report me but he gave me a thoroughly deserved bollocking. I did not like cheating. I found throughout my career that Clerks of the Scales, for the most part, are fair and understanding. They all do a great job and in my day I think they recognized that the bigger a jockey was the harder it was for him to do some of the weights. If they knew you had been struggling, they would often turn a blind eye, but God help the jockey who abused this understanding. I have done so in my time, even lining the cheating boots with racecards so that I could ride in them without hurting my feet, but I would never consistently take advantage of a Clerk of the Scales.

I went back to Petersfield from Sandown that evening with Bridget to have dinner with her brother, Bill, and stay overnight with him. The following morning, I got some weight off and drove back to

Sandown alone, having arranged for Bridget and Bill to join me there later in the day.

In the Fairmile Handicap Chase I had a bad fall on Lucky Edgar and broke my right shoulder. When I came out of the ambulance room there was no sign of Bridget or Bill, and I wondered what could have delayed them. I then had a telephone call to say that they had been involved in a car crash on the way to the races. Bill Smith kindly drove me back to Petersfield where I found Bridget, with several stitches in her face and terribly upset because her dog, Scout, had been killed in the crash. Apparently, a car had pulled out across the road from a public house car park, and Bill had no chance of avoiding it. He had hit it head on and, just before the impact, Bridget had jumped out of her seat towards him. Scout was sitting where her legs would have been and was killed outright. They were both pretty shaken, but they were extremely lucky not to have been killed themselves.

It was a black day for the Biddlecombe family because I learned then that Dad was in hospital with a fractured skull and crushed pelvis, following a hunting accident that same day. Bridget and Bill had known of this but had been forbidden to tell me until racing was over. Dad recovered remarkably quickly from his accident and was soon riding to hounds as fearlessly as ever. Tony, also, had his leg in plaster, having had it reset all those years after his fall on Ascension. I really wondered what else was going to happen after that. Mother frequently remarked that she had 'buried all four of us'.

I was out of racing with my broken shoulder, and Ken White deputised for me, until I came back to ride at Chepstow on 11 March where, although I did not ride a winner, I felt fit and ready to tackle Cheltenham. Little did I know what that meeting had in store for me.

My increasing weight problem had prompted Fred Rimell to search for somebody to take my place at Kinnersley. I had told him that I would like to turn freelance at the end of the season, and Bill Smith was an excellent choice as the new stable jockey to complement Ken White. Fred and I agreed that this arrangement would be a strictly private one, and that any announcement relating to it would be made at the end of the racing season.

While I had been on the sidelines, a potentially outstanding young horse, Comedy of Errors, owned initially by Ted Wheatley, had come to Kinnersley. Ken White had won the Radcliffe Novices' Hurdle on this brown five-year-old at Nottingham on 19 February, but had then been beaten on him on 29 February at Doncaster by The Bugler, a comparative outsider.

I was offered the ride on Comedy of Errors in the Gloucestershire Hurdle on 14 March, the first day of the Cheltenham Spring Meeting.

Fred's orders were to 'get him jumping, get him relaxed, but the main thing is, get him to jump, and don't come before the last'.

When the tape went up I dropped Comedy in nearly last, not too far, but right in behind the others. Despite my efforts to keep him there, he pulled hard and jumped his way towards the leaders. At the top of the hill I was going so easily that I could not believe it, and I had to drop Comedy into third place. Going to the second last hurdle down the hill I saw a good stride. When he landed he was in the lead and running very free. I thought to myself, 'Hell, what do I do now?', and then decided to let him run from the bend. I let him go. He was a big backward horse, but he ran well in the heavy going. As we went up the run in he began to wander. I still thought I was going to win when he looked, as a green horse will often do, up the chute leading off the course. As he did so, Noble Life, a complete outsider ridden by Tommy Murphy, caught me in the last few strides to win by a neck.

There was a hell of a row after that race. Mercy and Fred thought I should have won and nothing I could say would alter their minds. The following day, the newspapers were busily announcing that I intended to turn freelance at the end of the season and that Bill Smith would be first jockey at Kinnersley. I do not know who was responsible for this leak to the journalists concerned. I was extremely put out about it at the time because my agreement with Fred that this would not be made public until the season was over had been betrayed.

I never rode Comedy of Errors again. He developed into an exceptional horse and, as is well known, went on to win many good races including the 1973 Champion Hurdle and the Irish Sweeps Hurdle, ridden by Bill Smith, plus the 1975 Champion Hurdle and the 1974 Irish Sweeps Hurdle, with Ken White in the saddle.

Coral Diver was simply flying in the 1972 Champion Hurdle on the following day but he was knocked sideways and put out of the race when Dondieu, ridden by Bob Davies, fell and broke his neck, bringing down Canasta Lad and Garnishee. Coral Diver lost his momentum but picked his way through the fallen horses to finish seventh to Bula and Paul Kelleway.

The third day of the Cheltenham meeting was a miserable affair. I finished way down the field in the George Duller Hurdle when I rode

Bannon's Star for Josh Gifford; in the Mildmay of Flete Chase I pulled up That's Life, trained by Denys Smith; then I rode North Pole in the *Daily Express* Triumph Hurdle. This was a decent horse which Ken White had ridden to victory in the Victor Ludorum Hurdle at Haydock on 4 March that year, when I had been laid up with my broken shoulder. I had ridden North Pole earlier at Haydock and Wolverhampton in January, when he had won in great style. He was a dark bay with bags of class about him, rather flat-racey but a superb jumper. His owner, Chris Cleary, was a slightly-built, dapper Irishman who was a cheerful individual and a very good paymaster after a winning ride.

North Pole started favourite in the *Daily Express* Triumph Hurdle, and Bill Smith was asked to ride Zarib as he could do the weight far more easily than I could. Going to the last I could see Zarib in the lead and knew that Bill was going to win. As Zarib crossed the line, skilfully ridden by Bill, with North Pole well behind in fifth place, everything crystalized in my mind. I knew then that my period with Fred and Mercy Rimell, nine long successful years, was virtually over. As a freelance, Fred would seek me out when he needed me, but that was the actual moment which sealed my career at Kinnersley.

Gay Trip was given 11 stone 9 pounds to carry in the 1972 Grand National on 8 April, which was quite enough for him to hump around Liverpool. He started as second favourite at 12–1, with L'Escargot the clear favourite at 17–2. We took part in the usual parade before the huge crowds and then cantered down to the start. When they let us go, Gay Trip set off with characteristic enthusiasm. Fred had given me orders to go round the inside as far as I was able, as this was how Pat Taaffe had ridden Gay Trip to win two years before. Going to the first fence I was two horses out from the rails and Gay Trip jumped it cleanly. He made nothing of the second, but at the third fence L'Escargot was baulked and knocked over, and I was right behind him when it happened. As L'Escargot was getting to his feet, Gay Trip jumped into his hindquarters, which brought him to a standstill. Johnny Francome, riding Cardinal Error, who had also been baulked but had scrambled over the fence, was mixed up in this debacle and he saw me trotting away from the third fence to get back into the race again. I must have lost a good ten lengths. As the race continued I began to make up ground steadily, making no mistakes, and going down the back I eased out and still kept making ground quietly.

As Gay Trip jumped the Canal Turn he began to hang right-handed a little. As he jumped Valentine's he was beginning to hang even more as the weight started to tell. I had walked the course beforehand and picked out some good ground right on the rails but I could not get there because there were two horses in the way, so rather than struggle with him I decided to let him drift out and keep free of trouble.

Going over the Melling Road, Gay Trip was hanging like a pig. Jumping the second last I thought, 'Only one more to go and then there is the long run in – what shall I do with him?' At the last fence, Well To Do and General Symons took off alongside, with Black Secret and Gay Trip just behind them. Gay Trip cleared the last and as he had been hanging for so long, I decided to let him go as I felt he would go faster that way than hanging, as he had been doing, towards the whip. It would have been much easier had he hung away from it. Once we reached the rails by the 'elbow' he straightened himself up and began to run on with tremendous courage. I was gaining on Graham Thorner and Well To Do and really thought I was going to catch him to win my first Grand National. But the weight finished Gay Trip. He went under by two lengths, giving 22 pounds to the winner.

As I pulled up, all I could think about was Gay Trip, who had run his guts out in that race. I did not have any feelings of disappointment about coming second, neither did I question whether or not I should have won. It did not worry me because I knew I had done nothing wrong in the race.

Unfortunately, my stable did not share my view. There were long faces, with the exception of Tony Chambers, who congratulated me and asked me to share a bottle of champagne with him after I had changed.

David Coleman interviewed Graham Thorner and me after the race with his usual cheerful professionalism. Graham Thorner was very emotional over his win and I thought to myself that it was I who should be crying! As it was, I just felt that I had been unlucky to come second. The Grand National has never affected me emotionally.

Nobody believed me when I said that I had been hampered at the third fence. I watched the film of the race on the BBC replay and the *Movietone News*, but both reports missed the incident. I can only say here that it did happen, that I lost ten lengths and, in doing so, probably lost the Grand National. As for Gay Trip, he displayed such courage, not only by getting back into the race but by coming second with so much weight on his back, that I could feel nothing but admiration for this magnificent horse.

Almost immediately after Liverpool, I had the chance to ride in the Freight Services Champion Hurdle at Pietermaritzburg, Natal. Stan Mellor had originally had the invitation to go to South Africa but he was unable to accept, and suggested that I take his place. I was due to ride Coral Diver in the Scottish Champion Hurdle on 15 April, which was the same day I was to leave the country. I mentioned my invitation to race in South Africa to Bryan Jenks and he urged me to go. 'The chance of a lifetime,' he said. 'Take it.'

So I told Fred that I would not be riding Coral Diver after all. I knew the old horse would run well for Ken White, and indeed he won the race, but by that time I was on the way to sunnier climes.

Just before we left England, Bridget told me that she was expecting our first baby. She had delayed starting a family because she thought it could be harmful to a child to know that its father was at risk almost daily. My vague intimations that I might soon retire, and the fact that I was finding it very hard to keep my weight down, persuaded her to take matters into her own hands. I have always loved children and I was delighted by the news.

The invitation to ride in South Africa had come from Gavin Brown, who handled the public relations department for the Jockey Club in South Africa.

When Bridget and I arrived, after an enjoyable but tiring flight, we were given the VIP treatment. We were greeted at the airport and immediately interviewed on radio. After that we were taken to one of the top restaurants for lunch before going to our hotel, which was magnificent. Bridget did not feel too well, but she joined me in another radio show which was rather like 'Desert Island Discs'.

The track at Scottsville was superb, with sauna boxes attached to the racecourse buildings. In the R4000 Champion Hurdle I was to ride Courtly, a nine-year-old that had won a big race in the Cape earlier, and I rode him schooling in the early morning with his stable companion, Stormy Sky. The ground was very hard and, because of this typical going, only one race meeting a year is held on the track. The training facilities in South Africa were excellent when I was there, with coloured lads, wearing hardly any clothes at all, exercising the horses amid acres of cane fields. The apartheid policy was explained to us as soon as we arrived, and I soon discovered that the coloured people attending the races had their own enclosure, although little coloured boys were then allowed to lead the horses up.

The hurdles were portable, twelve in all, with the one in front of the stands being jumped only once and then removed before the horses came round again.

Courtly started favourite in the race, and was going well when Adam's Apple, ridden by K. Hall, stumbled and unshipped his rider going to the last hurdle. As Courtly rose to the last, Hall got to his feet and I hit him with my horse, sending him flying under the rails. He was unhurt but it brought Courtly to a standstill. He ran on again to take third place behind South Wind and Stormy Sky who dead-heated for first place. I had thoroughly enjoyed myself, and everyone seemed very pleased with the result, despite the collision.

Unlike the English, the South Africans have a break for tea before racing again afterwards, and then they have an early dinner. Everyone was most hospitable. Bridget was given a beautiful dress, and we were taken to see the stud farms and the game reserves. I went to a snake farm and was horrified when a huge python was draped round my neck and shoulders. It was cold and clammy and smelt awful! There were plenty of barbecues laid on for us during our visit and I must say we crammed an awful lot into that fortnight. I would not have missed it for anything.

The flight back was terrible. We stopped off at Johannesburg, which was very different from the beauties of the Cape Province. Contrary to our uncrowded aeroplane from Heathrow to Durban, the plane taking us home was crammed full of people and screaming children. They were the worst eighteen hours I have ever spent in my life, and Bridget hated every minute of it as she felt sick.

Soon after our return, we bought The Moores Farm, which adjoined our own house, with the intention of taking in horses for trainers on a livery basis. The Moores, which had belonged to Mrs Annie Mears, daughter of Mrs Brotherton, had twenty-five acres, a house, and a large covered school, together with sixteen loose boxes. We had the advantage of the wide expanses of common land which form Corse Lawn, which could be used for exercising, and the whole place was perfectly suited for our purposes. I now had a suitable place where I could train horses when I retired from racing, and everything looked set fair for us. Bridget, who had returned to show jumping for a short while before starting our family, intended to keep her horse, Klonk, and continue both with her competition work, and to expand her interest in horse breeding.

Meanwhile, I faced the remainder of the 1971–72 season with renewed zest. I had returned from South Africa feeling refreshed and able to view things in their proper perspective. Although I heard intermittent mutterings about my being 'past it' and had been told by several people that I should give up riding and do something else, I knew I was not finished.

Now, all the old determination to prove to myself and to others that I could still ride winners with the best of them came flooding back. Trainers who had not approached me when I had been retained by Fred Rimell asked me if I would ride for them when I started my first season as a freelance. Other trainers for whom I had ridden for years were quick to offer me rides in the future. I would have to sweat harder, diet harder and ride harder to stay anywhere near the top, but I resolved above all else that I would do so.

During my time in South Africa, Bill Smith had been beaten on Inishmaan at Ludlow in the horse's first race over fences. Fred Rimell asked me to ride him in the White Lion Novices' Chase at Chepstow on 6 May as I knew the horse so well. He jumped superbly, made all the running and won easily. I was pleased that he had made the transition from hurdles to fences so well and that his first win over the bigger obstacles had been with me in the saddle.

I was well out of the running for the championship that year, which was won by Bob Davies with eighty-nine winners. My total was fifty-eight. But I ended the season with a good win on The Pantheon, at Uttoxeter on 29 May; then I rode Bryan Jenks' Straight Boy to win at Worcester on 31 May, and at the last meeting of all, Inishmaan came up trumps in the June Chase at Stratford on 3 June to win by half a length.

Over the top? I felt terrific!

15

A Fresh Start with Fulke Walwyn

As a freelance jockey I must confess that, at the start of the 1972–73 season, I felt rather vulnerable. I no longer had the protection of a big stable or the security of a retainer. The major National Hunt trainers had their own stable jockeys and I knew that I would have to rely on spare rides from Fred, Josh and Fulke Walwyn when these became available. Otherwise I had to depend upon old friends and any trainers who needed me if I were to earn a good living. Bridget and I had our own horses at Corse Lawn and could easily have expanded that side of our lives more profitably.

But racing was the very stuff of my existence and my only constant worry was my weight. Other than that, I was ready to take on the best of them.

Once the season got under way I forgot my misgivings because I immediately began to kick home winners. I rode Solrex to win for Fred at Newton Abbot on 29 July 1972 and scored on Quick Brew, trained by Ted Fisher, at the Devon and Exeter meeting on 2 August. Ted was still training horses for Frankie Vaughan and I rode his Billymague to win twice that autumn.

Inishmaan won over fences at Fontwell on 17 August then I went down to 'Gifford' country to ride Bedouin for Guy Harwood at Plumpton on 28 August, where he won the Junior Novices' Hurdle. Bedouin was a difficult horse to ride. He had a habit of running out or refusing, so Guy decided to bring in the 'heavy brigade'! I rode Bedouin to win four races at the start of the season, including the Wyld Court and Tom Masson Trophy Hurdle at Newbury on 20 October 1972

Barbara Lockhart-Smith, who had trained Sartorious years before to enable me to win my new tooth, asked me to ride Christmas Dream at Southwell on 29 August. I had not ridden for her for ages, but she was another supporter from the past who gave me yet another winner as a freelance, having forgiven me for the Arrow Trout affair! Then I rode a few winners for the late Dick Holland from Shropshire.

My happiest moment was when I rode Coral Diver to post at Wolverhampton on 25 November 1972 for the Yellow Pages Long Distance Hurdle. He had just come right. It was a good class race, and the distance of 2 miles 7 furlongs was just right for him now that he was getting older. He went as well as ever. He was brilliant. I was so proud of the old horse, who went into the lead from the eighth and cantered in, pulling up. It was marvellous to ride him again.

That October, I had been given a private retainer by Martin Vickers to ride two horses he had in training with Toby Balding, Big Valley and I'm Happy. The latter seemed to have the makings of a good horse and I won several races with him. He appeared to have something wrong with his back and never reached his undoubted potential. However, I had a grand ride on Big Valley in the Newent Handicap Hurdle at Cheltenham on 9 December.

It must have been a good omen because the next day Bridget presented me with our first daughter, Laura. I was so proud that I celebrated the occasion with rather too much champagne. Some people said that it would have been nice for me to have had a son at that time, but I was only too happy that our baby was normal in every respect. Sons and daughters are all welcome as far as I am concerned.

When I went to Ascot on 16 December 1972 I remembered Coral Diver's performance in the Yellow Pages Hurdle and anticipated another glorious ride on him in the Long Walk Hurdle over 3 miles 2 furlongs. I thought he would be a certainty. He was carrying top weight of 12 stone 5 pounds and was up against some good horses, including Highland Abbe, an out-and-out stayer.

Turning into the straight, Coral Diver was going well within himself but when he started to climb the hill with all that weight on his back, I could feel him fading under me. He could not give any more and was completely exhausted. I could not believe it and hated to see him so distressed. Highland Abbe won by two lengths from Bourdon, with Coral Diver a further eight lengths behind, third. I was very unhappy after that race. The old horse had been asked too big a question.

Kempton and bad falls went hand in hand for me and the Boxing

Day meeting that year was no exception. There were six runners in the Holly Handicap Chase, and I rode Potentate for Gifford in this race, a horse of which he thought a great deal. I was lying up with the leaders going to the thirteenth when Potentate slipped up on take-off and dived into the fence. We were both rattled up and bruised after that. I bought a bit more ground in the William Hill Christmas Hurdle which followed when Kelanne, going like hell to stay with Canasta Lad and Jeff King, fell at the sixth. This time I did not get off so lightly. My right shoulder felt very sore but I did not have time to have it X-rayed as the next day I flew to Ireland with Fred Rimell to ride True Luck in the Irish Sweeps Hurdle at Leopardstown.

I could only finish sixth to Captain Christy, trained by Pat Taaffe and ridden by Bobby Beasley. Afterwards, Fred hinted that my two falls at Kempton had rendered me unfit to ride, which was untrue, but I was in some pain. A visit to the clinic on my return revealed I had sprained my shoulder and collarbone but nothing was broken.

In the New Year, I rode Bruslee for Michael Scudamore, a really grand sort of horse that put me in mind of Mill House. I rode him at Windsor on 2 January in the Montem Novices' Chase, just to get him jumping nicely, and although he crashed through one or two he showed a lot of promise. Mike gave him plenty of time to come to himself, and he went on to win the 1974 Mackeson Gold Cup.

King Flame started favourite in the Western Long Distance Novices' Chase, at Cheltenham on 4 January. He ran very freely with me and fell at the ninth. I fractured my collarbone, injured my right shoulder blade yet again, and was out of racing for a week.

The proverbial ill wind then blew kindly in my direction. With Barry Brogan in bed with influenza and Richard Pitman riding at Kempton for Fred Winter, Fulke Walwyn approached me to ride the unpredictable Charlie Potheen in the Great Yorkshire Chase at Doncaster on 27 January 1973.

Richard Pitman had already won the Hennessy Gold Cup at Newbury on this horse on 25 November 1972 and reported that he was quite a tearaway. I had previously seen Stan Mellor carried over the rails by him at Cheltenham.

Charlie Potheen was a wild ride. He jumped left-handed, hung left-handed and was only run on left-handed tracks. On his day he was a smashing horse but quite horrific to ride. He was also a notorious front runner and in my view he never gave himself a real chance as he tended to panic early on in his races.

In the Great Yorkshire, Tommy Stack was on another front runner in Clever Scot and, as we went to post, I said to Tommy, 'Don't chase me, please.'

When we set off, however, I was being run away with by Charlie Potheen with Tommy Stack taking me on. Charlie Potheen hit the first hard but it did not stop him. He just kept going at an almighty gallop which I will never forget, it was so relentless. Going to the first open ditch I said to Tommy, 'If we miss this they'll never find us – they'll have to dig us up!'

We both jumped it safely and cracked on, hammer and tongs. Charlie Potheen jumped well until the open ditch after the water when he made a second mistake, insufficient to check him but he stopped pulling, which enabled the rest of the field to come to him. Spanish Steps took the lead at the fourteenth fence and I thought all was lost, when Charlie began to run on again. From somewhere he had found the strength, some would say, the courage, to battle it out with Spanish Steps to win by four lengths. He was a very tired horse afterwards and was his own worst enemy in that he took so much out of himself in nervous energy.

Fulke Walwyn was elated, as was Charlie Potheen's owner, Mrs B. Heath, but I dismounted with mixed feelings. He was a real character but certainly not everybody's ride! I was as pleased as everyone else at the result, and the speed at which that race had been run had given me a memorable experience.

Shortly afterwards, Fulke Walwyn asked me if I would ride for him on a friendly basis the following season, as Barry Brogan was relinquishing his post as first jockey. I was elated. To ride for Fulke Walwyn as first jockey, even without a retainer, at this stage in my career, made me feel a new man. I now had a fresh challenge before me and the thought of riding for the Saxon House stable kept me going throughout the remainder of the season.

On 5 February 1973 I took an old school friend of mine, John Street, to Plumpton racecourse where I was to ride Judy Millar's grey mare Sea Tan, trained by Ted Fisher, in the Hickstead Novices' Hurdle.

John Street was in the sand and gravel business and was also travelling head lad for Johnny Haine. He would do anything for anybody and he loved his racing.

Sea Tan was brought down at the third hurdle by Jackaroo, which fell heavily with Doug Barrott. My fall was particularly nasty, with Sea Tan lying on top of me for several seconds. I was in a great deal of discomfort and when I went back to the weighing room I felt thoroughly ill. I was advised not to ride again that day and Lady Aitken took me into the bar and bought me a couple of large drinks which only made me feel worse.

John Street found me afterwards and I was in such misery that when I saw him I said, 'Oh, God, John – let's go.'

He almost carried me to the station and when we reached London he took me straight to the Park Street Clinic to see Alun Thomas. He could not touch me – I was in such pain – and he booked me into a nursing home nearby so that I could have a scan. John Street was tremendous. He went out and bought me some pyjamas, a toothbrush and some books, and stayed overnight in order to see how I was the next morning. I thought him a true Christian.

I had slight concussion through being struck on the head in the fall; bruised right ribs and a badly bruised liver. The latter injury caused me so much agony that I seriously considered retiring from racing before I killed myself. When the pain ceased, I dismissed these thoughts, but that was a worrying fall for me. I was in the nursing home for three days and out of action for almost three weeks.

I did not know then that John Street had heart trouble. He had a heart attack at Christmastime 1980, and I went to see him in hospital, taking with me magazines full of pictures of such well-endowed nudes that I thought he would have another attack through laughing so much. He came out of hospital, arranged to meet a friend for a New Year's Eve drink; sat at the bar to wait for him, having ordered himself a lager and some crisps; and dropped dead. I could hardly believe the news. He was a kind and generous friend to me and I had lost him. I will never forget John Street.

I returned to ride a winner on Daniel Boon for Richard Head at Warwick on 22 February in the Banbury Handicap Hurdle. Actually, I dead-heated in a fierce race to the line against young Roger Rowell, Auriol Sinclair's protégé and stable jockey, riding the favourite, William Henry, Auriol being one of the first lady trainers to obtain a licence in her own right.

After a victory on Mrs B. Heath's Barnard from the Walwyn stable in the Sussex Novices' Chase on 28 February at Lingfield, I won the Burford Novices' Chase at Newbury, on 2 March, riding Ballyhoara Hill for Michael Scudamore. I thought the fences might be a bit big for this horse, but he jumped well, got the distance of 3 miles, and Michael was delighted. It was great to ride a winner for him because he had done his utmost to put rides my way throughout the season.

I was getting into my stride again, winning the Hylton Chase at Worcester on 7 March on Mr T. Winterton's Pattered. He was a nice horse, trained by Earl Jones, and just trotted up, and went on to win good races, including the 1974 Welsh Grand National, ridden by Ken White.

I was now riding more horses for Fulke Walwyn and at Chepstow on 10 March 1973 I had my first ride on Sea Tale, also owned by Mrs Heath, in the final of the John Player Hurdle Championship. Sea Tale was one of the prettiest horses I ever sat on. He was grey, with dappled quarters and a gorgeous flowing white tail. He was as good as he was handsome and had won several times, but at Chepstow he was no match for Dark Sultan, ridden by Ron Barry, who made all the running to beat me by five lengths.

I had met 'Big Ron' when I had ridden up north, and also when he rode a few horses for Fulke Walwyn. He was similar to Tim Brookshaw in that he was as hard as nails, would take any ride and was an exceptionally good rider with a style all his own.

He was the one jockey who found the key to The Dikler, one of the hardest-pulling chasers in training. Ron rode him for Fulke Walwyn in most of his races and he established a great rapport with this horse.

In all the years I had known Josh Gifford I had never had a serious argument with him, but at Cheltenham on 13 March 1973 we came close to falling out. He had engaged me to ride Avondhu in the National Hunt Two-Mile Champion Chase. I had ridden this horse at Cheltenham on 8 December and found that he hated the track, having both fallen and refused there in the past. There were only six runners in the race and they set off at a good clip. I gave Avondhu a hard ride for about a mile, realized it was useless, and just hacked round for the rest of the way.

When I came in Josh was seething.

'You should never be allowed to have a licence – you couldn't ride a bloody bike!' he roared at me, with Althea in the background looking unhappy and asking him to calm down. I turned and walked away from Josh because I think that if I had said anything to him I should have hit him, which would have been awful. He was particularly upset as Avondhu's owner was watching the race on television and it was obvious to anyone that I had not given the horse a ride. As I walked away I turned to Josh and said, 'I suggest you get your licence back and ride the bloody thing yourself.' Josh was right in his accusation, but I knew that Avondhu should never have run at Cheltenham.

We were good friends again within hours of the incident, but it was unfortunate all round.

The 1973 Gold Cup gave me, for a fleeting moment, a memory which still stirs my blood. When Charlie Potheen jumped the second fence he gave me such a sublime, magical feeling that it took my breath away. He stood off so far and got so much height that he seemed to go farther and farther, and I hardly felt him land. Going to the last, I was behind The Dikler and Ron Barry, and Pendil, with Richard Pitman. Pendil, who seemed certain to win, was caught on the run in by The Dikler, and I finished third behind these two good horses. Charlie Potheen was a bit outclassed.

Liverpool was my next main engagement but I had no ride in the Grand National that year. In the Coronation Hurdle on the Friday afternoon, Tom Dooley, which I had ridden several times unplaced, fell two hurdles from home, bouncing me on both shoulders and kicking me on the left one as he got to his feet. I picked myself up feeling dazed, and after a quick Scotch with my Liverpool doctor friend I was taken to have an X-ray in Liverpool. Subsequent X-rays in London confirmed the Liverpool plates which showed a fresh fracture of my left shoulder blade and a cracked collarbone.

I went back to Southport that night and, on the Saturday, Lord Sefton invited me to watch the Grand National from the comfort of his box. I saw Red Rum win the first of his three Grand Nationals but I cannot say that I really enjoyed the race as I was feeling so poorly.

As a result of my fall on Tom Dooley, I was out of racing for the rest of the season. Ron Barry became champion jockey for the first time in his career with a total of 125 winners, beating Josh Gifford's record. Ron was to be champion again the next season, with ninety-four winners, just ahead of Richard Pitman.

My rain of personal blows was not over. I was sitting at home watching the Whitbread Gold Cup on television, which was run at Newcastle that year, when I saw Doug Barrott take a horrific fall on French Colonist at the fifth fence. He later died of his head injuries without gaining consciousness and the news was a terrible shock. Doug had been stable jockey to Josh Gifford since he first started training, and he was one of the nicest, most cheerful men you could wish to meet.

It was a sombre gathering of jockeys and friends who attended the memorial service for Doug Barrott on 15 May 1973.

My own bad fall, and then the tragedy of Doug Barrott's death, worried Bridget to the extent that she began to urge me to retire from racing while I was still in one piece. I could see her point of view, especially now that we had a daughter, and although I was loath to give up, I applied for a permit to train racehorses at Corse Lawn. I already had some paying customers in the yard, with horses from Ian Balding and Robert Armstrong, plus a few others from people who had sent them to me to be broken in and schooled, which they had insufficient time to do themselves.

Bridget had several animals she had bred, and the whole business was in her name as I had my own profession as a jockey. I knew of other permit holders who kept two yards, one in their wife's name and one in their own, and I was not even doing that. Although I had everything on my premises that a would-be permit holder should have in the way of training facilities and personal experience of horses and racing, I was refused permission to train on the grounds that Bridget had a 'livery' yard on the same premises. To me, a horse 'at livery' was one which was kept for its owner to take hunting and for which a fee was charged. I was keeping racehorses and schooling them for other trainers, or resting horses that had developed bad legs on the racecourse.

I was disgusted at the decision, but was forced to accept it. Bridget was particularly disappointed when my application for a permit was turned down as she thought that this time I was really going to settle down.

Inwardly, I was thrilled at the prospect of another season in the saddle, and the thought of riding for Fulke Walwyn as first jockey put all thoughts of becoming a trainer out of my mind for the time being.

16
My Final Season

When I rode as first jockey to Fulke Walwyn in my final season, I took on a new lease of life. I knew that I would only ride the best horses and those carrying heavier weights in decent races. It was Fulke's policy to have several good lads in his yard who were only too willing and able to ride the novice horses, leaving his number one jockey to take the cream of the rides. This meant that the rigours of wasting would, in most cases, not be necessary, although I would have to keep my weight in the region of 10 stone 12 pounds.

Fulke Walwyn had served for a short time in the 9th Lancers as a regular soldier. Perhaps because he was an ex-cavalry man, he was thorough in every aspect of his training programme. Nobody questioned his decisions and every lad in his yard afforded him the greatest respect, and rightly so. He knew the character and quirks of each horse and trained it accordingly, accepting any faults he could not change, and working on those which he could eradicate with great patience.

He was a first-class rider in his day under National Hunt Rules, riding as an amateur from 1929–36 and as a professional from 1936–39. He won the 1936 Grand National on Reynoldstown and took out a licence to train in 1939.

The Second World War played havoc with racing, but as soon as hostilities ceased, Fulke Walwyn became leading National Hunt trainer in 1946–47, 1947–48 and in 1948–49. He was to regain this title in 1957–58 and again in 1963–64.

He had numerous successes on the flat, especially when he trained for Miss Dorothy Paget, but it was Fulke's equal ability to turn out winning hurdlers and steeplechasers that quickly placed him among the top flight National Hunt trainers.

During the eight years he trained for Dorothy Paget, he won the Cheltenham Gold Cup in 1952 with her Mont Tremblant, ridden by Dave Dick, a horse which also won the Grand International Chase at Sandown. Fulke won his second Gold Cup with Madame K. Hennessy's Mandarin in 1962, ridden by Fred Winter, and took it again in 1963 with Mill House, ridden by Willie Robinson. He was to secure his fourth victory in this race when Ron Barry won in 1973 on The Dikler.

In the Grand National, Dorothy Paget's Legal Joy, ridden by Michael Scudamore, came second to Teal in the 1952 race, but in 1964 J. Goodman's Team Spirit and Willie Robinson won the race for the Saxon House stable.

Although he trained in Lambourn when I knew him, he was almost another 'local' to me, as he was born in Wrexham and lived for some years near Abergavenny; his father was Joint Master of the Monmouthshire Hounds for some years before the outbreak of the Second World War.

Fulke Walwyn knew every horse in his yard. After evening stables, he would go round the boxes, with his head lad carrying a wicker basket full of sliced carrots, and each horse was given a final titbit before settling down for the night.

He was a terror for repeating his orders. He would ring me up the night before a race and give me a string of instructions, which I had had when schooling anyway, and on the morning of the race he would give them to me again, and when I went into the paddock, I had the same orders drummed into me! It reflected his extreme conscientiousness as a trainer. He produced his horses to the minute, and so fulfilled his side of the bargain. Now it was up to his jockey to carry all those months of thought and preparation to a successful conclusion. It was this thoroughness that made him, in my view, such an outstanding trainer.

Fulke had a little terrier called Rags which he adored. Rags went everywhere with him, sitting in the Land-Rover to go to the top schooling ground and 'rodgering' our anorak sleeves, while Fulke chewed his chewing gum and took not one jot of notice. We used to squeeze Rags, or try to kick out at him to make him stop, to no avail. When we left the Land-Rover, the groundsman would take Rags for a walk on a lead, and when the horses were being ridden up for their morning's work, Rags would bark at them incessantly. Fulke would say, 'Shut up, Rags,' which made no difference at all, while the horses skittered all over the place. If anybody had touched the dog, Fulke would have shot them!

When we returned for breakfast, there was a chair put ready for Rags, and a little plate on the table, also for Rags, and Fulke would sit down and enjoy his boiled or scrambled eggs, at the same time feeding this dog, which had given us such a hell of a time all morning, with tiny pieces of bread and butter. We would watch this performance with mute rage, but it was amusing really, and Rags was quite a character.

I did not have to wait long to ride my first winner for Fulke that season, as Spitsbergen, owned by Lord Hesketh, who also had a share in Charlie Potheen, came out on 22 August 1973 at Worcester to win the Aberdare Handicap Hurdle.

The big surprise for me that afternoon was when Fearless Fred, sound enough to race again, won the Newport Chase with Johnny Burke, then an amateur and later to ride as first jockey for Fred Rimell. Fearless Fred ran twice more, carrying the fearsome weight of 12 stone 5 pounds to come second in the John Tilling Chase at the Devon and Exeter meeting on 30 August, and in the Somerset Chase at Wincanton on 20 September, when he broke down two fences from home and had to be pulled up.

Mrs Rose Jenks told me that when the old horse's fans saw that he was in trouble, they flocked to the rails to see if he was all right, not with morbid ghoulishness, but out of sheer concern. Some old ladies were in tears and more people went to inquire after Fearless Fred than went to cheer the winner. That was his last race and he ended his days in retirement.

No one could imagine how I felt when I wore the Queen Mother's colours for the first time at Chepstow on 6 October 1973, where I was to ride her Colonius in the Free Handicap Hurdle. I donned the blue and buff silks in the weighing room with a feeling of warmth inside. It was a tremendous privilege to be riding for Royalty, and especially for the Queen Mother. I tried to make light of it to the lads in the weighing room, remarking that the famous gold tassel bobbing from the black cap, which I could just see as I moved my head, might well knock me out if I was not careful. Deep down I felt a marvellous, glowing pride. It was such an honour to ride for this great lady.

I started favourite, but although Colonius ran well he was headed on the flat by Bill Smith, riding Bumble Boy for Bill Marshall. They won by four lengths from Swift Shadow, ridden by David Mould, with Colonius half a length away in third place.

Swift Shadow won the Wyld Court and Tom Masson Hurdle at Newbury on 26 October, beating me on Colonius again, this time by a hefty six lengths.

The following day I had an unholy ride on Charlie Potheen in the Hermitage Chase. This was his first run of the season and he was up against another great horse in Crisp, ridden by Richard Pitman. Quite early on in the race Charlie started to hang with me. I had to pull with alll my might to stop him from running out at the first in the straight. He tried to duck out, but I kicked him on and over it. When he came to the last ditch he was full of running but he had cocked his jaw on me by this time, and I had to pull him right off the runway at the side of the fence to get him into any sort of position to jump it. He half looked sideways, intending to go out, and then he just galloped into the ditch. It was one hell of a fall. Fulke Walwyn said it was one of the worst he had seen. I hurt all over, and Charlie Potheen was never the same horse afterwards, having dislocated several vertebrae in his neck and back.

Yet another trip to Alun Thomas, and more X-rays, showed that I had fractured the ends of four left ribs. True to form, the next ride I had was a winner when I rode Nelson Boy at Stratford on 15 November in the Countryman's Novices' Hurdle.

On 15 December I had the leg up on the Queen Mother's big grey, Inch Arran, at Ascot. He was huge – he must have been over 17 hands in height and had the most enormous hooves. He was a tough horse, a little past his best then, but at his peak he must have been a very exciting ride. David Mould had won a lot of races on him, and I rode him when he was coming to the end of his racing days. He was a bit head-heavy, but jumped round in a thundering, purposeful manner to come fourth in the Dunkirk Chase.

Having ridden several times for the Queen Mother and been unlucky, I was hopeful of riding my first winner for her when I went out on Tammuz on 18 December at Warwick for the start of the Hampton Novices' Hurdle.

This was some horse, quite a strong puller, and during the race I waited with him until I took it up going to the second last. He was cruising, with his ears pricked, and he flew it. I was well clear of the rest of the field when Tammuz just clipped the last and landed on his knees. After years of experience I usually knew whether a horse was going to fall or stand up in that situation. This time, I thought Tammuz was going to fall and decided to bale out. At the very last second I decided that he was not going to fall and that I would do better to hang on, by which time it was too late. I was gone. My first thought was, 'Thank goodness the owner is not here!' I felt that I had let the Queen Mother down badly, but after a few words with Sir Martin Gilliatt I stopped worrying.

I travelled to Kempton on Boxing Day where I had two rides for the Queen Mother. This time, Her Majesty was present and knowing this, I was even more aware, as royal jockey, of my duty to rise to the challenge and ride a winner for her.

It was a great feeling to stand in the paddock with the Queen Mother and Fulke Walwyn. She would listen to Fulke's orders and ask him how certain horses had run in their previous races. Then she would ask me how I thought the horse would run, and I would reply, 'I think he has a very good chance, Ma'am, he schooled well at home the other morning,' or perhaps I would tell her that I had ridden him schooling and that he would be better for the race. She genuinely loved her horses, and would listen intently to any comments made about them. When I had said my piece, I would touch my cap to the Queen Mother and walk away, with a nice light feeling as I left the paddock – one of happiness, really.

Colonius was unplaced in the Boxing Day Handicap Hurdle, but I was full of grim determination when I rode Isle of Man in the Yuletide Hurdle, the last race of the day. I had ridden him at Cheltenham on 7 December, to come second in the Bristol Long Distance Novices' Hurdle, but I thought he would stand a good chance over this shorter distance of 2 miles.

I let him make all the running, although Kempton was a bit sharp for him. He was a bit on the leg at that time, but was very fast and pulled hard. He made a slight mistake at the second last and I remembered the fall on Tammuz. 'Oh, God,' I thought, 'will I meet the last right or wrong?', but although he practically knocked the hurdle out of the ground, he stood up and ran on to win by eight lengths.

It was such a thrill to win that race. I had met the Queen Mother before when she had presented me with trophies; I had spoken with her in the paddock before I went out to ride her horses, but to come into the winner's enclosure having won for her was something special. Whenever I rode a winner for her, she never failed to speak first of all to the lad who had looked after her horse and led him up, to congratulate him, which to me was a heart-warming gesture. I would then take the saddle off, and exchange a few words with the Queen Mother and Fulke, before weighing in.

It was gratifying to see Her Majesty's obvious pleasure at Isle of Man's victory. The Queen Mother knew racing form much better than most people, and she was not only a good winner but a generous loser. That win on Isle of Man made up for all my previous disappointments on the royal horses.

On 29 December 1973, I rode Game Spirit for the Queen Mother for the first time at Newbury. I had followed David Mould on this horse in earlier years and never dreamed that I would ride him for Her Majesty. David told me that Game Spirit was a smashing ride and even advised me how best to ride him, which I appreciated.

I rode him to post for the Weyhill Handicap Chase and he felt good under me. In the race he was electrifying, pulling quite hard but jumping with terrific energy. He was a joy to ride. He took the lead two fences from home and ran on to win from Richard Pitman on Soloning by two lengths.

Meanwhile, a big, strong chestnut horse had arrived at Saxon House from the United States. He was a nice horse owned by Charles Bird, bred originally in Ireland, and his name was Amarind.

Soon after his arrival I rode him in a schooling session with two other horses at Fulke's where there were two sets of fences, the baby ones set alongside a hedge, with no open ditch, which were fun to jump two or three times. Then you had to jump the big fences, three of them, full size, standing alone with deep wings and including one large open ditch. I hated jumping these.

I had jumped Amarind over hurdles but never over fences. I had been out the night before and was not feeling very special, but Amarind jumped the baby fences perfectly. As we turned into the big fences I felt my heart sink. The novice horse fell at the first, the lead horse ran out at the second, and I was left all by myself going to the third, which was the big ditch, thinking, 'Do I pull out or do I kick on?' I decided that as Amarind had jumped the other two fences fluently I might as well jump the last, but that momentary hesitation on my part was conveyed to him in a flash and he made a tremendous leap at the fence, hit the top and went down on his knees, shooting me over his head.

Dave Dick had once schooled a Gold Cup horse for Fulke and fallen off in much the same way. He told me that Fulke had gone spare. I remembered this as I lay on the grass and realized that this was far worse. There were three horses, not one, galloping about loose, which was unheard of when schooling for Fulke, and he was, as Dave had foretold, beside himself. The other lads came running over to me because I was still on the ground, but I was not hurt – just creased up with laughing and a little frightened to get up!

I had my first ride on Amarind on a racecourse on 1 January 1974 in the Broadway Hurdle at Cheltenham, and came third to David Mould on the favourite, Moyne Royal. Amarind was more of a steeplechaser to my mind, and that was a nice run round for him.

Sea Tale, who had come close to winning in his earlier races, finally made it on 2 January 1974 at Cheltenham, giving a spectacular display of jumping to win the Ernest Robinson Handicap Hurdle.

At Sandown on 4 January I rode Tammuz in the Metropolitan Novices' Hurdle. It was a dream of a ride. His jumping down the back straight was unbelievably quick and he cleared the second last in front to canter in six lengths clear of my old associate Terje Dahl on the Polish horse, Dubler. Terje had sent some horses over to Toby Balding that season so that he could ride in this country.

At that meeting I rode Isle of Man in Division II of the Metropolitan Novices' Hurdle. He was running away with me when a faller at the second saved the situation by almost bringing me to a stop. Isle of Man, too, jumped superbly, pulling into his bridle and standing off a long way. He hit the last quite hard but quickened to win by two and a half lengths from another Scandinavian, J. Skjoedt, riding Sasha. I will always remember my 'Royal Double'.

On the second day of the Sandown meeting I rode Potentate for Josh to bring off what some friends consider to be one of my most improbable wins. I was well behind the rest of the field without a chance when I managed to conjure up a wonderful run on the inside to win the William Hill Handicap Chase by three quarters of a length from Richard Pitman on Credibility.

Pitpan, a lovely French-bred colt, rich mahogany in colour with lop ears, made my day at Windsor on 19 January 1974 in the John Player Hurdle Championship Qualifier.

The race developed into a battle between Bill Smith on Hill Top, trained by Fred Rimell, and who was strongly fancied by the Kinnersley stable, and myself on Pitpan.

I was waiting on Bill all the time and, going to the last, I saw a good stride, as did Bill, who came to me at this point. We both jumped it well and on the run in Pitpan started to drift across towards Bill. I tried to pull him off and ride hard to the line, and eventually straightened him, drawing on every vestige of strength I had left.

I beat Bill by a length, and in doing so had ridden the 900th winner of my career.

After the race, Fred Rimell came up to me and said, 'Well done.'

'Thanks very much,' I replied, for here was Fred, generous in defeat.

'Thanks to me,' Fred added, 'half those buggers came from my stable – you'd better buy me a bottle!'

The champagne was flowing anyway, masses of it, provided by the executive.

Fulke Walwyn insisted that I made the correct weight to ride Zellaman in the Ladbroke Club Handicap Hurdle at Kempton on 26 January. They went a great gallop and I thrust him at the last, hoping for a wonderful jump, which he gave me, and then drove him for the line, with my whip sending him on, and my left hand almost by his ears, to win by half a length. As I pulled up I felt severe pains in my stomach and everything seemed to be far away. I had difficulty in dismounting as my legs had turned to jelly and the course doctor diagnosed stomach cramp due to exhaustion. The wasting had taken its toll of my body once more, and I had no more rides that afternoon.

In the Wincanton Challenge Cup Chase on 31 January, my only opponent was a friend of mine, Norton Brookes, who lived near Stratford. He was riding Crystal Gazer for David Nicholson and I was on Game Spirit. I felt the responsibility weighing very heavily on my shoulders. Game Spirit lost his footing a bit going to the first as the ground was rather loose and, after that, I concentrated purely on getting him round. Game Spirit made all and won, but he was never going well at any stage. Subsequently, this horse died of heart trouble, and I sometimes wonder if he was aware of this then undiagnosed disorder which may have given him palpitations when the going was not true under his feet.

Among other dire warnings Dave Dick had given me about making mistakes when riding for Fulke Walwyn was a terrifying description of what happened when you rode a losing race when he thought you should have won.

'If you ever get beat on a fancied horse of his,' Dave said solemnly, 'he is a terrible man. He will be miserable and give you a dreadful bollocking. The only thing to do, if that happens, is to look at him, laugh, and walk away.'

I had been beaten on one or two and nothing had been said, but at Windsor on 20 February 1974, I came third on Pitpan in the Curfew Novices' Hurdle. Fulke was obviously annoyed. He growled at me, not giving me time to explain that Pitpan had made two mistakes which nobody had seen. In the middle of it all I remembered Dave's advice, and momentarily saw his wicked face in my mind's eye. The thought of him made me chuckle and I had to walk away. Fulke stood there and watched me go. Afterwards, he called me out and I thought to myself, 'Oh, Christ! – now for it.' But all he said was, 'Now, Terry, what did happen?'

I told him, and he listened intently before going off and having a large vodka. I was to discover that Fulke Walwyn rarely lost his temper and when he did it flared up and down in a moment and was then forgotten.

After my reprimand I rode Game Spirit to win the Fairlawne Chase later that day, followed by another victory on Barnard, and all was well again.

Brantridge Farmer, trained by Fulke, put up a smashing performance in the National Spirit Hurdle at Fontwell on 26 February, which he won by fifteen lengths from Paul Kelleway on Red House. I felt certain, after that race, that he would win the Champion Hurdle for me at Cheltenham in March, thereby fulfilling one of my remaining ambitions.

At the beginning of the season, Bridget had told me that she was expecting another baby. Despite enjoying every moment of my racing, my domestic pressures, as the months went by, resulted in a great deal of heart-searching. My racing was my life, but I also had my young family and wife to consider, and I decided to make this my last season.

When I told Fulke and Cath Walwyn that I intended to retire at the Cheltenham meeting that spring, I do not think they entirely believed me, knowing that I had made similar declarations in the past. I did not want to let them down, especially as they had given me such a generous opportunity to remain at the top, but I had reached my decision and was determined to stick to it.

After I had won on Finmoss at Wincanton on 7 March, I thought to myself that I should have retired there and then, on the course where I had ridden my first winner all those years ago, on Burnella. Finmoss was a difficult ride, would not race without blinkers and nobody else could win on him. I had a terrific reception from the crowd when I came in after the Fonthill Novices' Hurdle, with several people questioning my decision to retire this season when I was riding so well, but my mind was made up.

I did not want to give up, but all the circumstances conspired to force my hand and there was no turning back.

One of the most historic occasions on the social scene that month was the Piper Heidsieck Champagne dinner held in London to celebrate the fiftieth anniversary of the Cheltenham Gold Cup. Among the many famous guests present were twenty-five men who had all won the race and I felt honoured to be one of them.

On the morning of the first day's racing at the Cheltenham March meeting, I woke up determined not to leave my favourite racecourse without riding my last winner there. I went through the usual routine and arrived at the course just as I had so many times before.

Things did not start too well for me as Isle of Man ran too freely with me in the Sun Alliance Novices' Hurdle on 12 March and I was unplaced behind Ron Barry on Brown Lad.

One of my chances of winning at that meeting in my own mind was on Amarind in the National Hunt Two-Mile Champion Chase which followed. I had ridden him at Wincanton for the first time over fences in the John Bull chase on 17 January, when he finished fourth to The Dikler. At Cheltenham we went a fair gallop and he was going very nicely until two out when he fell heavily, giving both of us a thorough bone-shaker. As I got to my feet my only thought was 'I've *got* to ride a winner before I go — somehow.'

Brantridge Farmer was waiting for me in the paddock before the Champion Hurdle the next day and I thought 'This must be it,' remembering how he had run for me earlier. He went off at a tearing pace and was going well until, opposite the water jump, he was suddenly off the bridle and fading rapidly. He would not have won a selling plate, let alone the Champion Hurdle! I was so down-hearted, for I would never have another chance to win this race for as long as I lived.

When I went out on Sea Tale for the Lloyds Bank Hurdle I think I rode one of the best races round the *inside* of Cheltenham that I have ever ridden. There were lots of runners in the race and I hit three wings with my leg as we jumped. I never gave one inch away. But to my dismay I found that through being so stubborn I was being shut in by the others. I could not get out, and when there was room to get out, I knew that I would have to go round the rest of the field and lose my place going up the hill. So, I stayed where I was, and the only time I pulled out was going to the last, which Sea Tale absolutely pinged. He had been foot perfect and extremely brave. I had saved a lot of ground but I should have pulled out. I never rode a race like that before and I should have won on Sea Tale.

In the Cheltenham Gold Cup on 14 March I had the choice of rides between Charlie Potheen and Game Spirit. I think I was unpopular with Mrs Heath when I chose to ride for the Queen Mother. Photographs were taken of me with her in the paddock before the race, and the papers were full of my 'last Gold Cup' and riding for the Queen Mother. 'Come on, Game Spirit, I want a Happy Ending' was one of the headlines that morning, and the words were echoed in my heart as I went to post for the Gold Cup, wearing the Royal colours for the last time ever.

When the tapes went up, we set off and, going down the hill, I noticed Richard Pitman on Pendil tracking Bob Davies on High Ken, who was a patchy jumper.

'Don't get behind that bastard – he'll go arse over head in a minute,' I warned him, but I was too late. Before Richard could digest what I had said and change his position, High Ken had gone and, in falling, brought down the mighty Pendil who had started favourite at 13–8 on. This debacle at the twentieth fence momentarily checked Game Spirit but did not stop him. Going to the last, Bobby Beasley on Captain Christy ploughed through the fence from its roots to the top. I thought, rather unsportingly, 'Oh, good – fall, and bring down the other one,' which was The Dikler! My thoughts would not have pleased Fulke had he known. It did not happen and I came in third, twenty-five lengths behind the winner, on whom Bobby Beasley had crowned his tremendous comeback to racing.

Bill Smith, riding Charlie Potheen, almost caught me on the run in. He was making his transition to Fulke Walwyn's stable to take over from me, having stayed with Fred Rimell for almost two years.

I had a wonderful reception when I came in. I cannot remember what I said to the Queen Mother after that Gold Cup. I was feeling rather full up. I know I told her that Game Spirit had run a wonderful race, which was true, on ground which did not suit him, and had survived a minor interference. She congratulated me, and afterwards she sent me some signed colour photographs which are among my most treasured possessions.

No sooner had I survived that emotional moment than I was faced with another when the jockeys with whom I had ridden for years presented me with a superb watercolour of a 'two horse match'. I was overwhelmed.

I could come nowhere on Bumble Boy in the County Handicap Hurdle. He had no chance against the winner, True Song, but I had been offered the ride by his owner, Pat Gallaher, who was hoping to give me a victory at my last meeting. It was a gesture that I found most moving.

When I weighed out for the Cathcart Chase, the last race I was to ride in my life, I went through the usual routine, feeling steady in my mind, and when I walked into the paddock, nobody said much to me. I had the leg up on Amarind, whom I thought was none the worse for his fall on the first day, and rode him out towards the course behind Richard Pitman, who was on the favourite, Soothsayer, to parade before the stands. Richard turned to me before we reached the course and said, 'Go on, Biddles, you go in front – it's your last day.'

'No,' I replied, 'carry on, it doesn't matter.'

'Go on,' he insisted, reining Soothsayer left-handed to allow me to pass.

'Well, thanks, Pip,' I said, and edged Amarind past him onto the racecourse.

I had no idea that so many people had stayed to watch me ride in my final race. It was such a surprise to me and when they caught sight of me the cheering was deafening. I could not believe it. Why on earth should anyone care that Terry Biddlecombe was retiring from racing that afternoon? As I turned and cantered to the starting gate, with the light fading on the racecourse, the cheering was still ringing in my ears and I felt a constriction in my throat as the full realization of what was happening dawned on me. Never again to ride at my beloved Cheltenham, cradled beneath the Cotswolds, or hear again the roar of a crowd of people who loved not only horses and racing, but everyone connected with the game – including me it seemed.

I do not think I have ever been so aware of the irresistible fascination Cheltenham has always held for me. It had caught me in its spell since that first tragic incident in my life with the death of Or Massif; seen my greatest triumph when I won the Gold Cup with Woodland Venture, and witnessed many of my worst disasters. I knew I would never be free of its magnetism nor ever wish to be as long as I drew breath.

We reached the gate and lined up as usual. I remember thinking to myself that Amarind would have no chance, having had a fall already at the meeting, but he jumped with enormous courage. When we got to the top of the hill, David Mould came alongside me on Clever Scot and said, 'Biddles, if I'd got enough money I'd square all the other jockeys up in this race just to let you win.'

'Great, Dave – now why don't you bugger off and win yourself?' I replied tersely.

He galloped on, grinning at me as he went, knowing that my curt reply reflected my pent-up feelings. I went on down the hill with Amarind jumping cleanly for me but well out of the race. Jumping the last, I felt a sudden sense of relief. As I passed the post in fifth place, Richard Pitman having won with Soothsayer, the tears blinded my eyes as the nostalgia of the occasion, mingled with nervous and physical tiredness, swept over me. The shouts and cheers from the crowd as I came in were tumultuous. I slid off Amarind, unsaddled and went into the weighing room with the noise of that astonishing farewell still audible as I sat down, just for a moment, before taking off my colours for the last time.

But more was in store for me. I was walking round in the weighing room without any clothes on, trying to collect myself together and change, when everybody started coming in! I did not know what was happening until someone produced a bottle of champagne, and friend after friend from all walks of life filled the room. Lady Aitken had arranged a champagne reception for me as a surprise, and it was a fantastic party.

When eventually I reached home, I was deflated. I did not want to drink anything but I had a few to be sociable with people who called in to wish me well.

Later, I sat in my chair with a large Scotch, thinking about everything for a long, long time. Then I went to bed. My career as a professional steeplechase jockey was over.

17
This Is My Life Now

When I woke up the next morning the world had gone – vanished. I mooned about the place, doing the horses and not really thinking very clearly. With Bridget heavily pregnant, I was kept pretty busy but the sense of anticlimax was dreadful.

The racing fraternity had seen to it that my final goodbyes had not been said at Cheltenham for on 25 March the World Sporting Club invited me to be Guest of Honour at a Grand Dinner and Boxing Evening at Grosvenor House, to mark my retirement.

What an evening that was! Chaired by Lord Oaksey, who said so many nice things about me that I almost regretted the occasions I had ribbed him on the racecourse, I was presented with a superb onyx-based chandelier on behalf of the Directors of the World Sporting Club.

It is at this point that I should like to pay tribute to the late Jack Solomons who did so much for racing. Evenings such as this one were frequently laid on by him for jockeys who had won big races, or become champions, and they were all at his own expense. He was a great old friend, much missed by those of us in racing who appreciated his generosity, and also by the boxing fraternity. Jack loved his boxers.

On 16 April 1974 I attended a luncheon in Birmingham for the presentation of the Midlands Sportsmen of the Year Awards. I drove up with Bill Smith, and Ken White acted as chauffeur to Fred Rimell, who was to receive an award also. We all had a very good time and Bill and I drove back, feeling very merry, to Corse Lawn.

It was a great afternoon and we decided to back a pony that Bridget had bred. We tacked it up, Bill got into the saddle and the pony bucked him off. It galloped all over the place, breaking the tack, and Bridget was furious. When we got back to the house she told us that we were not going to have any dinner that night and, feeling like two naughty schoolboys, we went off to have a few jars and a Chinese meal in Tewkesbury. When we returned, the house was quiet, Bridget and Laura were asleep, and we slunk off to bed. The next morning I felt a bit guilty, and to make amends I decided to chain harrow the two paddocks close to the house. I was not feeling very well after our night out and had just finished the harrowing when Bridget called out to me that I had to catch a train to London. I suddenly remembered a telephone call from the BBC some weeks before when I had been asked to take part in a weight-watching programme entitled 'Fit not Fat'. I had accepted a fee with expenses, but forgotten all about it until this moment.

When I went into the house, I noticed my clothes laid out neatly on the bed, with a matching tie. Bridget had never done this for me in her life, and after the previous day's misdemeanours, it was even more puzzling. Anyway, I changed, caught the train to London, and met the BBC representative and an attractive model, as had been arranged, at the Hilton Hotel. I was told that I could eat and drink as much as I liked before going to the Savoy Baths to see how much I could lose, before returning for another tuck-in at the hotel. I thought this was a splendid idea and proceeded to eat everything in sight accompanied by plenty of champagne and several Gaelic coffees, with a secretary making a note of everything I ate and drank before we set off for the baths.

The BBC cameramen and producers waiting to film my slimming feat at the baths were all rushing about when we arrived, worrying that the condensation would harm the cameras, and were generally agitated. As soon as the main producer saw me he said, 'Right, come on through here would you, please?' indicating the hot room.

'No,' I replied, firmly, 'we've got to do the job properly, I must go into the steam room first,' which I did, for twenty minutes. They looked very taken aback, but I knew how to waste better than most people and I sat in the steam room feeling really good. When I came out, I was almost rushed into the hot room where I saw four figures with towels over their heads. I said to one of the cameramen nearby, 'What are these bloody fools doing?' and, with that, one of them unwrapped himself and I recognized Eamonn Andrews, clutching a microphone in one hand and a large, red book in the other.

'Terry Biddlecombe, This is Your Life!' he announced, looking very flushed. I had been conned into the baths by his team! When the other figures removed the towels from their heads I saw the grinning faces of Scudamore, Macer Gifford and Tim Brookshaw. They were all feeling the heat, especially Eamonn. They had not bargained on my going into the steam room first, and had been forced to wait in the hot room for about half an hour longer than they had anticipated, which I thought was very funny.

After the initial surprise, I said to Michael, 'If I had seen your fucking feet first, I would have known something was up.' Michael was renowned for his peculiar feet, and they could not have belonged to anyone else!

After the initial niceties, Eamonn Andrews said frantically, 'I've got to get out of here, what do I do now?'

'Jump in the cold plunge,' I suggested, which was nothing new to me. It nearly killed Eamonn because the water was freezing, and he was no sooner in than he was out again – gasping!

It was a great evening, and the family had kept the secret for months. When we returned to the studio, Bridget appeared, looking very smug, and I knew then why my clothes had been so carefully laid out! It was a marvellous reunion with the family and old friends: Mother and Dad, Tony, Doc Wilson, Dave Dick, Fred Winter, Fred Rimell, Bob Davies and Sue, Josh Gifford, Pat Taaffe, Joe Ballinger, and a greeting from Frankie Vaughan, who was in Canada at that time, reminding me of our first meeting in the Turkish baths in Torquay.

To crown it all I had a message from Her Majesty Queen Elizabeth the Queen Mother, wishing me well for the future, which was presented to me by Sir Martin Gilliatt.

Ten days later, on 26 April 1974, Bridget gave birth to our second daughter, Elizabeth, and once more I overdid the champagne

Nevertheless, I was depressed. I regretted my retirement with a mixture of anguish and resentment. I would say, on reflection, that it took me a year to adjust to the vacuum which had replaced my routine as a steeplechase jockey. I rarely went racing and could not make up my mind where my future lay. As the summer drew to a close and the new National Hunt season sprang to life, I could stand it no longer, and took Bridget to Barbados for three weeks in October 1974. I wanted to lie in the sun, and think.

On the day we arrived home from Barbados, I had a telephone

message asking me to contact Julian Wilson at the BBC who wanted to see if I had the makings of a paddock commentator. It seemed like a gift from heaven at that moment – a chance to get back into racing, if only as a spectator.

My first effort was to take place at Ascot, with about twenty-four hours in which to brush up my form. I was very out of touch with racing and I sat up all night, trying to cram all the information I needed into my head, but I could not concentrate. I turned up at Ascot and in the first race there were twenty-three runners. I became flustered, mixing up somebody's name with that of his father, and forgetting which switches I had to pull in order to hand over to the other commentators. I had never worn earphones before and it became a nightmare. By the fourth race I was improving, but I did not get the job. I defy anybody, with that amount of notice, to become a polished paddock commentator literally overnight! I have, however, worked with Julian Wilson at most of the televised Cheltenham meetings, summing up races, and generally commenting upon their outcome.

It is common knowledge that my marriage gradually disintegrated. We both tried to make it work and went to Barbados again in 1975 to get away from the routine at home.

I then decided that I would try once more for a permit to train a few horses of my own at Corse Lawn, but again my application was refused. Had I applied for a full licence, it would have entailed enormous expense and I was not prepared to venture deeply into such an undertaking when my marriage was still very shaky.

Soon after I had been denied permission to train for the second time, I could see no future for us and neither could Bridget. We parted on good terms.

In 1976, Gary Newbon of Midlands ATV approached me and asked me if I would like to do a racing 'spot' once a week on his sports programme. I said that I would love to, and have continued to work with Gary, who is the programme presenter, Billy Wright, the sports programme producer, and the rest of the team since August 1976. We get on very well together. I thoroughly enjoy my television work, which has given me a fresh interest and enabled me to keep in touch with racing and racing people.

Since my retirement from racing I have continued to break and school racehorses for outside trainers, and to qualify horses for racing, including Fred Rimell's 1976 Gold Cup winner, Royal Frolic, and The Pilgarlic, which was given to me by Cecil Haynes' widow, now Mrs

Poole, and which came fourth in the 1981 Liverpool Foxhunter's Steeplechase ridden by Nigel Twiston-Davies.

When Coral Diver finished his racing days, Bryan Jenks made a gift of him to me and I had him in my yard for about four years. It was marvellous to have my old favourite after all the triumphs we had shared and he ran well in point-to-points before finally retiring. Sadly, he had to be put down in 1980.

During the time I was writing this book, I had the great misfortune to lose Fred Rimell, who died in the summer of 1981. This was a poignant loss for me as we had been associated not only during my time with him as a jockey, but right to the end of his days. He was a good friend, and I owed him much of the credit for my success as a jockey as he produced so many fine horses for me to ride to victory.

Since his death, whenever I have met old associates at race meetings they speak of Fred as though he were still with us. They cannot believe that his familiar rotund figure will no longer be seen on the racecourse. He was a tremendously alive man, always jovial, always quick to offer anyone a cigarette, or a quick 'livener', and appreciative of a pretty woman. His humour and warmth are greatly missed; he was a vital cog in the racing machine. The sudden and tragic death of Tim Brookshaw, also, distressed everyone who knew him.

Two years after my marriage broke up, I met a wonderful girl by the name of Ann Hodgson at a party, who at that time was working in the haematology department at Gloucester hospital. We became friendly, fell in love, married, and now have a baby son called James. I have never been happier. Ann is a marvellous cook, a splendid mother, and keeps me young-hearted with her youthful optimism. We both love horses – in fact we share many interests – and with a new future ahead of us there is so much to live for.

I am still a comparatively young man with many ambitions yet unfulfilled. Some of them I will never realize, such as winning the Champion Hurdle, or beating Stan Mellor's record of 1034 winners. My final total was 905, with my last winner being Finmoss at Wincanton where I had started my career with Burnella in 1958.

After I had retired I was made a life member of Cheltenham Racecourse by the late Major General Sir Randle Feilden, which was a great compliment. The Wincanton executives, whose course also held such wonderful memories for me, instigated 'The Terry Biddle-combe Steeplechase' in my honour, which is run every October, and

I have rarely missed a chance to see its outcome.

My thanks must go to my family for their constant support, especially to Mother for her warmth and kindness to me, my family and friends, and to Dad, for encouraging me in my racing career.

To racing itself I can never be grateful enough. It has enabled me to meet many people and make lifelong friendships. I have seen more of this country and of others than I would ever have dreamed possible. It has been my privilege to ride some of the best horses in training for some of the finest trainers in the business, and thereby experiencing sufficient thrills to last three lifetimes.

That is a debt I can never repay.

Career Record

Season	1st	2nd	3rd	Unpl.	Total
1958–59	8	8	5	46	67
1959–60	18	24	20	129	191
1960–61	18	19	40	136	213
1961–62	39	33	35	231	338
1962–63	41	37	26	183	287
1963–64	56	51	33	230	370
1964–65	114	86	76	255	531
1965–66	102	78	59	232	471
1966–67	83	62	32	184	361
1967–68	68	49	31	132	280
1968–69	77	59	48	187	371
1969–70	89	63	37	158	347
1970–71	72	56	44	173	345
1971–72	58	50	27	141	276
1972–73	41	31	35	89	196
1973– 14 March 1974	21	17	14	38	90

Index